Working Together in Theatre

WORKING TOGETHER IN THEATRE

Collaboration and Leadership

ROBERT COHEN

First published 2011 by
PALGRAVE MACMILLAN

Palgrave Macmillan in the UK is an imprint of Macmillan Publishers Limited, registered in England, company number 785998, of Houndmills, Basingstoke, Hampshire RG21 6XS.

Palgrave Macmillan in the US is a division of St Martin's Press LLC, 175 Fifth Avenue, New York, NY 10010.

Palgrave Macmillan is the global academic imprint of the above companies and has companies and representatives throughout the world.

Palgrave® and Macmillan® are registered trademarks in the United States, the United Kingdom, Europe and other countries.

ISBN: 978–0–230–23981–4 hardback
ISBN: 978–0–230–23982–1 paperback

This book is printed on paper suitable for recycling and made from fully managed and sustained forest sources. Logging, pulping and manufacturing processes are expected to conform to the environmental regulations of the country of origin.

A catalogue record for this book is available from the British Library.

A catalog record for this book is available from the Library of Congress.

10 9 8 7 6 5 4 3 2 1
20 19 18 17 16 15 14 13 12 11

Printed in China

*To the thousands of theatre artists in
all areas with whom I have worked with
over the past fifty years*

CONTENTS

ACKNOWLEDGMENTS

I have been privileged to work with hundreds of professional theatre workers for more than fifty years, and I'm indebted to all of them for the collaborations in which we have engaged and from which I have learned.

For this particular book I would like to thank many such colleagues whom I have queried directly and who have directly aided me in this project:

Ramy Eletrebe, Cameron Harvey, Janet Swenson, Jaymi Smith, Vinnie Olivieri, Luke Canterella, Holly Poe Durbin, Catherine Zuber, Scott Lehrer, Donald Holder, Jerry Patch, Jo Winiarski, Jeff Greenberg, Gabor Tompa, Mihai Maniutiu and Cliff Faulkner.

PREFACE

There are many books on the subject of the various theatre arts: acting, directing, scenic design, playwriting, and so forth. I've written six (five on acting, one on directing). But there are few books on how all these people work *together,* and that's what I've set out to do in this one.

My goal is to examine how creating great theatre requires not only great work by many individuals but also a great 'working together' of specialists in many different fields. People come to this work for many different reasons, and usually from a broad variety of backgrounds, but for their work to truly bear fruit it must be consolidated into a collective and seamless whole. And this, I find, takes two things often seen as opposites but which are equally essential: collaboration and leadership.

I've included in this book the work experiences of literally hundreds of people, many that you have heard of and many that you haven't, but all whom have devoted the bulk of their lives to the producing of what they hope and expect will be theatre performances that will live in the minds of those who see them for the rest of their lives. The performances I cite are almost all from professional venues, mainly in the live theatre but sometimes film and television, since it is anticipated that the majority of this book's readers will either already be working professionals in these arts, or will be persons hoping and/or training to become so.

The book is divided into three parts.

- Part One is introductory. Its two chapters include a general overview of the relationship of **collaboration and leadership** in creating theatre, and a study of the two basic forms of theatrical organization in which they are commonly represented: the **ensemble** and the **hierarchy,** respectively**.**

- Part Two divides the process of theatrical collaborations into four stages, which, while often overlapping, have a loose chronological structure. First is the **preparation stage**, where a producer and director, and often a playwright, translator or dramaturg, originate the basic ideas of a production. Second is the **planning stage**, where designers enter the project and join with the director to collectively create the production "on paper," (actually, these days, mostly on electronic files): sharing ideas, images, sounds, and written descriptions that indicate how the play will look and sound, who will be in it, and how, where and when it will be put together. Third is the **production stage,** where actors and stage managers join the team in the rehearsal hall, business and publicity staff members get to work in their appropriate offices, production staffs move into shops and studios to create the scenery, costume, props, wigs, sound cues and other production aspects, and technicians move into the theatre, hanging and wiring the sound speakers, focusing the lights, and installing the scenery and machinery created in the shops. Fourth comes the **presenting stage,** where stage managers take over many of the controls and everything is put together on the stage and played before an audience.

- Part Three is a concluding chapter that discusses the modes of communication that may be employed at every level of this complex but highly integrated process which, apart from scale, is pretty much the same in professional theatres around the world. An appendix that details some of the methods discussed in parts one and two follow.

Exercises appear at the end of Chapters 3, 4 and 5, which can be used by individuals or groups to experience, hands-on, some of the methods and techniques that can lead to successful collaborations and leadership in actual practice.

And to the reader: all citations are identified in endnotes, arranged by page number, at the back of the book.

PART ONE

INTRODUCTION

Family Theatres / Theatre Families

"No one … not even geniuses … ever makes it alone," says Malcolm Gladwell in his best-selling *Outliers*. This truth permeates this book, which has only one goal: to help theatre artists learn to create great art *together*.

The chapters that follow are not about aesthetic or intellectual goals, but rather about the process of working as a unit. Every theatre production, though sometimes headlined by a world-renowned director or one or two famous actors, is put together by a great many people, numbering from the dozens to the hundreds. And when these people work together they can, as a collective, attain artistic heights that none could attain independently. "If the theatre is not about the interaction of people, it's about nothing," says Joe Dowling, former head of Ireland's Abbey Theatre and now of Minneapolis's Guthrie Theatre. "Theatre," Dowling continues, "can never be solely about concept, ideas, intellectual pursuits – it has to be about the way in which the people relate to one another."

People in a theatre or film company, therefore, must work closely together. In doing so, they often call themselves a "family." Indeed, one of the most common comments theatre artists make when accepting Tony or Academy Awards is praising their fellow artists in the project by saying, "We were a family!"

There would rarely be a need to say this in previous centuries, however, because until the seventeenth century, *real* families created most theatre. The troubadours, *jongleurs,* mimes, and *commedia dell'arte* troupes that toured Europe from the Dark Ages through the Renaissance were almost entirely blood-related artistic collectives, with elders handing down their duties and roles to their descendents from one generation to the next. Even the celibate monks who created liturgical dramas at the start of the second millennium were members of lifelong "brotherhoods,"* as were the craft guilds that created the mystery plays of the European High Middle Ages. In the late sixteenth century, it was two real brothers, Richard and Cuthbert Burbage, together with their father, James, and their fellow Warwickshire countryman Will Shakespeare, who came together to create the greatest theatre and dramatic repertoire known to the English-speaking world. A century later, the young Jean-Baptiste Poquelin assumed the stage name of Molière and, together with four members of the Béjart family (one his mistress and another afterwards his wife), founded the *Théâtre Illustre* in Paris, which became the greatest theatre company in that country's history. Meanwhile, half a world away, eleven Japanese families were developing a unique and popular dance-drama style into the *kabuki,* which for the past four centuries has been Japan's leading theatrical art.

And in the nineteenth century, a Russian teenager named Konstantin Alekseiev gathered his relatives together and, with them, created the Alekseiev Circle, a family company whose amateur productions entertained Muscovites in the Alekseiev home and country house, leading Konstantin to take the name "Stanislavsky" and co-found, with Vladimir Nemirovich-Dantchenko, the Moscow Art Theatre, which went on to revolutionize acting throughout Europe and, eventually, the United States.

These were all, at least initially, *family* theatres. Some continue to reflect their family heritage: In Japan, the same eleven families that ruled the *kabuki* in the seventeenth century continue to dominate it today. In France, Molière's *Illustre,* which was consolidated with others into the *Comédie Française* not long after his death, is still known as the "House of Molière," and its permanent company members call themselves not artistic partners but *sociétaires,* implying a social and not just a professional linkage.

---

*"Brotherhood" remains a term that designates certain unions, such as the United Brotherhood of Carpenters and the International Brotherhood of Electrical Workers.

But blood-linked family theatres are extremely rare today. In America, the tradition is upheld mainly in the circus – as exemplified by the Zoppé Family Circus, founded in 1842 and now run by its founder's great-great grandson, Giovanni Zoppé, who grew up performing with his father, mother, wife, two siblings and their spouses. We're "just like the circus was 100 years ago," said Giovanni in 2005, as he took the reins from his father.

Members of such real family theatres did not acquire their theatrical skills by training at drama schools or university theatre departments, as most theatre artists do today. Rather, they learned their skills in apprenticeships with their family-led troupes. Tradition has it that William Shakespeare's first theatre job was looking after the horses of wealthy patrons when they attended his company's performances. Before he was invited to play before King Louis' court and become France's most famous actor-playwright, Molière had honed his craft touring his company through rural villages in Southern France for some thirteen years. What training such artists received came not through courses of formal instruction but through continuous performing – often passing the hat for their supper when not being chased out of town. This called for an extraordinary commitment and group loyalty, for which family ties are the surest component.

Non-family theatres created in subsequent centuries in many ways followed the family model, forming large companies of actors who lived in the same city and performed at the same theatres, working with many of the same colleagues year after year. Many in such companies married and performed together, including Alfred Lunt and Lynn Fontanne, Henry Irving and Ellen Terry, and Hume Cronyn and Jessica Tandy, while others created family acting dynasties, such as the Booths, the Barrymores, and the Redgraves.

But there has been a sea change in theatre production since the mid-twentieth century. As a person who has been directing plays since 1957, I have watched these changes evolve with fascination.

First, theatre has diversified geographically, particularly in America. In the 1940s and 50s, the American professional theatre simply meant the New York professional theatre. To be sure, there were the seeds of a regional American theatre movement being planted – Nina Vance's Alley Theatre in Houston, Margo Jones's Theatre 47 in Dallas, Zelda Fichandler's Arena Stage in Washington, Herb Blau and Jules Irving's Actors' Workshop in San Francisco – but that was about it. Apart from those venues, anyone wishing to create professional theatre and be paid for it had to move to New York. Now, however, there are nearly *2000* professional theatres in the United States, about 150 of them operating on budgets of anywhere from one to thirty-some million dollars. And these theatres are broadly scattered throughout every state and large city in the nation. Such diversification is good in many ways, but – since the vast majority of theatres outside of New York present only limited runs of, typically, three to seven weeks – it has also led to actors, designers and directors working mainly on short-term, single-production assignments rather than on yearly (much less lifetime) contracts as was commonly the case in earlier generations. And while single-show ensembles may bond into what participants may *call* a family at Tony Awards time, such pseudo-families are, in most cases, decidedly short-lived.

European theatres companies, maintained through most of the twentieth century on a permanent or semipermanent basis, often with ample government funding, have also moved toward single-production contracts in the third millennium. Prominent European actors and designers worldwide now receive attractive offers from other theatre, television and film companies from around their continent – and even around the world. In our now-global economy, permanent companies are rapidly giving way to independent theatres where relative strangers come together for short work periods to produce single projects.

Second, as the theatres are diversified, so are the artists they engage. Today's professional theatre practitioner has probably received his or her basic training in a university graduate program (particularly in America) or a theatre conservatory (particularly in Europe) or a commercial school in New York, London or Los Angeles or other large city, rather than a long-term professional apprenticeship or internship – which, today, is almost always very brief (measured in months rather than years), usually unpaid (even lacking a housing allowance), and can thus normally only be a brief midway step between the classroom and the profession. So the "family of strangers" that gathers today to mount a twenty-first-century production is also educationally diversified: its constituents comprise a varied assortment of independent artists who have been trained in different schools, in different cities, in different ways, and by different teachers. Moreover, they have usually received intensely *specialized* training in just a single theatrical discipline: as an actor, perhaps, or sound designer or stage manager or a projection designer. If they are trained in a university, they will sport MFA degrees in their specific discipline: an MFA not in "Theatre" but in "Costume Design." And when they then become professionals, they will join specialized professional unions,* which oversee the rights pertaining to their particular discipline and protect their members from real or imagined subjugation from artists in other professional unions.

Specialization existed in the past, of course, but not so rigidly. Thespis, whom Aristotle considered the world's first actor, was also the playwright and director of his early Greek tragedies. Aeschylus and Sophocles wrote, directed and often acted in their plays, and designed them – and perhaps their stage machinery – as well. Shakespeare and Molière acted in their own works as well as the works of other writers; probably both also directed their plays – Molière definitely did. Indeed, until the twentieth century what is now called directing was in fact normally executed by the production's playwright or leading actor.

So in contrast to their predecessors over the past two millennia, theatre artists today are also diversified *professionally* into separate artistic disciplines. This can lead to isolation of the various artists – what in France was ridiculed as the "arthritis of specialization" when it threatened to throttle the more free-form avant-garde theatre of the early years of the twentieth century, when distinguished easel painters, including Pierre Bonnard, Edouard Vuillard, and Pablo Picasso were routinely designing scenery for theatre and dance.

Finally, artists who hope to make a living in today's highly mobile and geographically diversified theatre must become individually *competitive* if they hope to make a living. No longer able to rely on a family connection to begin or sustain their careers, today's artists must compete avidly for a foot in the door, an audition or portfolio review,

---

*The unions, basically, are Actors Equity Association (AEA) for Actors and Stage Managers, SDC (the Stage Directors and Choreographers Society, as recently renamed) for Directors, and the United Scenic Artists (USA) for Designers – with USA members segregated into more than a dozen specific branches, including those for Scenic Designers, Costume Designers, Lighting Designers, Sound Designers, Projection Designers, Scene Painters, Art Directors (for films), Storyboard Artists, Computer Artists, and Art Department Coordinators, among others. While Stage Managers are currently represented by AEA, they have different (and higher) salary scales than do the actors in that union.

a production assignment, a union membership, and then continuing (and hopefully growing) recognition – in the press, in the media, and by word of mouth – on a larger and larger scale for the rest of their careers. Since today's theatre is broad-based, they must embrace its diversity of locales, styles, and performative media. Which means that unless they snare a permanent position at a regional theatre, or national attention in film, television, or star assignment on Broadway, they must "go on the move," competing to establish reputations in multiple media and separate locales. They must compete broadly for their livelihood, and they must do so throughout their careers. And they must make friends – without making rivals or enemies.

But all of this requires the most serious attention to "working together."

For today, families don't make theatre; theatre makes families.

1

Collaboration and Leadership

Collaboration and Leadership: the key words of this book's subtitle. Are they allies or opposites? Does one contradict the other, or does one *require* the other? Let's look at them separately first.

Collaboration

"Theatre is a collaborative art." How many times have you heard that? Hundreds probably. Maybe thousands.

Well, it's true. And even though obvious, it bears repeating. If a sales clerk daydreams at her post at Macy's one afternoon, the store won't close down forever, but if the actor playing Mercade – who is suppose to arrive with the news that the king is dead – fails to make his entrance in the final scene of *Love's Labor's Lost*, the play simply cannot continue, for his unexpected announcement instantly reverses everything that's been happening up to this point.*

---

*This is not a random example. Fifty years ago I was in a production where exactly this happened. The actor, absorbed in a book in the dressing room, simply forgot to enter. While the actors ad-libbed in panic, I ran offstage as if hearing someone call me, then, not finding him, ran back onstage to explain to my fellow-actors that I had "just seen Mercade" who had told me that the king was dead. The play went on, but the actor's career, to my knowledge, did not.

Yet the actor playing Mercade is not the only person who could create this theatrical catastrophe. If the stage manager has failed to call him up from his dressing room in time, or failed to flash the off-stage cue light that signals his entrance from behind a see-proof and soundproof door he is to enter through, the play may likewise come to a dead halt. Or if the wardrobe assistant had mistakenly taken Mercade's costume back to the costume shop for repairs ten minutes beforehand, or if the scene shifting crew had failed to unlatch the door after moving it into place during the previous scene change, the entire performance could be ruined, and no one would talk about anything else after the curtain call. In the theatre, *everybody* must pull his or her own weight, and pull it *all the time* or disaster may follow.

So full collaboration among all members of the theatre company is essential and essential all the time. No job in theatre is too small to engage everyone's attention. Actor Willem Dafoe has won two Oscar nominations for his work in films, but his career is centered on his stage work at the experimental Wooster Group theatre company in New York, which calls itself an "ensemble of artists." How did he join the group? "I just wanted to be with those people... I literally walked in there and said: 'I wanna work with you guys.' And they said: 'Okay, well you go and sweep in the corner,'" Dafoe explains. Film and Broadway star Denzel Washington describes his attitude in similar fashion: "What I learned working with directors like Jonathan Demme, and what I now try to create, is community feeling. We're all in it together. I can grab the bucket and pail just like the next guy. Nobody can get to work earlier than me. And I like that."

For there's nothing like sweeping and scrubbing the dressing room floors – and doing it *well* – to remind you of how much effort and affection (and often humility) goes into collaborating with others in the creation of great theatre art. Indeed, most of the persons who work in theatre love doing so. Not every minute of every day, of course, but almost always *they come back for more* – whenever they can. Few theatre artists retire voluntarily. Many, when they are between well-paying assignments (Broadway shows or films, say), work for free. As this book was being readied for press, Broadway stars Bernadette Peters and James Naughton were spending a full week rehearsing a staged reading of composer John Kander's new adaptation of *The Skin of Our Teeth* in New York, for which they received only the bare minimum (and union-required) scale salary. "People in the theater are just very generous," Kander reported afterwards in the *New York Times.* "They do readings all the time, usually just as favors. Then they get their $300 and they go home." Their fee for doing this commercially would surely be in the five figures.

What theatre has retained from those centuries when it was largely a family business is that its best artistic work almost always comes out of well-tuned *working relationships.* These need not be social relationships, but they are personal, and they are equally or even more intense than social relationships because they are fiercely dedicated to achieving specific artistic goals, maintaining clear and honest communications, and aimed at a wholly integrated collaboration.

Such collaborations (the word is a compound of "co" and "labor" – thus indicating "shared work") may make the work process more comfortable than non-collaboration would, but that is not the reason why I wrote this book, nor is it the reason you should be reading it.

Dynamic and free-flowing collaborations make theatre art *successful* – not just for the artists involved, but for their audiences as well. So while this book deals with what in many quarters might be called theatre ethics, it does not presume to preach morality. It is, at heart, a *practical* book. Its principles are not designed just to make the theatre pleasant, but to make the theatre *great.*

There's an immensely practical, even economic reason for you to learn the art of successful theatrical collaboration, too. Your career will absolutely depend on it! Why? Because at the end of a production, the overseeing producer and/or artistic director will almost certainly hold formal or informal "exit interviews" with most or all members of the artistic team. These interviews will not be held to assess the talent, skills, or reliability of those who worked on the show, since the interviewers will have already made such judgments themselves; what they really want to know is *how well you worked with others* on the team. So they will ask you about the others – and they will ask the others about you. And make no mistake about it: your professional future may well depend on what the responses of your collaborators will be. A director, designer, actor, or other member of the team who is described by other colleagues as, for example, argumentative, sullen, unhelpful, distant, selfish-minded, crude, impolite, unappreciative, pouty, arrogant, or overly self-absorbed will, you may be sure, have trouble getting rehired for the next show or following season.

Such persons may even fail to receive good reports when other theatre companies call to check their references.

Of course, having a key role or a design assignment in a show that gets thrilling reviews, sold-out houses, and nightly standing ovations can compensate for a good deal of flack from your exit interviews (theatre being, at least in part, a commercial business), but even if you are lauded to the skies for your talents you may be a toss-up in a future employer's mind if your lack of collaborative skills are reported to have made your colleagues miserable. For despite what you might read in the gossip columns, the theatre artists who succeed over a lifetime career are inevitably *the ones that draw the best work out of their artistic partners, and who have their own best work drawn from them by the same people.*

It's a reciprocal process, a win-win situation for all involved, and it pays off in the seamlessness of the final product. Your ability to collaborate will prove essential for your creation of collective theatrical art, as well as for the furthering of your individual artistic career.

No one understands the importance of this better than those who initiate theatrical productions and engage theatrical artists: producers, artistic directors, play directors, and casting directors. Should you, as an applicant for a part in – or a position on the artistic staff of – a production, come off brilliantly in your audition or resume/portfolio review, the producers' and/or directors' next steps will be to consult with your previous colleagues. And their first (and sometimes only) question will be, ninety-nine times out of a hundred: "How was he/she to work with?" Your talent and skills will have caught their attention, but they already know about those things from the reviews and photos and videos: what they really want to know at this point is *how well you work with other people.* And whether you can easily integrate yourself with the company they are assembling.

Absolutely no one is hired into a professional theatre or film company without this sort of one-on-one background check of their collaborative and cooperative abilities. And a negative assessment of these attributes – or even a tepid "well, I guess he's OK…" – will probably send them back to their long list of other applicants.

And the worst thing about failing to be rehired for this reason is that you will never know *why* the axe fell on you. Nobody will ever tell you that they didn't ask you back, or recommend you to a colleague, simply because they thought you were difficult to work with. You may spend the rest of your life wondering why, after all the good reviews and standing ovations you received, they never called you up for their next season or forwarded your name to another theatre. The reasons for such silence are both personal (no one wants to be considered a tight-ass) and legal (no one wants to be sued for "attitude discrimination"). You'll be left in the dark, wondering why your audition or portfolio didn't meet their standards and without ever realizing that *they* weren't the problem: *you* were.

In sum, your ability to collaborate effectively, willingly, enthusiastically, and unreservedly is nothing less than a career *requirement*. It is also the definition of what it means to be a "professional" in the performing arts.

But, you may say, "I don't have a collaborative instinct." Don't worry, no one does. As the Tony award-winning director/choreographer Twyla Tharp explains, "Collaborators aren't born, they're made…a day at a time, through practice, through attention, through discipline, through passion and commitment – and, most of all, through habit." That's one of the primary goals of this book, not only to provide you with collaborative skills, but also with the collaborative habit.

Does this mean, however, that great theatre art evolves solely from people who are always sweet-tempered, gracious, gentle, undemanding, and soft-spoken? Lord, no! Almost all great theatre artists are, at least at times, opinionated, strong-willed, and individualistic, sometimes aggressively so. Disagreements, criticisms, demands, disputes, challenges, arguments, and rebukes – all intensified with the inevitable stress of approaching deadlines and mounting fiscal pressures – are endemic to artistic work everywhere in the world.

And for this reason, the free collaborative spirit requires at least a general set of boundaries – and a focus toward collaborative *goals* as well as skills. And this can come only through some sort of leadership.

Leadership

Leadership is not contrary to collaboration. It is in fact crucial to it.

Leadership is what organizes the collaboration. It gives it focus, discipline, boundaries, and orientation. It combines ideas with goals, visions with imaginations. Leadership helps collaborators find common ground between varying ingredients of imagery, dramaturgy, intellectuality, philosophy, and social viewpoints. It also involves practical matters: setting targets, timetables, and budgets; cultivating good relationships and healthy attitudes; inspiring imagination, creativity, commitment and "going the extra mile."

Leadership does not reside solely in the top ranks of an organizational chart; it permeates collaborations at every level. It includes mentoring: the passing down of experience from a senior to a junior – and sometimes from a junior to a senior. It includes sharing, as with those personal experiences of individual members that may contribute to the deeper fabric and texture of a production. And it includes discipline, insuring that work is executed as well and as quickly as possible – and negotiating the proper balance between these two, often contradictory, goals.

Where does such leadership come from? You read in the introduction about the theatre company as "family," but notice you did not read that it is always a "happy family." Families are rarely if ever wholly harmonious. Rivalries, quarrels, and even violent separations are relatively commonplace, and so are the battles within a theatre: One can only imagine the turmoil in Molière's company when he spurned his wife to marry her younger sister at a time when all three were acting in the same productions!

Family theatres had family leadership, generally from a patriarch – father or father figure – who assumed the role of producer/director. In the Zoppé Family Circus, fathers handed down the leadership through seven generations. In the all-male *kabuki*, fathers introduce their fully costumed sons to kabuki audiences in a public ceremony when they are children; when they grow up, the sons assume their father's roles and eventually their stage names – yet they must still ask their father's permission to make even minor changes in the actions or gestures that their characters perform in their inherited roles.

And while there are no longer actual family theatres companies of note in Western theatre, there are "virtual family" companies of the current era that are based on similar principles. Members of the Living Theatre, which was founded in New York by husband and wife team Julian Beck and Judith Malina in 1947, continue to live together, eat together, perform together, and share their political agenda with audiences around the world today, with Malina continuing at the company's helm at time of writing. Another virtual "mama" is off-off-Broadway's doyenne, Ellen Stewart, whose "Café La Mama" (now the La MaMa Experimental Theatre Club), founded in 1961, remains an important avant-garde producing unit still under Stewart's leadership.

Without a true family, however, leadership cannot be simply inherited. Nor can it be simply "assigned." Yes, a director may be appointed, and a producer who funds the production must be listened to. But real leadership, though it may begin with an appointment or a bank account, must eventually be earned – and thereafter maintained.

For leadership is a quality, not a title. It is vision: the ideas, goals, and imagination that spur a production and guide it through to completion. It is integration: finding a common ground for the many different inputs of collaborators – intellectual, emotive, imagistic, philosophical, and dramaturgical. It is organization: setting targets, timetables, and budgets; cultivating relationships and healthy attitudes; inspiring imagination, discipline, and creativity. And it exists not solely within the topmost ranks of a theatrical hierarchy, but permeates and shapes collaborations across the entire spectrum of the theatre production team.

A summary: collaboration and leadership

In combination, and only in combination, collaboration and leadership are crucial to theatrical production. They are as two sides of the same coin: Collaborative energies blend dozens of diverse and idiosyncratic talents engaged in the arts of performance, and leadership aims this coalescence of artists toward their focused goal. At its best, effectively merging these seemingly opposite goals can produce performances that are seamlessly integrated and forcefully propelled, that develop maximum theatrical impact, and that you and everybody who sees them may remember for the rest of their lives.

However in order to create such mergers, theatre companies must create organizational structures that make them possible. And, this is the subject of the following chapter.

2

Ensemble and Hierarchy

Collaboration and leadership are two fundamental qualities of human interaction. In the theatre, these come in the forms of two types of organizational structure: the ensemble and the hierarchy.

Like collaboration and leadership, ensemble and hierarchy are also two sides of a coin. And while you can separate the two sides of an Oreo cookie and still eat each separately, should you slice a coin in two you would destroy its value, as neither side would be legal tender. And so, while it is customary to say that some theatre companies are "ensembles" and others are "hierarchical," the fact is that all theatres are a mixture of both – but mixtures with significantly varying percentages of each.

And so we will begin by discussing each separately.

Theatre ensembles

Were you to translate the title of this book into French, it would be *Travaillant Ensemble,* for *ensemble* is simply the French word meaning "together."

Yet in the world of theatre, *ensemble,* in both French and English, has come to have a more powerful meaning, connoting not merely a joint project but a familial relationship in which all members of a theatre-producing group interact not just professionally but also socially and emotionally. In this sense, ensemble is a long-term relationship; a day-in, day-out collaboration in shared living, thinking and creating.*

A dedication to such an ensemble can provide lifelong satisfaction to those individuals who accept it, and can also do much more: throughout the centuries, the ensemble model has led to the highest levels of theatrical art and creativity.

Successful ensembles

In the United States, Chicago's ensemble-based **Steppenwolf Theatre** is one of the country's leading regional theatres, having achieved and maintained extensive national and even international exposure. Founded (mainly by high school seniors) in 1974, it has since spawned a large number of internationally distinguished actors, including John Malkovich, Gary Sinese, Joan Allen, and John Mahoney, and productions that have traveled from the Chicago home base to Broadway and the West End. But among theatre practitioners it is equally celebrated for its lifelong commitment to "ensemble collaboration and artistic risk," and for its creation of what the company calls its "permanent ensemble" of actors, directors, designers, and playwrights who share the same theatrical goals and dreams.

Steppenwolf's multiple prize-winning *August: Osage County*, for example, was written by one company member (Tracy Letts), directed by another (Anna D. Shapiro), and, at its 2007 Chicago premiere, was performed by nine other members, including one of Steppenwolf's founders (Jeff Perry), and the playwright's father (Dennis Letts). When it went to New York later that year, with its company largely intact, it won the Tony, Pulitzer, Drama Desk, Drama League, and both New York and Outer Circle "Best Play" and/or "Best Production" awards, with *New York Times'* critic Charles Isherwood calling it "the most exciting new American play Broadway has seen in years," and attributing its success to Steppenwolf's commitment to its family-like ensemble, saying, in part:

> Great ensemble acting always adds up to more than the sum of
> its parts. It transports and transforms, and it illuminates the vital

---

*Do not confuse this use of the word ensemble with its use to refer merely to a group of actors ("the ensemble") playing the chorus, or multiple small roles, in a single production.

importance of collaboration in the complicated art of making theater. ... [Many of] the men and women playing the fractious Weston
family in "August" ... have worked together for years at Steppenwolf
in Chicago. ... They are already an artistic family. Knowledge of one
another's rhythms, styles and strengths is without a doubt among the
many factors infusing the production with a cohesion that is crucial
to its effectiveness .... The ferocious honesty of the acting keeps us in
tense thrall, convinced at every moment that beneath the boiling surface of the play lies painful truth.

Isherwood's remarks help to explain the astonishing power of successful collaboration in the theatrical arts, which makes the theatre
more than simply the sum of its many parts. And much of the world
had a chance to see Steppenwolf's success with this show, which went
to London in 2009, and toured the United States in 2010, in each venue
with most of its Steppenwolf cast and management team intact.

There have been other outstanding models of theatre ensembles,
founded not by literal families but by figurative ones: like-minded
individuals whose love of theatrical creation was more than desire
to build their individual careers. Some such ensembles date back to
the waning years of nineteenth-century Europe. In France, André
Antoine, a clerk in the Paris gas company, formed the *Théâtre Libre*
("free theatre") in 1887 with some of his fellow employees, creating, with his amateur ensemble, a new theatrical realism that capti-
vated audiences for a decade. In Germany, Otto Brahm's *Freie Bühne*
(also "free theatre") followed Antoine's model, as did J.T. Grein's
Independent Theatre Society in England. These ensembles were
essentially amateur theatres, outside the commercial theatre framework and playing mostly for subscribers only, but they revolutionized
the theatre of Europe and later America. One must remember that
the French word *amateur* comes from its original meaning, "lover,"
and should not merely be considered its now-degraded definition of
"nonprofessional."

It was Stanislavsky, however, who consciously brought the notion
of ensemble acting to the broader attention of Europe and America
in the twentieth century, creating, with his **Moscow Art Theatre**, an
expansive movement dedicated to the destruction of the star system
and the redevelopment of an ensemble ethic based on artistic rather
than pragmatic reasons. "There are no small parts, only small actors,"
Stanislavsky declared, famously, and he spent the rest of his life seeking an intense "communion" (his term, as translated by Elizabeth

Hapgood in *An Actor Prepares*) of artistic sharing within what became for decades Russia's greatest professional acting company – and one of that country's outstanding design and production venues as well.

Stanislavsky established the ensemble model for a long time to come. His planning and rehearsal process consisted of long, exploratory gatherings for each production, with members collectively experimenting with every scene and moment of the play as they tried out different interpretations, stagings, make-ups, costumes, bits of business, and acting styles. Nor was the ensemble limited to working together in the theatre building. Actors and designers would go into the regions and neighborhoods where their productions were set to deepen their appreciation of the play's milieu. They joined with their directors in researching the world of the play, and made every rehearsal an opportunity for discussion, debate, and experiment. Such rehearsals could go on for a year or more: for an adaptation of Dostoevsky's *The Village of Stepanchikovo*, Stanislavsky conducted 196 separate rehearsals – and then abandoned the production because he felt he had not been able to reach a satisfactory standard.

Other companies followed Stanislavsky's lead. Jacques Copeau's **Théâtre du Vieux-Colombier,** founded in Paris in 1913, began each season with a summer retreat in the country, returning to Paris for lengthy rehearsals – again lasting a year or more – as well as for classes, discussions, and company meetings. America's first great ensemble, the **Group Theatre**, was founded in New York in 1931, when Lee Strasberg, a devotee of Stanislavsky, and Harold Clurman, a disciple of Copeau, decided to create their own version of such ensembles.* Like its mentioned predecessors, the Group held retreats in the country where all company members would participate in classes and dramatic investigations, exercises and improvisations, following which the members would return to New York for a season of rehearsals and professional stage productions. The company's stage work, however, was interspersed with company meetings, where Group members – including actor/playwright Clifford Odets, actor/director Elia Kazan, designer Mordecai Gorelik, and future acting teachers Stella Adler, Morris Carnovsky, Sanford Meisner, and "Method Acting" guru Lee Strasberg – who went on to become the longtime leader of the Actors' Studio – would argue about, shout about, and vote upon virtually

---

*Producer Cheryl Crawford was a third co-founder.

every issue faced by their membership, from play selection to casting to artistic leadership. Such intense collaboration does not come easily, however. As Stella Adler, one of the Group's founders (and later Harold Clurman's wife), was to explain, "The actors of the Group had to be strong to survive the hardships involved. And there were those who survived and those who were destroyed."

Results achieved by the Group proved an early indication of the stunning results modern ensembles achieve. Arthur Miller, recalling their productions from when he was only a playwright-to-be, remembered mostly "the beauty of the Group Theatre's productions ... and the special kind of hush that surrounded the actors, who seemed both natural and surreal at the same time. To this day I can replay in memory certain scenes acted by Luther and Stella Adler, Elia Kazan, Bobby Lewis, Sanford Meisner, and the others.... When I recall them, time is stopped." It is surely no exaggeration to say that the Group Theatre revolutionized the American theatre in the same way that Antoine, Copeau and Stanislavsky revolutionized the European one.

The Group has its direct heir, perhaps, in the previously mentioned **Wooster Group**, named after the street in New York's SoHo district where they create and perform exciting theatre to this day. This newer "Group" emerged from scholar/director Richard Schechner's Performance Group of the late 1970s, and since then has been directed by its cofounding member, Elizabeth LeCompte. The distinguished stage and screen actor Willem Dafoe got his start there, and continues with the company, recalling that, "I was attracted to the Wooster Group when I saw these people [and] the way they made it work. It was a romantic way of life to me." And just how does the Wooster Group work? Its ensemble is broader than the Group's because it includes virtually everybody in the production process. "We all get in the room," Dafoe continues. "All the technicians. All the actors. The designer, the director, even to some degree, the administrators are all in that room.... They're there to serve the thrust of what's going on." An even larger level of collaboration has been the basis of the **Cornerstone Theatre,** founded by Bill Rauch and Alison Carey in 1986, which, though now based in Los Angeles, often merges its own company members with large numbers of local residents of cities, towns, and farming villages around the country, developing original productions – usually adapting classic plays to the political and social situations of their performance venues – and performing them in unique sites: an abandoned iron foundry in Pennsylvania, the basement of a city hall in West Virginia, a woman's prison in Northern California, and on an Indian reservation in Nevada, among many other like locales.

Theatres dedicated to ensemble have also continued to flourish in many government-funded national, state, and city theatres in Europe, where lifetime contracts (comparable to professorial tenure) for theatre artists have been maintained, permitting the maintenance of permanent theatre companies. The **Comédie Française** in Paris has already been mentioned, as it seeks to retain at least certain aspects of the classical style it has been showcasing for more than 300 years. The **Berliner Ensemble**, founded by Bertolt Brecht in 1953, continues to promote Brecht's unique "epic theatre" style in the German capital, and maintains many of its Stanislavsky-like, yearlong rehearsal rigors in presenting an increasingly expansive repertoire of plays. Jerzy Grotowski's **Theatre of Thirteen Rows,** founded in the tiny town of Opole, Poland in 1958, attracted a band of intensely committed collaborators and became globally famous when Grotowski's emotionally searing productions and "poor theatre" techniques were showcased at international festivals in the following decade, bringing his work and reputation to Europe, and soon after to Asia and the Americas. Russian Director Lev Dodin, Artistic Director of St. Petersburg's **Maly Drama Theatre** since 1982, tackles plays of profound social and political investigation, and oversees a large company – with 56 actors on year-round contracts – that he describes as "an ensemble" that has "a collective soul."

And two companies in Paris, with their founding directors each still at the helm at time of writing, have had remarkable success in creating sheer collaborative genius. The ***Théâtre du Soleil***, founded by Ariane Mnouchkine and some of her fellow theatre students in 1968, is collaborative to the extent of close social intimacy. Company members live, eat, and work together for years at a stretch. Their entire theatrical repertoire (both texts and productions) is created from lengthy investigations and improvisations involving all members of their large company of actors, designers, musicians, and technicians, along with Ms. Mnouchkine herself. In addition to directing, Mnouchkine performs a variety of duties. She is often at the front door taking tickets during the performance; when she is asked to do press or television interviews, she accepts only if other members on the production team are invited to accompany her, and are given equal exposure. The Soleil collaboration even involves the Soleil audience, who are often invited backstage to visit the actors at their makeup tables before the show, and onto the stage for cookies and soft drinks and a chat with the performers during the intermissions. Each company member at the Soleil, including Mnouchkine, receives the identical salary, and each participates in the production's technical work – some shifting scenery in one scene and acting in the next – as well as cooking the company meals and sharing the housekeeping chores. The intense collaboration has certainly paid stupendous rewards in this case: the *Soleil* is internationally renowned for its masterful and sublimely acted productions, both at its home theatre (the Cartoucherie, an abandoned munitions factory in the woods just outside Paris), and at major theatre festivals on all continents. Collaboration, Mme. Mnouchkine makes clear, can work wonders.

And Peter Brook's Paris-based **Center for International Performance,** which creatively adapts and produces literary classics from around the world (*Shakespeare's Sonnets,* the *Mahabharata, Carmen*), together with new plays – some company-created – developed in Africa, the Middle East, and other non-Western locations, is another company that believes deeply in ensemble, and has displayed its splendors worldwide since the 1970s. Brook has written extensively of his beliefs in creating plays in free-flowing mutual collaborations, generally with a semipermanent collective he has assembled from internationally known theatre artists:

> Sets, costumes, lighting and so on find their place naturally as soon as something real has come into existence in rehearsal. Only then can we tell what music, form and color need to enhance. If these elements are conceived too soon, if composer and designer have crystallized their ideas before the first rehearsal, then these forms impose themselves heavily on the actors and can easily smother their ever-so-fragile intuitions, as they feel for deeper patterns.

All of these ensembles – from the traveling vagabonds of the Middle Ages, to the sublime theatre companies of Shakespeare and Molière, to the modern European ensembles of Stanislavsky, Brecht, Grotowski, Brook and Mnouchkine, and the American ones like the Group, the Wooster Group, the Living Theatre, Steppenwolf, La Mama and Cornerstone – are creations of theatre artists dedicated to working fluidly and passionately *together,* and extracting the best artistic efforts from each other. Achieving their artistic goals year after year, and creating permanent identities in their communities over decades or even (in the cases of Molière and Stanislavsky) centuries, are the most profound achievements of theatrical ensembles.

And yet...

And yet virtually no plays are created in what could be considered a purely ensemble format. Collaboration includes, but is considerably more than, co-laboring and cooperating.

Cooperation – which we were all taught in elementary school – is a less intensive term, referring to occasions where a number of persons share tasks on a relatively equal basis. It seems the same but it isn't. Cooperation is what happens when everyone pitches in to set up the campsite or wash the dishes after Thanksgiving dinner. Such work sharing is a lovely social act, often an altruistic one, but as we will show later, it is quite unlike collaboration, which is a complex integration of specialized and creative activities. Collaboration requires organization.

This should be no surprise. Tap "Get organized" into a Google search box and you will get five million hits. "Getting organized" is one of the great urgencies of twenty-first century life. And organization requires at least a minimal level of *hierarchy*. Indeed, collaboration barely exists – and almost never flourishes – without some form of organizational hierarchy. Garry Hynes, the first woman to win Broadway's Tony Award for directing, began her career by creating, with a group of her school friends, the Dublin Theatre of Galway –the first professional theatre in Ireland outside of Dublin. How did she do it? "I think I had an instinct toward organizing, toward groups of people and the organization of them – I think that was the instinct initially," says Hynes. Making art means, to at least some extent, doing business; indeed, as Irving Berlin's immortal lyric reminds us, "there's no business like show business."

Hierarchies

If we know anything about organizations, it's that they have organizational charts. Generally, these are illustrated in pyramid form, with those persons of highest authority at the peak and those of lowest rank dispersed at the bottom. In the military world, such organizational pyramids read downward: the Generals on top, then the Majors, then the Lieutenants, then the Sergeants, Corporals and Privates in that order – with many sub-steps (e.g., Major General, Private First Class) in-between. In corporate pyramidal structures, CEOs are at the apex, while beneath them follow the CFOs and COOs, then the Vice-Presidents, the Directors, the Managers, the Heads, and finally the Workers. The corporate chart will also include, on horizontal lines that branch at every step, various Assistants, Associates, Adjuncts, Consultants, and bearers of other high-sounding titles that serve those to the left and right of them on the chart.

Such complex vertical charts illustrate standard hierarchies where, essentially, the people at the top direct those beneath them, and those at the bottom report to those above. However, these charts appear so forbiddingly authoritarian – even dictatorial – in theatre organizations, and seem so contrary to the notion of collaboration, that most companies shrink from making them public – or even writing them down on paper for internal consumption. Some refuse to even admit that such hierarchies exist.

But they do exist. As Willem Dafoe noted about the Wooster Group, in virtually the same breath as his comment cited in the previous chapter, "Everybody can participate, but the truth is there's a very strong central figure, and, like any group, a *natural hierarchy* starts to form." And that's why the first sentence on the Wooster's current website describes the company as "an ensemble of artists under the direction of Elizabeth LeCompte," which means that the ensemble is *under* a person who provides it *direction* – thus making clear that the relationship is vertical: with a director on top and an ensemble *under* her.

Hierarchical power structures – whether overt or covert, legally founded or emerging "naturally" from a group – are simply essential for any company's longevity, and that certainly includes theatre companies. And despite their very true commitments to collective decision-making, all the ensembles mentioned in the previous chapter have or had such structures. In fact, most were popularly – if not officially – known not so much by their actual names as by their leaders' names; for example, "Antoine's," "Brecht's," and "the Becks'." And while Mnouchkine's Soleil is perhaps the most deeply collaborative among today's active ensembles, it is often simply known as "Mnouchkine's," and Ms. Mnouchkine, indeed, is the only original member who has remained with the company to the present day.

The Steppenwolf Ensemble, while certainly living up to its self-description as "committed to ensemble collaboration," makes no effort to hide its administrative and artistic hierarchy which, on its website, lists, reading downward in order of importance, an Executive Artistic Board, an Artistic Director, an Executive Director, and then fifteen separate Directors (Finance, Operations, New Play Development, Special Events, Casting, Marketing, Development, Foundations and Government Relations, Corporate Relations, Special Events, Traffic, Marketing and Communications, Young Adults Program, and Technical), followed by nine Managers, then dozens of individual Assistants, Associates, Supervisors, Crew Chiefs, and Masters. This is a huge and highly structured organization; certainly a far cry from Gary Sinese and his high school buddies getting together in 1974 to mount a production in a church basement.

It turns out that while the creation of an ensemble usually begins with like-minded individuals eager to work together and share authority, such groups cannot continue beyond two or three productions purely through mutual good will, democratic decision-making, and mutual sacrifices. And the reasons for this will become clear in the balance of this chapter.

Specialization, oversight, supervision, and management

Why must theatres organize hierarchically? Why can't everyone simply share all the responsibilities together, or in alternation?

The answer begins with a need for *specialization*. Since individuals differ in skill levels (Jack paints better than Jill, Jill sings better than Joe), groups that aim for excellence quickly realize the need to maximize their members' unique abilities and minimize their flawed ones. And so they naturally arrange for the best painters to do the painting, the best singers to do the singing, and the best person to play Hamlet – with only secondary consideration (if any at all) as to what the individual company member personally *wants* to contribute to the production.

By so doing, they create a *division of labor* in which members' contributions depend more on their talents and skills than on their individual desires.

But such a division of labor at the horizontal level requires a division of authority on the vertical one: *somebody* has to make the decision as to how to *allot* the various duties – and thus assure that the labor is divided in a fashion that is complementary ("I wash, you dry") rather than duplicative ("I wash, you wash") – not to mention contradictory ("I wash, you soil"), or capricious ("I wash, you watch me").

And the person who makes these decisions will naturally assume an *oversight* role that spans both washers and driers – or, in the theatre, electricians and carpenters, cutters and drapers, actors and stage managers. And that somebody will also assume a higher position in what will become – through this very process – a hierarchical structure of authority.

Oversight, of course, means a "view from above," or a "super-view" or "super-vision" – that shortens to "supervision." Thus *supervisors* (literally "overseers") are created from the simple necessity of getting dishes washed and dried in a quick and orderly manner.

Is this inevitable? Yes it is. Even if all decision-making could be democratically decided by majority vote, with no one taking a supervisory role, *somebody* would have to organize the voting process, which at the least must include scheduling the meeting, creating the agenda, calling for nominations and votes, counting the ballots, announcing the results, and then implementing the decisions and evaluating whether those decisions were good or bad. So Dafoe's "strong central figure" arises, whether one likes it or not, and a hierarchy, if not already established by outside forces, emerges.

Supervision and oversight, in short, are necessary corollaries to the division of labor. Wherever there are a multiplicity of specialized workers, supervisory roles and their inherent higher authority will always emerge – at least if the group is to continue, and certainly if it is to thrive.

And in theatre, this division of labor is huge, since theatrical work contains dozens of individual craft specialties, such as acting, directing, lighting design, carpentry, fabric draping, sound design, projection design, fight choreography, and dozens of others as well, some yet unnamed.

And these specialties are indeed *special*. Each has its own well-crafted techniques and jargons, each develops common practices and ethics, and many have become independent trades with their own professional unions, guilds, societies, and associations. Supervisors – and all upper levels of theatre management – must oversee not only a spectrum of such specialized workers in separate areas, but a spectrum of their different trade union agreements as well.

And individual areas have their internal vertical hierarchies as well: differentiating among masters (e.g., master carpenter), journeymen (journeyman carpenter)* and apprentices, with the hierarchy insuring that those most experienced (the masters) oversee those less skilled and experienced (the journeymen and apprentices).

Hierarchies, indeed, provide the essential structures of *management,* which can be broken down into several horizontal areas: time management (the schedule), money management (the budget), facility management (the buildings and equipment) and personnel management (human resources). Theatre artists, to be sure, often recoil at such hierarchical terminologies, which are derived from the business world. Hollywood and Broadway actors frequently rail at the "suits," that is, the executives, who descend from their corporate headquarters to rule on budgets, schedules and even (to the actors' even greater horror) casting. And no theatre artist that I am aware of has ever taken the title of CEO. But, high-sounding artistic manifestos to the contrary, no long-term theatrical collaboration has been able to avoid creating such a hierarchy, either explicitly or implicitly. Apart from the theatre's amalgamation of individually specialized trades, its need for its artists to make a living, its need for its productions to open on time, its need for box office income and/or government, foundation or donor sourced funding – and usually its need for all of the above – creates a multiplicity of critical challenges that only skilled management can fulfill. Trying to meet any of these demands simply through a series of company meetings and majority votes would be disastrous: the company would simply fly apart from the centrifugal force of wild and whirling words.

So a focused and measured centripetal (i.e., pulling *toward* the center) force must be created to hold the artistic collaboration together and give it focus and efficiency. With circling planets, the centripetal force is the sun's gravity; for circling theatre artists, it is only the "strong central figure" who, when filtered down through a well-articulated hierarchy, provides a company's leadership and maintains its efficiency and focal point.

---

*The terms master and journeyman, though etymologically male, are used for women as well as men.

Thus the counter-balancing forces of hierarchy and ensemble, like those of gravity and escape velocity, keep the "theatrical planet" spinning in a steady orbit, neither exploding into space nor imploding into itself.

So just how does this happen in the theatre?

Hierarchies in the theatre: titles

While the professional theatre company has no CEO, the person at the top of its artistic hierarchy will usually hold the title of *Artistic Director* (*AD*), or there will be a somewhat shared top platform consisting of the AD, who will handle all artistic matters, and an *Executive Director* or *Executive Producer* to take care of the administrative ones. In a university theatre, the artistic and administrative matters may be handled by a single Dean or Department Chairperson, or may be shared between a number of campus officers or administrative/faculty/student committees.

But such titles can confer quite different levels of authority from one theatre environment to another, and the authority of any of so-titled individuals can be challenged. For the fact is that *no title is absolute*, and no assignation of authority is all-powerful. Titles, after all, are only words on paper, and these can be "assigned" only so far – as even "absolute rulers" such as King Charles I discovered on the scaffold, *le roi* Louis XVI at the guillotine, and Romanian dictator Nicolae Ceausescu as he faced the firing squad. Professional Artistic Directors are themselves subject to the approval of the Boards of Directors that oversee them, as well as subject to withdrawal of funding from foundations, donors and governmental agencies, and are finally subject to general acceptance of their work by the theatergoing public. Authority – which is a quality, not a title – may be granted, but such grants are always provisional. To be effective, authority must be earned and thereafter must be continually sustained.

Moreover, leadership in the theatre does not and cannot exist solely at the top of the hierarchy, but is in fact suffused throughout the organization. For, as we shall see, artistic directors inevitably delegate leadership roles to many persons: directors (play directors, musical directors, technical directors, fight directors), designers (scenic, costume, lighting, sound, projection, properties), and managers (production managers, stage managers, house managers, company managers, business managers). And these persons delegate leadership roles to many others, both officially, as with crew chiefs, dramaturgs, and master technicians, and unofficially to actors – particularly to those leading, distinguished and/or senior actors who are deeply respected by other members of the company for their talent, skill, and wisdom. Even collaborators on the same horizontal level may informally find the level tilting diagonally in places, as when a more experienced actor or carpenter mentors a more junior one. For although most theatre practitioners in our times have received formal training in schools, colleges, or conservatories, much of their hands-on training will still occur on the job, where they can perfect their skills under the eyes of experienced elders in their fields – as virtually all theatre artists were trained in the past.

And absolutely everyone within a production hierarchy will, for at least a moment or two, have an inherent leadership role when they become the sole master of their particular part of the performance. When Bernardo says "Who's there?" at the beginning of *Hamlet,* the actor playing that role is the person that everyone in the audience stares at and listens to; indeed, although there may be forty actors in the cast, the *entire production* hinges upon the player of Bernardo at that moment. And when the console operator executes the "fade to black" lighting cue, he or she *alone* concludes the play – for everyone on stage, off stage and in the audience. It is "just" a simple light cue, one might think, but for the board operator it is one of many crucial – and magic – moments where she holds the entire production, and everybody in it, in her hands.

In a larger sense, a large share of leadership in many theatrical productions – and even more in film and television work – is often shared not just by titled officers but rather by a company member who, because of his or her abilities or reputation or personal charisma, assumes a *de facto* level of leadership that is altogether "off the chart." Well-recognized stars and recurring cast members of long-running television shows, for example, often wield a more tangible leadership role during rehearsals than the show's director (who may be hired for a single episode) or even its executive producer does. And young actors may at times covertly seek the counsel not of the director but of a more experienced actor with whom they share the stage.

For these reasons, theatre hierarchies, and the modes of communicating within them, tend to be far more fluid and consensual than those in military or corporate enterprises. A general may simply order his troops, a CEO may brusquely mandate assignments to her underlings, but communication in today's theatre organization rarely means rigid commands from above or baleful acquiescence from below. Virtually all present-day producers and directors seek not merely to tell people under them what to do, but rather to animate, to induce, to aim, and above all to *empower* the artistic team they lead, with the theatre hierarchy running horizontally as much as vertically much of the time, and at times rising up instead of plunging down. Indeed, as the world has become more globally connected, and communications faster and broader – and in the world of weblogs, Facebook and Twitter, more unfiltered and democratic – boss and worker, teacher and student, professional and amateur speak with increasingly equal voices. In all the arts today, leadership tends to be more evocative than prescriptive, more inspirational than disciplinary.

Nor is climbing "up" a hierarchical ladder – usually the major career aspiration of military leaders and corporate executives – a major goal for the vast majority of theatre artists. For what does "up" mean in theatre? Few directors dream of climbing "up" to the role of producer; if anything, career moves between those two fields tend to go "down" with, for example, successful producers such as Hal Prince in theatre and Rob Cohen in film eagerly moving from the producer's office to the director's chair when they got the chance – on the grounds that it was more exciting to direct plays and films than to produce them. And few successful actors seek to move full-time into directing; for those that do, it may even seem a step "down" if what had drawn them to the theatre originally was the thrill of creating a performance on stage, rather than laboring to analyze a script or block a crowd scene.

Nor does climbing the theatre's hierarchical ladder produce the economic payoff familiar in the corporate world. Starring film actors receive far higher pay than do their directors or producers and, in most regional professional theatres, the disparity of incomes between the top and bottom of the ladder is nothing like its corporate counterpart: which in the theatre might be eight to one between the Artistic Director and the Assistant Stage Manager, vis-à-vis a thousand to one between the corporate CEO and the secretary in the global corporation.*

So while hierarchies and the authority they organize are as crucial in theatre as in other multi-worker activities, they are normally – and *necessarily* – less rigid, less dictatorial, less vertical, less formally structured, and less all-defining than almost any other sort of organization.

But they do exist, and indeed they coexist with the theatrical ensemble.

How does that work? It works because theatre is a very special art. Unlike most businesses, and even unlike most other arts, it is uniquely human.

So collaboration and leadership, and ensemble and hierarchy, are not really two sides of a coin, as I suggested earlier. They are two sides of the human animal. And you can't take them apart without killing the animal.

A human art

Theatre is an art that people make not out of canvas and paint, or marble or musical instruments, but out of themselves.

Theatre is made *by* people, *for* people, and is *about* people. And it engages its people in two-way *interactions* – both across the footlights with its audience and among those on and backstage themselves.

Moreover theatre is fundamentally *about* such interactions. Human interactions constitute both the *work* of the theatre and the *play* (the playing) of drama. For persons actively engaged in theatre, the process is both work and play; it is both working hard and playing hard.

And so the creation of theatrical art is a very special kind of activity, with some quite surprising characteristics. And each of these characteristics helps define how collaboration and leadership may best be pursued.

---

*Fewer than half of America's professional actors, for example, earn incomes above the national poverty line from their acting work in any given year. See my *Acting Professionally* (with James Calleri), seventh edition, Palgrave Macmillan 2009, for a complete analysis of actor incomes in the United States. Incomes for directors, designers, and other theatre artists are not noticeably different from these.

A numbers game

More people than you might expect are required to "put on" even the simplest of plays.

I am looking at the theatre program for Claudia Shear's autobiographical drama, *Blown Sideways through Life*. This is a one-woman show: a ninety-minute play with a single set and a single actor, written and performed by Ms. Shear, which premiered at the tiny Cherry Lane Theatre in New York's Greenwich Village, where I saw it several years ago. It made her famous.

But what always amazes persons unversed in theatrical practice is the number of individuals listed in Ms. Shear's program for this "one-woman" performance. There were, in addition to the one-woman (Ms. Shear) herself, eight producers, a director, four designers (set, costumes, lighting, and sound), a composer, a choreographer, a production stage manager, two general managers, three press representatives, a company manager, an assistant stage manager, an assistant director, an assistant to the general manager, a production manager, a technical director, two assistants to the producers, an assistant technical director, an assistant set designer, an assistant lighting designer, three painters, a production electrician, a production photographer, a legal counsel, an accountant, a comptroller, two management interns, the theatre's general manager, a house manager, a box office treasurer, an assistant treasurer, a house carpenter, six business firms (general management, insurance, advertising, banking, payroll service, press representation), and three production firms (scenery, lighting, and sound).

And, after all this, the program awards "special thanks" to fifteen additional persons and institutions.

So this little, off-Broadway, solo show required no less than seventy persons and nine firms – in addition to the sole author/performer – to make its way to the public. And that figure doesn't include the ushers, the ticket takers, the concession personnel, or the maintenance crew. The bottom line: It takes a village to raise a child and a hundred people to put up a one-woman show.

And if it takes a hundred people to mount a one-woman, one-set, one-act, off-Broadway show, what does it take to mount the Broadway *Phantom of the Opera*, or, for that matter, the Oregon Shakespearean Festival *Richard III*? We're talking *multiple* hundreds for these more ambitious theatrical enterprises.

And these are individual human beings, each with ideas and emotions, and each *connecting with the production* in both an intellectual and emotional way. And since the production may ultimately be thought of as a "success" or a "failure," each will also be linked forever with the success or failure each believes he or she will have in part created.

Persons who are versed in practical theatre, of course, will find nothing unusual about this. Putting on a play is never a solo activity: it always involves lots of people doing lots of things, and a lot of people deeply caring about how these things "come across" to those others who make the effort to come and see it. And the theatre involves the close *collaboration* of these persons, since what they do must come out in relative harmony. Moreover, they execute many of their tasks in a precise order of progression: For example, the lighting crew cannot focus the lights until the scenery is in place but the scenic crew cannot install the scenery until the lighting instruments have been hung. Similarly, the actors can't rehearse on stage while the scenery is being installed, or when the lights are being hung, or while the audio technicians are establishing sound levels, or while the painted floor is drying.

Multiply these examples with the dozens of units and scores of individuals that must have access to stage time, actor time, director time, and anybody else's time; and you can understand why management and precise scheduling are absolutely crucial to this "creative art" we call theatre.

Of course all major enterprises involve large numbers of individuals doing many things in some sort of organized manner. Running a restaurant, mounting a military invasion, arranging a wedding, putting out a magazine, building a rocket ship: all of these activities involve dozens, hundreds, or even tens of thousands of people working together. And all such enterprises demand organization, management, and good collaborative skills for all involved. There's nothing very special about that.

What makes *theatre* collaborations so special – and there is no doubt that they *are* – is the compilation of seven individual factors:

- the *diversity* of the theatre's skills
- the *creativity* inherent in art
- the *fictive* world of drama
- the *emotional* world of theatre
- the *terror* of personal exposure

- the *seduction* of celebrity
- the *inviolability* of the performance schedule

These factors – particularly in combination – bring with them unique demands. Their extraordinary nature requires that collaboration in the theatrical arts be far different than it is in the army, the restaurant, the factory, or the corporate boardroom.

Let's look at them individually.

The **diversity** of the theatre's skills

Few if any fields of endeavor employ such a broad array of talented individuals as does the theatre. Even in Ms. Shear's one-woman stage piece we see specialists in the general areas of stage, costume, lighting and sound design, acting, directing, creative writing, stage management, choreography, painting, musical composition, structural engineering, acoustics, photography, electronics, human resource management, law, finance, accounting, and public relations. These are all high-level professional arts or skills – major universities give advanced degrees in every one of them – and yet they must be integrated into a single work.

There are also highly sophisticated technical crafts involved: computer programming, mechanical engineering, carpentry, electronics, fabric cutting, fabric draping – as well as some relatively unsophisticated tasks – floor-sweeping, clothes washing, and toilet-scrubbing, to name a few. These must work in complete concert as well.

And productions larger than Ms. Shear's may involve additional workers; for example, conductors, projection designers, instrumentalists, casting directors, lyricists, orchestrators, musical directors, hair and wig designers, dressers, dance captains, company managers, understudies, property masters, winch operators, fight directors, prompters, sound mixers, wardrobe supervisors, dramaturgs, research advisors, speech and dialect coaches, acting coaches, singing coaches, and script assistants. Film and video productions start with these folks and add yet others: camerapersons, continuity persons, set dressers, editors, sound boom operators, cable grips, location scouts, caterers, web designers, and many new positions created alongside each new technological advance.

Few human activities require the integration the work of such a varied spectrum of trained, professional workers toward a *single product* (normally a play production or a film), and rarer, outside the theatre or film worlds, is the sole supervisor that must oversee such a broad range of highly specialized yet necessarily intertwining arts and crafts.

The **creativity** of the artist

In most large-scale group enterprises, such diverse groups of specialists are organized – often rigidly – into efficiently disciplined hierarchies. We've already mentioned the military operation that, for example, must integrate the work of pilots and foot-soldiers, gunners and cooks, medics and engineers, strategists and supply officers, by creating a vertically arranged command and control structure, with the command coming from on high (the commander-in-chief), and the control exemplified by rote-drilled "grunts" at the very bottom.

But as effective as military, factory, and corporate models might prove in air strikes or auto manufacturing, they inevitably fail when applied wholesale to theatrical situations. Why? Because such organizations need not coalesce the creative imaginations of artists. Many a business executive, having bought into a film company or joined the Board of Directors of a regional theatre, has learned this lesson the hard way. This is not, of course, because artists are holier than foot-soldiers, assembly line mechanics, magazine editors, or wedding consultants. Nor are they divas whose every whim and worry must be entertained; nor does the term "creative artist" elevate actors, designers, stage technicians, or (least of all) directors to planes that are above the rules of law, or codes of ethics, or demands of moral responsibility. Theatre artists are subject to as many legal, moral, social, and (if they are unionized) professional codes as are marines, accountants, plumbers, and construction engineers.

But artists are hired not just for their practical skills but also for their *imaginations*. Any actor who plays Hedda or Hamlet, as well as any designer, director or technician who makes a contribution to that character's environment, makes a *creative* investment into such a project. And imagination – which springs at least partly from unconscious resources – is both personal and ephemeral. It cannot simply be commanded via hierarchical authority. Nor can it be schematically organized on a corporate flowchart. All experienced theatre producers know this.

And so there is a limit to the way in which creativity and imagination may be shaped by a command and control administration, or along the models of the corporate ladder or assembly line.

Discipline may be ordered, to be sure, but the deepest levels of artistic achievement can only be *evoked* – and in large part that evocation must come from within *the artist's own creativity*, comprising his or her wildest imagination, deepest aesthetic sensibility, and wellspring of artistic passion. No theatre veteran would doubt this.

The **fictive** world of theatre

While it has one foot planted firmly in the real world, the theatre's other foot is equally ensconced in the worlds of fiction and fantasy. And, if anything, the theatre's fictive world is the dominant one.

There may have been a real Hamlet, a King Oedipus, a Lady Macbeth – and there certainly *was* a real Anne Frank, a Roy Cohn, a Richard Nixon – yet the world of theatre is fundamentally fictive, in which actors dress and behave other than as they normally do in their "real" lives, or even as did the "real" persons they in part represent. Actors appear onstage not as themselves, but as part of larger dramatic and aesthetic patterns contrived, at least in part, by others, including playwrights, directors, and designers. And this contrivance has as its goal the creation of a major theatrical impact – measured (in the best instances) in terms of its life-defining conflict, transcendent romance, side-splitting comedy, inspiring heroism, soaring poetry, ennobling despair, or whatever artistic splendors its creators can generate through their collective creative imaginations.

The stage, therefore, is the home of evil and saintliness, adventurism and miracles, epochal romance and murderous revenge. It's where Medea murders her babies, Othello his wife, and Romeo and Juliet commit double suicide – and also where Peter Pan flies, Franklin Delano Roosevelt walks, Helen Keller speaks, Hermione lives, Prior Walter ascends to heaven, and Macbeth's witches vanish into thin air. It is part tragedy, part glory, and part fantasy – sometimes all together.

The disparity between these fictions and the far grittier world of theatre *work*, however, is the source of much difficulty, for the fantasy, romance, and magic of the stage, and the heroic struggles of its dramatic characters, inevitably bleed into the real lives of those charged with recreating this fictive experience. The late nineteenth/ early twentieth century director/teacher Konstantin Stanislavsky said that the actor must "live the life of his character on stage," but the fact is that actors have *always* lived the lives of their characters on stage. A Greek actor named Aesop was so overwrought in playing the role of Orestes, Plutarch tells us, that he ran his sword through a stagehand, killing the poor fellow. The American actor John Wilkes Booth was so swept up in the fantasy of *Julius Caesar* in which he had recently played Mark Antony that he went into Ford's Theater and assassinated President Lincoln in his box seat. Theatre history is indeed replete with tales of actors playing lovers replicating these roles in real-life, so much so that eighteenth-century French commentator Pierre Rémond de Sainte-Albine wrote, in his 1747 *Le Comédien,* "love scenes are never represented so vividly as when the actor and actress...are really in love with each other." The gossip columns of current American film stars show us how Sainte-Albine was writing not only for his time but also for the ages.

But an equal problem for the actor is not living the character's life onstage but letting go of it *off* stage. For once you put on the sword of Henry V, or rise to heaven as you're burned at the stake as St. Joan, it may not be so easy to soundlessly defer to the apprentice costumer who is lacing you into what you at first think are too-high-heeled shoes or a too-tight corset.

For, dramatic *characters* are rarely nice. More often they are cruel, threatening, ferocious, imbecilic, or wacko. Or they're seductive, teasing, sultry, mysterious, or mesmerizing. Often they even assume iconic or supernatural stature; sometimes they rise from the dead, other times they throw thunderbolts from heaven. *Charisma*, not politeness, distinguishes great stage characters – "sacred monsters" (*monstres sacrées*) the French call them – characters who excite us, scare us, awe us, and tempt us. This charisma cannot simply be acquired – much less projected – simply by "doing what you're told." It's almost the opposite.

And yet, while great dramatic characters exude charisma as they live their fictive lives in stylized worlds, the actors that play them, and those who work with them on the stage, must settle into the more mundane tasks of collaborative labor. Is there a discontinuity here? No – but only when we understand and master the skills of collaboration.

The **emotional** world of theatre

A play's characters don't just behave. They *feel*. And while almost all dramatic characters can (and should) be seen to have emotional responses to the actions they engage in, the principal dramatic characters of every play must be seen to *convincingly* experience intense emotions: love, grief, worship, suffering, exaltation, and the like – and to do so night after night. Indeed, the world's major dramatic characters (Hamlet, Hedda, Blanche, Willy, Prior Walter) are almost always portrayed at the highest moments of crisis they will experience in their entire lifetimes. And so they cry real tears, tense real muscles, brighten into extravagant grins, and, in at least one case, blush bright red on a precise cue.* At the deepest level, these "behaviors" cannot simply be faked. The best actors – and this has been remarked upon since the time of Plato – experience true epiphanies of feeling, which may lead to profound emotion in the audience as well.**

And it is virtually axiomatic – although there are occasional arguments to the contrary – that actors really *do* feel the emotions of their characters. The maxim of Horace, more than two thousand years ago, is that "in order to move the audience, you must first be moved yourself." Stanislavsky was only the most famous of the thousands of actors and teachers and directors who have repeated this maxim during the past two millennia.

Emotion runs high in other professional fields as well, of course. Sports, law, medicine, business, and the military are every bit as emotional as are the theatre arts – and sometimes more. But theatrical emotion is based on fiction, not fact. Marines raising the flag at Iwo Jima may have performed a symbolic (and therefore theatrical) act, but they faced real bullets when they did it. Their weighty feelings had little in common with the actor's preparation for the emotions of

---

*In 1974, I saw the great Hume Cronyn play the role of an aging writer in Noel Coward's *A Song at Twilight*. The role called for him to silently read a love letter he had received in his youth and – alone on stage at the end of the play – break into a crimson flush, conveying the play's crucial revelation and its climax. Cronyn's blush could be seen in the back row. In an interview, Cronyn swore that he had used no "technique" to create this effect, but merely experienced the emotion of the character.

**See my "Be Your Tears Wet: Tears (And Acting) in Shakespeare," *Journal of Dramatic Theory and Criticism*, Winter, 1996.

his or her role, which takes place in an only-imagined environment. And theatrical emotionality is often the *goal* of performed theatre, not merely a consequence or by-product. The emotions of the operating room stem solely from the urgency of the surgery; they are not part of the aesthetics of medicine.

But how do emotions come freely into play in theatrical performance, yet still get turned off safely when the performance is done? How can the onstage crying, screaming, and clawing come to a sudden close when the actor heads into the wings? How does a performer avoid overidentification with his or her roles, and with the emotional overwhelm that may follow? These questions, like those in earlier passages in this section, point to the special problems and special nature of theatre – and of theatrical collaboration.

The **exposure** of the theatre artist

Few persons are so exposed as are performers. As dancer/director/ choreographer Bill T. Jones colorfully explains, "A performer secretly believes there is nothing worth doing other than performing... standing in a glorious arena, a circle of transformation, a black void with artificial sunrises, sunsets, tiny vortices of light, screaming shafts of illumination striking [him].... A world wherein he's completely exposed." But with that exposure comes a price. After the performance, Jones writes, "the performer knows waiting. The waiting for well-wishers, friends, sponsors. Waiting with anticipation when one feels good about the evening, dreading a look of disappointment or an avoided glance when the evening did not go well.... Poor performer. He or she will never be satisfied."

For along with the plaudits comes the inevitable specter of ridicule – both in terms of the artist's professional skill and his or her personal life. After all, theatre artists, and particularly actors, are far more visible publicly than your average, law-abiding doctor, lawyer, or plumber. And sometimes the ridicule that accompanies the job can get pretty raw. Although booing, hissing, and throwing spoiled fruit may be rare today, published criticism can be devastating. How would you like your work to be called, in a daily newspaper read by tens or hundreds of thousands of people in your community, "mediocre, banal, and pathetic," a phrase I picked up from a play review in this morning's newspaper? Or to read remarks about your physical decrepitude, boring personality, lack of talent, or obnoxious voice in the postings of a weblog that will be read around the world, and be highlighted in Google searches of your name for, perhaps, the next decade or two? Yet actors, playwrights, directors and (though to a lesser extent) designers and technicians face this possibility every time they encounter a review of their work. How would you like to hear a critic reporting, on a national network television program, that while watching your performance as Cleopatra you "occupied the spare time in several of her speeches by counting her teeth." The actress who may have happened upon that review of herself on YouTube is a longtime Royal Shakespeare Company star.

We live in increasingly skeptical and iconoclastic times, where the public delights in scandals and personal attacks, and a hyperactive press corps, abetted by shock journalists, radio talk shows, TV evangelists and public officials thrive on bringing down the (presumably) mighty.

This vulnerability is intensified for actors, who appear before the public, no matter how costumed or made-up, essentially as themselves. An actor is utterly defenseless against the acidic drama critic who assaults his or her body, face, voice, skills, and even intelligence. Nor can actors easily redeem themselves from such assaults, as it's probable, at least for stage actors, that more people will read the review than see their performance. And actors, directors, and playwrights who become celebrities have even more to deal with: the dreaded hordes of paparazzi who follow them to the doors of their homes, or cars, or even into public rest rooms to get the lowdown on their divorces, miscarriages, weight gains, and private sorrows. It's no wonder that when you type the two words "paparazzi" and "violence" into Google's search engine, you get two million hits.

Such regular, detailed, personal, and public exposure to harsh criticism is a peculiarity of all artists, but legendary in theatre and film. Author/actress Diana Rigg once wrote a best-selling book, *No Turn Unstoned,* that compiled a horrifyingly amusing collection of such insulting critiques. One of Rigg's most painful examples, regarding an actress who played six different roles in a production and read, about herself, that "she cannot change her face, which is that of a worried hamster." How would you survive this attack? How would you escape the psychological timidity of fearing future attacks from the same critic – or others trying to emulate him?

Fear of personal exposure – as opposed to a fear of the entire show going down in a sea of bad press – often leads to a self-protective attitude that can seriously weigh down any spirit of free-flowing artistic collaboration and creativity that the theatre artist has developed up to this point.

The seduction of **celebrity**

On the other side of humiliation, though, is the equal curse of over-adulation. Some think that the attractiveness of the one compensates for the despair of the other, but the seduction of praise carries its own dangers, which may be even worse than the fear of derision.

Theatre artists – particularly actors, directors, prima ballerinas, and opera singers – are especially vulnerable to the lure of celebrity and its attractions. Indeed, though few of us admit it, that's one of the reasons why many of us want to be artists: to become a "star" shining resplendently above the madding crowd. (OK, so this isn't you. It's just the person next to you.)

Yet, as Cassius says, "the fault, dear Brutus, is not in our stars, but in ourselves, that we are underlings."

Let's face it: we (I the author and you the reader) are underlings. And yet the stars are in our eyes – and often in our fantasies – or I wouldn't be writing and you wouldn't be reading these pages.

And why shouldn't actors and directors and designers have their heads in the stars from time to time – particularly knowing there's always the possibility of walking up to the Academy Award stage to seize your statuette and praise your friends and family in front of a global audience?

The life of a theatrical artist is difficult enough to sustain without at least some light at the end of our tunnel – and it had better be a brilliant light if it will draw us through the necessary years of struggle that artistic careers customarily require. That light is the roar of the greasepaint and the smell of the crowd; it's the standing ovation, the glowing review, the Tony; it's the legendary salaries, exotic travel, fans and groupies, public admiration, and, maybe, even aspirations toward the highest political positions in the nation as have, in past decades, become demonstrably within reach. A certain amount of fantasy is probably necessary to maintain at least a tiny connector line between obscurity and celebrity, between the unemployment line and the post-Oscar celebration.

So the task is to heed the wisdom of the old pop song: "Don't let the stars get in your eyes; don't let the moon break your heart!"

For the fantasy to be a star can lead into the temptation to *act* the star. This is what used to be called, with a judiciously raised eyebrow, "artistic temperament." As in "she's very temperamental." As in, "I'll never work with *her* again."

Today the word "temperament" has gone into disfavor: the equally discreet jargon now is "attitude." But by any name (and "diva" or "prima-donna" remain current as well), it is tantamount to an early artistic demise.

And, of course, it's based entirely on a misconception. For true stars rarely if ever behave in the cavalier, flamboyant ways we usually see in gossip magazines, TV talk shows, or movies about "theatrical folk." Showing up late, showing up drunk, staging tantrums in the dressing room, publicly trashing one's costars and colleagues: these are almost always publicity fictions, many derived from 1940s movies about Hollywood.

On the contrary, the vast majority of theatre and performing artists – from headliners on down and in all media – show up on time (or ahead of time). They are sober, they are polite, they are professional, they are prepared, they are generous with praise to their coworkers, and they are pleasant to be with in virtually all public situations – or they are fired.

There are exceptions, of course, but there can be no question about this single fact: *No one has ever been hired by a present-day theatre company because they were temperamental.* No one has been hired because they threw a big scene in their last show, or because they carried on like Norma Desmond in *Sunset Boulevard*. Even if they are *playing* Norma Desmond, they will rehearse like Glenn Close; which is to say they will be the "four Ps": professional, prepared, polite, and pleasant (as well as brilliant).

The lure of celebrity, and its dangerous consequence of "attitude," is often the gravest threat to theatrical collaboration, because even more than the fear of ridicule it tends to isolate the artist from the artistic project and from the other artists in the project. Many angels – but only one human – can stand on the head of a pin, or on a pinnacle, and a collaborative human enterprise needs more than a pinnacle on which to stand. It needs ample shared space where people can work together – which is, of course, the subject of this book.

*The **inviolability** of the performance schedule*

It is ten minutes before curtain time for *Hamlet* and hundreds of people are taking their seats in the house, while three or four dozen more – actors, technicians, and stage managers – are in the dressing rooms and backstage, preparing for the show to begin. But wait! The actor playing Francisco is nowhere to be found! He only has eight lines in the entire play, but they all come in the opening moments, and without a Francisco, the show cannot start! And no understudy has been called to take the role!

It is not merely a theatre cliché that "the show must go on"; it is a necessity. In this day of baseball strikes, union slow-downs, pilot sick-ins, and factory lockouts, the classic show-biz motto prevails, and prevails absolutely. There's just too much at stake: the substantial loss of box office revenue, the alienation of the theatre company's subscribers, and the demoralization of the entire cast and crew who do show up, ready to go.

So while planes are late, plumbers get the flu, professors forget appointments, and psychiatrists go on vacation, the show will – indeed must – start on time: "running late" (a despised contemporary phrase in theatrical circles) is simply not in the vocabulary of professional performing artists. And persons new to the profession – last year's drama student who had had no problem in his college classes getting "extensions" for a late paper or scene presentation – may find himself out on the street for trying to carry this laxity into his post-graduate life.

Let's rub this in a bit with some actual facts. Broadway productions rent their (very expensive) theatres months in advance, and hire their artists – actors, designers, and technicians – on union-negotiated contracts. Delaying a Broadway opening, even for a single night, will cost the producer well into the six figures. Not-for-profit theatres depend on a base of loyal subscribers, who may be quick to cancel their subscriptions when their long-scheduled night on the town finds them turned away at the theatre door. Film and video productions are even more time-intensive than live theatre, for the basic studio charge – including cast and crew – can run into tens of thousands of dollars per *minute,* and the actor who calls in sick at the last moment can cost the production millions – and make headlines in the trade papers. TV episodes, therefore, wrap on Friday or heads roll, and film directors that can't bring their picture in on time become

Hollywood's lepers – and sometimes the subject of books they're not going to want to read (see Steven Bach's *Final Cut*).

So while theatre abjures many of the time-sequenced efficiencies of the factory assembly line, which have been endlessly parodied by plays such as *The Adding Machine, Morn to Midnight* and *The Pajama Game*, the performing arts are at least as clock-driven as are industrial corporations.

Creative imagination must, in the professional theatre, evolve within an efficiency-dominated schedule – which makes theatrical collaboration all the more necessary and intense. Problems that must be solved must be solved quickly; conflicts requiring resolution must be resolved immediately. In the onrushing American production calendar, there is little opportunity to defer these sorts of difficulties until tomorrow, much less until next week. Working relationships, which in a more leisurely business could be established delicately must, in the heat of rehearsals and performances, be forged speedily. For missed communications, unproductive arguments and ego-driven indulgences are not only annoying but also forbiddingly expensive. And to their perpetrators, they're professionally disastrous.

The symbiosis of the human art

So how do we weld the democratic and improvisatory nature of the artistic ensemble with the orderliness and focus of the theatrical hierarchy?

It is probably not coincidental that humans are born bilaterally symmetrical: two legs, two arms, two breasts, two eyes, and two ears. We are two-half bodies that combine to make far more than the sum of their parts. It's the same thing above the neck: our right brain (logical, objective) pairs with our left brain (intuitive, subjective). Neither half-brain alone, no matter how brilliant, can match the power of both in their symbiotic combination.

If we were to think, mathematically, of ensemble-based and hierarchical organizational systems as the ends of a continuum of structures, that wouldn't mean, in theatre, that the "ideal" fulcrum point would be precisely in the middle. For some productions, such as Mnouchkine's year-long projects mounted by a huge, semipermanent company with an open-ended opening date, the organizational structure clearly would favor the ensemble side. But for a professional regional theatre production with a three-week rehearsal period, a supertight budget, and a highly paid unionized cast and staff not used to working together, the hierarchy will be working overtime from play selection to closing night. And there is no question that most European theatres, particularly those that are nationally or municipally subsidized (such as the Berliner Ensemble, *Comédie Française*, Helsinki City Theatre, Romanian and Hungarian National Theatres), the ensemble format has, at least potentially, more room (and time) to operate, while in the American professional theatre, where plays are mainly staged as single productions with most if not all artists hired individually, the oversight of a hierarchy will be more essential.

But numerical percentages are of no real use here, for the only thing to consider is that *both ensemble and hierarchy must be in full play* – or there will be no play.

But that leads to a final question, often asked in drama schools: Should the creation of theatre be focused on process or on product? This, however, is in fact a surprisingly false issue, and can be dealt with quickly.

Process and product

It is true that process and product are often thought of in contradictory terms, with the notion that a process-oriented artist is a different sort of person than a product-oriented (or result-oriented) one. This is faulty thinking, however, since *nothing is a process unless it is aimed at creating a product.* "Process" is not merely "doing things." It is, as Webster's Third International Dictionary indicates in its first meaning, "a progressive *forward movement* from one point to another on the way to *completion.*" *Process* is at the root of "procession" which is a march *toward* something (as opposed to "recession," which is a march away from something). It is not aimless action – any more than a procession is aimless wandering.

What turns aimless wandering into a procession? Direction. What turns aimless action into a process? Leadership. How is leadership applied? By authority and inspiration.

It is misleading, therefore, to make moral distinctions between theatre artists who are "process-oriented" and those who are "result-oriented," because *all* theatre artists must be productive in – and understand the importance of – both areas. Any process, in order to progress, must have an aim, a direction, a goal. These need not be fixed from day one, of course. Most typically they begin as fuzzy thoughts that – after many stops and starts and about-faces – come into focus as the process proceeds. But that there *are* goals to be reached at the climax of the effort is essential to turn what may begin as a warm-up exercise to conclude as a true artistic achievement (from the French word *achever,* "to finish").

Process and product, collaboration and leadership, and ensemble and hierarchy are thus intrinsically and inescapably linked. No production can possibly succeed without some measure of both. Collaboration is the *horizontal* glue that holds an ensemble together and makes the work collective, mutually supportive, and the composite of many minds, bodies, and imaginations. Leadership is the *vertical* glue that gives the ensemble a direction, a focus, a goal, and a set of deadlines. The effective combination of the two can produce wonders; an overreliance on a single one can spell disaster.

And this all leads to what must be the theatre's first rule.

Rule Number One

Rule Number One for a *professional* theatre artist is that *your success is determined by the production's success – not the other way around.*

This is far from obvious to most theatre students, which is why I choose to call it Rule Number One, and place it before the specific discussions that begin in the next chapter.

Students come to their schools – from kindergarten to graduate school – as individuals. They are usually accepted by admission officers they will never meet again, and are then lumped in with other students most of whom they have never seen before.

And from the time they begin to be graded in elementary school, they realize that they are in *competition* with each of these other students: for respect, for attention, and for grades. To get a "B" means they have to be, at least in theory, "above average," which means "better than most other students," while to get an "A" means to be "outstanding" – or "standing out" from all the others. And if your instructors "grade on a curve," this maxim is no longer just a theory but a mathematical fact: your grade will go down precisely in inverse proportion to how much your classmates' grades go up – and vice versa.

So no matter how often you tell yourself "just do the best you can," and as much as your teachers and parents may impress upon you the need to share, to cooperate, and to work constructively with your fellow classmates, you know in your gut that if you want to succeed (in your grades, in your career, even in your love life), you must be *better* than most of them. You must do what you can to "stand out" from the pack in whatever way you can. And almost everybody in your school tries to do precisely this.

Obviously this system, which you have been living with for sixteen years by the time you graduate from college, does not exactly encourage collaboration, even if the teachers urge such upon you. And this competition for approval, grades and other advantages often affects, or perhaps even *in*fects, most beginning students in theatre.

Moreover, if you are planning for a professional theatrical career you will soon realize that you *must* stand out from the others – not just in your class, but also against students throughout the country. For the fact is – as you will soon realize if you haven't already – that the vast majority of career theatre professionals (and not just theatre wannabes) are *unable to make a living from their artistic work* in any given year. So you're going to have to be very, very, *very* good to make a living as a theatre artist – probably throughout your entire career.

If that weren't enough, you're surely aware that high school and college age students are smack at the point of finding, and creating, their individual adult identities – social, sexual, intellectual, and occupational – and that the competition in these fields can be even more ferocious, leading in some cases to bullying, gang warfare, binge drinking, school shoot-ups, and suicides. One hopes this rampantly competitive individualism doesn't play out too much in the high school or college drama production, but the fact is that most beginning theatre students first get involved in stage work not to subsume themselves in a sublime collective effort as much as to show off how great, brilliant, sexy, and talented they are.

Yet it's also a fact, which may surprise you, that a sustained career success in the professional theatre or film arts is almost always centered on an artist's *collective* rather than his or her individual achievements. For while there will always be great individual performances in mediocre shows, and stunning sets or costumes or sound scores in forgettable films or stage productions, the most *powerful single step for a career stage or screen artist* to make is to be a part of a truly great *production*.

Why? Because such a production will be seen more, admired more, and remembered more than any individual's single contribution to a poorly received production. A hit show that runs on Broadway or the West End for a year will be seen by nearly half a million people – including most of the producers, directors, casting directors, and art directors in and passing through New York or London. A hit film will similarly attract the attention of every producer and director in Hollywood, and a hit TV show will run for years, and perhaps go into syndication for the rest of the lifetimes of the artists who made it.

And why is this important? Because in professional theatre, film or television, your acting or design or directing in any project is also your audition or portfolio review *for the next one.* And if only a few people come to see your project – and your performance or your design or direction – you haven't just failed your audition or portfolio review – *you will never have had the opportunity to get one.*

For the fact is that having your name attached to even one such successful project *is, by far, the best single thing that can propel your artistic career forward.* Just having the *title* of such a project on your resume is an automatic eye-stopper for the person looking you over for some future job. It's the *great show you were part of* that becomes the true icebreaker for your first conversation with a producer or director or casting director who is looking over your materials. And this is why this is Rule Number One. For who will actually recall – or even be aware of – your great costume design for a show that closed during its first week, or your terrific performance as the star of a show that got otherwise terrible reviews?

Austin Pendleton, a very accomplished stage and film actor/director/playwright is still widely remembered in the entertainment industries as the "kid" who played the supporting role of Motel the Tailor in the 1964 Broadway premiere of *Fiddler on the Roof.* Yes, Pendleton was terrific in the role, but it was also a *great show* and everybody in New York came to see it, and then left singing "Wonder of Wonder, Miracle of Miracles" in Pendleton's nasal voice. If he had played the starring role in *A Girl Could Get Lucky,* which opened two nights earlier and ran only eight performances, Mr. Pendleton might still be waiting for his second Broadway role.

So it's essential that, while you may have hunkered down and concentrated on your own personal work on a school production, you must concentrate all your energy *on the whole project* in a preprofessional or professional one.

You must give yourself totally to that project, and live and die for it to succeed as a complete entity – and that every other person connected with it succeed as well – not just satisfactorily but *magnificently*. Only then will you have built up your resume in a way that can really propel you forward.

In one sentence then: If you want to be a success, it is absolutely necessary that *everybody working with you be a success as well*. Amateur theatre is often rife with backbiting, upstaging, catty remarks, second-guessing and the like. High school and college drama can be full of these things just as well. Just remember with such cases: *that's why they're amateur*. The pros know that this is career death. Great collaboration techniques are essential, not just to help you become liked by your colleagues (although that is certainly a very agreeable by-product), but also because it is vital for the establishment and furthering of your career. Of your *individual* career – and also the future of any project you undertake, and the ensemble of like-minded artists you can gather around you.

The word "techniques" is carefully chosen here, because being a great collaborator does not come naturally. It's not only high school and college students who are fiercely competitive but also most animals are: Just watch a litter of piglets fighting for their place at the sow's teat. We must be *trained* to be socialized – to "do unto others" and to recognize that a rising tide lifts all boats. But in an environment where just one person will get the year's Tony Award, or just six actors will come up with $25 million star contracts, it is often difficult to keep that socialization in mind.

Collaboration "technique," after all, is often nothing but a learned manner of maximizing *everybody's* contribution *to* a theatrical project in order to maximize everyone's individual benefit *from* the project. It is not simply an instruction to "be nice" (this book is called *Working Together* not "Making Friends") nor is it about "keeping your mouth shut" and stifling your ideas. It's to help you realize that maintaining and employing a critical perspective has nothing whatsoever to do with backbiting, upstaging, or making catty remarks.

Enough sermonizing! Now let's go into the details.

PART TWO

3

The Preparation Stage

Now we're into it: the study about how theatre actually works, and the specifics of the symbiosis of leadership and collaboration.

We'll start with the roles at the top of the theatrical hierarchy: those individuals who carry the labels of producers and directors. The preparation stage starts with at least one of them, and so, therefore, must this section of this book.

It is often difficult to draw a firm line between these roles, however, because they often overlap and are often, particularly in small-scale semiprofessional productions, occasionally combined into a single "producer-director." The distinction is even harder to draw in England, where until fairly recently the term "producer" was also the term for "director."

Moreover, the producing function is often an institution, such as a regional professional theatre company like Portland Center Stage or the Utah Shakespearean Festival, where there may be a variety of officers and boards of directors that share the role of producer, or a university where theatrical activity is produced by a Theatre Department or School of the Arts with an internal hierarchy of deans, chairs, artistic directors, and like officers. Even Broadway productions are, today, mostly produced not by an individual but a corporation (e.g., Disney) or a consortium of multiple producers.

So it is perhaps more proper, in many of these cases, to refer to a "producing entity," in which the role of the producer is assumed by a legally constituted institution, acting through its chief executive or a delegatee.

But we will begin by distinguishing the terms of producer (or producing entity) and director – at least to the extent that will be useful.

The producer/producing entity

Simply put, the producing entity, whether in the hands of a single producer or multiple or institutional producing group, initiates and then "produces" the show. This normally includes selecting or commissioning the play, raising and authorizing the expenditure of funds, renting or owning the theatre, and hiring or approving the hiring of the production's individual artists – including the directors, performers, designers, and crew that collectively comprise the production's artistic staff.

In addition, the producing entity (which for short we will henceforth call "the producer," even if corporate) has the final authority over the budget and business operations that every public or private enterprise must deal with: legal issues, accounting practices, tax filings, facility maintenance, public relations and publicity, fundraising, utilities and janitorial services, and all other activities that all businesses must practice – and that often aren't a whole lot of fun.

Finally, and often most importantly, the producer is responsible for the long-term health and viability of the company's permanent assets, which may include physical properties (a theatre building, scene and costume shops, a truck) as well as intangible ones (a subscriber base, an ongoing rapport with national and local funding agencies, a reputation among local theatre critics and reporters, a dedicated permanent staff, and, often, a cadre of loyal volunteers). And the institutional producer is also responsible for maintaining, and sometimes even enforcing, the sponsoring institution's stated "mission," if there is such a one, and particularly if this mission is formally spelled out in the entity's public literature and website. For protecting and building an institution's mission and assets are rarely major concerns of the individual directors or others further down in the artistic hierarchy, particularly those who are hired for only a single production. But they are invariably the primary goal of the producer, and certainly of the institutional producer who heads a permanent company and must look after its affairs not just for this production but, one hopes, for years to come. As I write this, the co-artistic directors of California's

South Coast Repertory are in their 46th consecutive year at their company's helm, where they continue to maintain and build upon their guiding mission, which has led them from the company's origins in an wharf-side stagehouse converted from a failed bait shop to a Tony Award-winning regional company with a multimillion dollar stagehouse and a repertoire of play premieres and other productions that have won Pulitzer Prizes and a revered national reputation.

Such producers fully oversee their staffs and are normally the *only* persons authorized to hire – or fire – artistic staff members, including the directors.

But directly below the producer is the individual who normally exerts the highest level of day-to-day, moment-to-moment, artistic leadership in a stage production. This is the director.

The director

Non-theatre people often think that a director's job is basically to block the actors and pace the action. These directorial roles are important, of course, but neither is the director's principal reason for being.

First, the play director directs in the same way that *any* director – such as a bank director or the FBI Director – directs: by *providing direction.* The director (derived from Latin, meaning "one who makes right" or "one who sets straight") gives aim, shape, and focus to his or her enterprise, whether it is a play, a bank, or a federal bureau.

But a play director does not just direct the play. She or he also directs its *players*: which includes not just the theatre's actors, but its designers, stage managers, stage technicians, and crews. Fundamentally, then, the play director directs *people,* not just productions, or ideas, or aesthetics. And these people often have quite different goals than do bank workers or FBI agents, since theatre workers rarely consider themselves primarily as just "employees" of the institution that hires them. Moreover, despite the hoary actor's joke (Director: Cross left. Actor: What's my motivation? Director: Your paycheck!), stage artists rarely work in theatre simply for the money. For although plumbers, paperhangers, and office workers usually retire as soon as they have the money to do so, few theatre people retire until they have to. Katherine Hepburn was performing at the age of 87, George Burns acted in films until he was 98, George Bernard Shaw was writing a play when he died at 94, and George Abbott directed his final Broadway production at 104. Absolutely none of them needed the money. Deep down, theatre people love their work – if and when they get it.

So what would be their incentive if not the paycheck? Mostly, it is a wish to create lasting and important works of art. Partly, one suspects, to fulfill childhood dreams, or other demands buried deep in their hearts. And surely to interact with a larger public – and other artists – at a higher level than simply the mundane activities of daily life. "What is a man," asks Hamlet, "if his chief good and market of his time be but to sleep and feed?" What is he indeed? "A beast, no more!" Hamlet answers. For most theatre people, sleeping and eating became trivial after they were first exposed to "the smell of the greasepaint, the roar of the crowd." For those bitten with the theatre bug, their first experience of live performance leads to an all but irresistible craving for more.

And therefore, a director charged with shaping theatrical collaborations must deal with the *subjective* desires of the artistic team, and with the *personal, emotional, and unconscious* drives stimulated in them by the special nature of this special art we considered in Chapter 2: its intensely creative, fictive, and *feeling* world, its near-inviolable schedule, and its unavoidable exposure to a public whose responses may range from extremes of adulation to condemnation. Leadership of this sort of enterprise takes a lot more than just "making right" or "setting straight." It requires skills that reach into the emotional hearts and unconscious minds of those being directed. And it should not be surprising, when collaborating theatre artists consider themselves a family, that they consider their director as a parent. As the young Elia Kazan said of Lee Strasberg when the Polish-Ukrainian guru was directing him in the Group Theatre: "[Lee] carried with him the aura of a prophet, a magician, a witch doctor, a psychoanalyst, and a feared father of a Jewish home."

So while theatre directors' strategies will always include providing rational "directions," these will, when executed by a master of this art, be backed by an authority that provides what great mothers and fathers provide: a feeling of protection, a wealth of encouragement, and the occasional burst of sheer inspiration. With these, the director will, in addition to staging and pacing the play, employ his or her personal gifts to *create and coalesce* – rather than to demand and browbeat – a fruitful collaboration of the other artists, and will lead them to *work together* toward clear and coherent goals that have been mutually developed. "You're the head coach," says film director Richard Linklater (*Me and Orson Wells*) about his craft, "and like a head coach, your job is to create an atmosphere where all your collaborators, every department head, every worker, every actor, the writers if you're working with them, can do their best work around the common goal, which is the best movie possible from this material."

Thus, the director's role is not to command an artistic collective to their duty, but to unite and aim them toward a shared challenge. To help them find what is unique, whole, pointed, surprising, and extraordinary about the production they are to create. To develop with them a work greater than the sum of its parts. And to create a living monument that can be seen as art, be enjoyed as entertainment, and become a source of pride to all its participants.

Great directors will seek to bring each member of the team to his or her highest point of creativity. Then they will do more: they will seek to bring him or her to a point higher than that; higher than they have previously achieved, and even a point higher than anyone has ever achieved. That they will seek this does not, of course, mean that they will achieve it, but that is not the point. Football coaches inspire their teams by asking them to "give a hundred and ten percent." Achieving 110% is impossible by its very definition, but it's the *effort* to exceed the possible that makes the good athlete great – and the good actor sublime.

And so, being handed the title of "director" does not, by itself, confer the ability to lead, but only the demand to do so. Directing in the theatre requires not mere titular authority but an authentic force that proves compelling, captivating, and charismatic. And such directors must do this without getting in the way. Like parents, they must inspire without stultifying, must challenge without inhibiting. They must lead the charge without draining the energies, the talents, the joy, and the commitment of those that follow them. And this is a very tall order.

In sum: Leadership is not simply awarded. It must be earned. And before that, it must be *learned*.

Autocrats versus democrats

The public image of the play director, unfortunately, is far from the notion of collaboration.

The classic image in the press, and in movies about the theatre, generally portrays the director as screaming at the cast, suing the producers, and/or storming furiously out of the rehearsal hall.

There is much more than a grain of truth in this image. George Clooney coyly says of the actor-director relationship (which he knows from both sides): "As an actor, it is collaborative, but as a director, it is a dictatorship!" Playwright Neil Simon recalls a rehearsal when director Mike Nichols, after an actress complained that his blocking might keep one part of the audience from seeing her, promptly "turned and whispered to the producer, 'Fire her.'" Nichols has even admitted to a time in his career when he "saw himself becoming a tyrannical bastard." Longtime *Cheers* and *Frasier* star Kelsey Grammar got so angry at one director in rehearsal that he hollered to him, "If you say the word 'fuck' to another actor in this company, I'm going to come down there and kick your ass!"

Other directors, mainly in the past century, have defended their right to be tyrannical. Elia Kazan, the often volcanic director of the stage premieres of *Death of a Salesman, A Streetcar Named Desire,* and *Cat on a Hot Tin Roof* (and an equal number of celebrated films), recalled that "every time I was a nice guy, cooperative, and yielding to the point of others, I had a disaster." The unrepentant Kazan went on to say that to be "accommodating, fair-minded, well-balanced, obliging, generous, democratic and co-operative" was only to practice "the seven deadly virtues for the artist." He perhaps learned this lesson from his mentor, Lee Strasberg, of whom he remembered, "Lee... had a gift for anger and a taste for the power it brought him.... His explosions of temper maintained the discipline of this camp of high-strung people. I came to believe that without their fear of this man, the Group would fly apart."

But the director-as-tyrant is pretty much yesterday's news. For while director-critic Charles Marowitz argues that "the zeniths [of directing achievements] have been achieved by men who were single-minded, dictatorial, autocratic, and often tyrannical," citing "directors such as Konstantin Stanislavsky, Vsevolod Meyerhold, Evgevny Vakhtangov, Max Reinhardt, Bertolt Brecht, Jacques Copeau, Jean Vilar, Tyrone Guthrie, John Dexter, Peter Brook, Richard Foreman, and Robert Wilson," he fails to mention that all but the last three persons on his "zenith" list have been dead for at least two decades, and of those three, all now in their 70s or above, each is internationally celebrated for his unique, highly innovative style of performance, and most of those working under them consider themselves disciples as much as collaborators.

For things have changed. Clooney followed his "dictatorship" statement by adding "... but if you cast the right people and lead them in the right direction, they will do right." Mike Nichols has turned himself around as well. During the filming of *The Day of the Dolphin*, Nichols explains: "I told the [Director of Photography] toward the end that I was not proud of the way I had treated the guys and I wanted to apologize. And he – a very mild man – said, 'It's too late for that.' It took my breath away. It made me realize that I had to put the brakes on completely ... that the director has an absolute obligation to treat people decently." And so he did, saying years later that he realized "an actor needs, above everything, to be able to trust [the director] because of the necessity to call on deep and sometimes frightening feelings. He needs someone to say, 'That's O.K., you're safe, nothing bad will happen from exploring those feelings." We doubt Mr. Nichols has a need to apologize these days.

Of course there are and will probably always be the "auteur" directors like those previously mentioned, Wilson, Foreman, and Brook, who have been and remain exacting and authoritarian. In his *New York Times* review of Foreman's 2009 *Idiot Savant*, chief drama critic Ben Brantley wrote, "People don't so much act in Mr. Foreman's productions ... as take orders." But those who work under these formidable artists are fully aware of their methods from the outset – and while these directors may be autocratic, they are not screamers. In today's professional theatre – and professionally oriented amateur, academic and community theatres as well – a director who screams, who berates, who storms out of the rehearsal hall, has almost entirely disappeared.

Indeed, longtime director/producer Hal Prince (with 63 Broadway credits since 1950, and still going) cleverly removes the contemporary director from the top of the theatrical hierarchy and locates him or her in its middle: "The director today is *at the center* of a circle of creative people." Not the top, but the center. This is a major distinction.

What has created this change? Many factors have intervened. Actors, designers, and technicians are today better educated and more intensely trained to professional standards than at any time in our country's history. Most attain professional status only after studying and working in a variety of schools and theatre companies, and in several different parts of the country (or world), and they bring to their professional work a broad knowledge of accepted standards – artistic, legal, and ethical – from a broad spectrum of experiences.

Even more important has been, particularly in America since the 1960s, the remarkable rise of interculturalism in the arts, and the simultaneous breaking of the "glass ceiling" for women, all of which has led to the opening up of leadership roles throughout the theatre ranks. Today, the American theatre scene is replete with black theatres, Latino theatres, Asian-American theatres, Women's Collective theatres, theatres for the deaf and for the blind – and in the "conventional" American regional theatre of the twenty-first century, at least a third of the directors and artistic directors are now women or they are persons of color – compared to less than 5% in the 1950s and before.

And those who hold leadership positions in the theatre today – particularly directors and artistic directors – are less likely than their forbears to have been raised with a single-minded focus on achieving dominant hierarchical status during their careers. Rather, they are far more likely to be eager to forge collective enterprises, companies where "working together" is itself at least as important – and maybe more – as is the goal of achieving individual fame or fortune.

These factors, and probably many more, have led to the rise of collaboration as a primary working model in theatre, and one making inroads in film and in the corporate world as well. Indeed, "collaboration is the buzzword of the new millennium," says Twyla Tharp. Today, in their classrooms from kindergarten to graduate school, young people are experiencing participatory learning and creating collective collaboration models that were relatively unknown to previous generations, and students training for professional theatre careers are becoming familiar not only with these learning methods but also with the union regulations and government oversight (in accord with local and national fair employment and anti-harassment laws) that are in place for them when they enter the profession. Tyrant directors may survive, or try to, but they will no longer face the cowering actor or trembling designer who would previously have given way to their ventings.

Moreover, the director now increasingly participates, at least in larger ventures, in a collective "directorate": a veritable assembly line of specialized directors that might include, depending on the work staged, a music director, a dance director, a movement director, a combat director, a text director, a vocal director, and often a codirector and assistant director. (That some of these "director" positions are more commonly called by other names – choreographers, fight coaches, speech coaches, vocal coaches, dramaturgs – only shows how titles can shift upwards within the theatrical hierarchy.) The director may technically stand atop this hierarchical heap, but the heap is no longer a conical volcano; it's more like a low and windswept dune. And when the production is an opera, the director's authority is ordinarily *beneath* the music director's, while in a television series it is almost always beneath the show's producers (who are often its writers as well), its stars, and even some of the actors in recurring roles, who know their character's intentions and back-stories far better than do the directors, who are often hired for just one or two episodes.

Thus today's young director rarely asserts the absolute authority of the young Nichols or Kazan. Quite the contrary, they often espouse the exact opposite. Acclaimed TV series director James Burrows (*Cheers, Frasier, Will & Grace, Gary Unmarried*) explains, for example, "On my set there is no hierarchy. Anybody can say anything they want. Any writer can tell me what I've done is wrong. Any actor can say, 'I don't believe in that piece of business' and not do it. Anybody can say anything. I'm not offended. I can say anything about anybody else and they're not offended." Veteran actor John Travolta says "this fable that directors take you aside and do all the acting for you … is the biggest lie ever. The great ones let you alone to create your vision."

But has the tide really turned so drastically? Probably not. If tyranny is a thing of the past, leadership remains fundamental to the theatre, and essential to move the collaboration forward. And directing is fundamental to combining the many arts of the theatre into a single work: into a work of art, not a work of arts.

So let's look at the details of how directors can implement leadership that supports – and doesn't destroy – collaboration.

Unto the breach!

We saw earlier that leadership in the arts cannot be imposed in military fashion – but that does not mean that we can't learn from martial models.

Actress Kathleen Chalfant had this to say about working with acclaimed contemporary director George C. Wolfe on the Broadway premiere of *Angels in America*: "He is a great general. I always thought if there was a war and you wanted to follow the person who would get through it, you should follow George. George is a fierce defender of his artistic collaborators. He defends them against the outside world…. He makes you feel safe, as though you are in his world and you go in his direction."

We could turn to military historians or group dynamics experts to give us some guidance on this, but an actor/director named William Shakespeare understood the process as well or better than anyone, so let's learn from him, a fellow theatre artist. Here's how Shakespeare's King Henry V begins his heroic rallying cry to his troops:

> Once more unto the breach, dear friends, once more!
> Or close the wall up with our English dead!

With these words, Henry leads his exhausted and heavily outnumbered soldiers into a final assault through the well-fortified French battlements of Harfleur. This is a leadership challenge if there ever was one: to inspire ordinary men to face death and carnage, then to face it a second, third, and fourth time, to boldly sally forth into a hail of arrows, a sea of swords, and a mob of armed and mounted warriors for – for what? For what Shakespeare in a less militaristic play had called "a little patch of ground, that had in it no profit but the name." A daunting task: Do you think you could do it?

Of course, Henry's a king, which title certainly gives him some advantage in this task. He has, as it were, titular authority to lead. But titular authority – even kingship – does not confer the ability to perform superhuman miracles. *Inspiring* others to risk their lives for what is essentially your (and not their) chosen goal is an extraordinarily difficult task, as much for a monarch as a menial. Soldiers are famous the world over for malingering, goldbricking, panicking, disappearing, deserting, and even for fragging (murdering) their officers. Suppose Henry simply said: "OK, chaps, if you don't mind, when I say three, how about charging over there into the cannon fire, OK?" The troops would suddenly disappear – not unto the battlements but in the other direction, into the French countryside.

But the miracle occurs! Henry's men make their charge, the English win, and the astonishing victory is a result of his extraordinarily masterful leadership.

How did Henry do it? Just look at his words – and learn from them.

> "**Once more** ..." – *it's final*: only one more time, men, then we got 'em!
>
> "...**unto the breach** ..." – *it's easy*: we've already done the hard part, guys, we've opened up a big breach in their stone wall. Now its just a matter of plunging in and mopping up flesh!
>
> "...**dear friends** ..." – *it's love*: I may be a king, but each one of you is dear to me and dear to our country. And each of you will be your king's dear friend and your country's beloved hero when we finish this final mop-up.
>
> "...**or close the wall up with our English dead**" – *or shame on you, you f-ing bastards!* If you don't go into the breach, if you don't return my love, if you don't care about being your country's beloved hero, you can just bury the corpses of your buddies in the wall and return home to face the consequences. Or maybe I'll just bury YOU!

Without yelling at anybody, yet also without pulling out a rule book, time clock, or job description, King Henry exhibits five fundamental tactics of leadership:

- energetic *commitment*,
- unbridled *optimism*,
- a *dismissal* of all difficulties,
- the *offer* of *love* (royal in his case) and,
- the *threat* of terrible *retribution* (death in this case) if such a magnificent offer is refused.

These are very powerful tactics. They include a delicately veiled threat, at the end, but are otherwise *inductive:* encouraging, engaging, buoyant, confidant, inspiring. They are tactics that make strong soldiers follow their leaders – not out of fear but out of hope, love, passion, fierce optimism, and a shared moral commitment.

Inductive leadership

Commitment and optimism lend energy: everyone wants to be on the winning side, and everyone knows that energy and optimism keep the project heading forward through the inevitable rough waters to come.

Dismissal of difficulties – "the game's afoot," he soon will say – makes clear it's do-able, it's only a game, a sport; it's even going to be *fun*, like rabbit hunting. Sharing the rewards and bonding with the team provide incalculable incentives: the offer of love, group affection, exaltation, even, for some, heavenly rewards. These incentives can inspire the sort of fearlessness known by warriors, even kamikaze pilots and suicide bombers. No reward system is stronger than this one; it is not merely inductive, it is seductive. When Henry, later in the play, says:

> We few, we happy few, we band of brothers –
> For he today that sheds his blood with me
> Shall be my brother –

every man in his army must feel the impulse to trade the risk of death on the field for the hope of bonding into an eternal brotherhood. They are now his kin, his blood brothers who have been seduced into following him "unto the breach" – which also adds, if you haven't caught it by now, a slyly sexual metaphor to the King's appeal to his (all-male) band of warriors.

Punitive leadership

But the threat of terror – not only death but also being left behind as so much mortar in a foreign wall – provides the alternate to optimism and is an instant catalyst for action. The bliss of success is underpinned by a nauseating fear of failure, humiliation, and eternal aloneness. Henry's soldiers may be lured forward, but they are also warned – if only by implication – not to retreat. And so are a director's fellow artists.

Since time immemorial, therefore, leadership involves both inductions and threats: the carrot and the stick, honey and vinegar, the lure of incentives and the fear of punishment. Which category of incentive is the better one? Italian statesman (and playwright) Niccolò Machiavelli posed this question, famously, in his tract *The Prince* in 1513, asking if a leader is better advised to be loved or feared. "It might perhaps be answered that we should wish to be both," wrote Machiavelli, "but since love and fear can hardly exist together, if we must choose between them, it is far safer to be feared," and this answer has resounded through the ages. But Machiavelli concludes his answer with this often-ignored caveat: "Only he must do his utmost to escape hatred." For the fact is, as Shakespeare and Machiavelli both understood, "both" is indeed the only correct answer to this fundamental question.

Leadership, in sum, is not achieved simply through rational explanation. It is indeed rational; but also psychological, as it touches our deepest emotions; cultural, as it plays on our most ancient loyalties; and biological, as it digs right down into our primal instincts.

Effective leadership, like Henry's, reaches our hopes and our fears simultaneously, turning us into jelly. As actress Chalfant said about director Wolfe, it compels us to follow, it defends us from others, it makes us feel safe, it gives us direction. It makes us *move* – and *be moved* – in response to its call.

For without reaching into the emotions, the passions, and the pre-conscious and unconscious minds of others, "leadership" is merely a word.

Specifics on theatre directing

So is the director – like Shakespeare's King Henry – simply a master manipulator of emotion? The answer is "yes" – but let us delete the word "simply."

Inspiring soldiers into battle or theatre artists into an original vision of theatre are mighty challenges. So we can leave Shakespeare now and just talk about theatre directors.

Directors succeed, of course, by their mastery of craft in their particular art: casting, blocking, pacing, and so forth. But in order to do that they must enlist large numbers of independently minded people into willing collaborations, just like King Henry and Fortinbras or, for that matter, Dwight Eisenhower and David Petraeus. And theatre directors don't normally have armies at their disposal as did these celebrated leaders and Machiavelli's *Prince* prototype, the ruthless tyrant (and son of the Pope) Cesare Borgia.

What directors do have, or can have, however, is the capacity to *ennoble* their co-workers, to offer a sense of communion, of excitement, of intellectual verve and emotional thrills, and even of fun. "I need to have fun in rehearsal," says longtime director Harold Prince. "I need the laughter, no matter how emotional things get. I shy away from contention."

By creating communion, excitement, verve, thrills, and *fun* into their collaborative work, directors put the entire group at the service of each individual, while still guiding each individual into realizing his or her deep responsibility to the group.

And the key to all of this is the notion of "mission" that defines the beginning and end points of the labor.

The mission

"Why are we here?"

Probably no moments are so crucial to the success of a production process as the key meetings when the director first meets the artistic staff and first meets the cast. "Why are we here?" is the question on everybody's mind. And, as previously noted, "Because we're getting paid" is never the complete answer.

But what propels process into product, and collaboration into result, is not just work, work, work: it is work with a *purpose*, work toward a *goal*. It is an adventure, an exploration, a call to a greater challenge. It is a *mission*.

Indeed, some of the great theatre figures mentioned earlier considered themselves missionaries. Several mentioned in previous pages – including Stanislavsky, Copeau, Clurman, Brook, and Grotowski – have published personal manifestos promoting their aesthetic, artistic, and/or socio-political ideals.

In the 1930s, the Group Theatre established what is arguably still America's foundational theatre ethic. The Group ended its existence more than seventy years ago, but it began the modern American theatre as we know it, becoming the first internationally acclaimed theatre company in America, and initiating an "American acting style" for both theatre and film that is stronger than ever today. Yet it was founded not simply out of an aesthetic desire to improve the art of acting, but with a fervid missionary zeal to reform American culture. In his autobiography, Kazan described the exemplary passion of the company's two founding directors, Harold Clurman and Lee Strasberg, with great clarity:

> Clurman inspired the Group ... by roaring defiance at the rest of the theatre world, relighting the fire for the members ... by the fervor of his passion as well as by the validity of what he said. ... Harold's face, as it filled with blood, looked as if it might burst ... .

> Strasberg … was the force that held the thirty-odd members of the the-
> atre together …. An organization such as the Group … lives only by the
> will of a fanatic and the drive with which he propels his vision. He has to
> be unswerving, uncompromising, and unadjustable. Lee knew this.

This was not merely a theatrical collaboration: it was a religious crusade, and its leaders – and members – were crusaders.

Kazan concludes, "an organization such as the Group … lives only by the will of a fanatic and the drive with which he propels his vision." These were passionate times, (Clurman's book describing the Group's history is titled *The Fervent Years*), in the heart of the Great Depression and the gathering storm of World War II, and the Group thrived in this climate. And while today's directors generally abjure roaring defiance and fanaticism, the visionary zeal that Kazan describes – whether voraciously expressed or quietly residual – remains a direc-tor's strongest foundation. Because vision does not merely instruct, it inspires.

"Cry 'God for Harry, England, and St. George!'," Henry V cries to his troops at the end of the speech quoted earlier in this chapter. It is the call to a great mission. With this near-musical peroration, Henry brings everything down to a single sound bite: it is easy to remem-ber, easy to chant, easy to follow – a rhythmic, crescendoing sonic boom. "Yes, you're doing it for me (Harry, his nickname), but you're also doing it for your country (England) and for your patron saint (St. George), who's now in heaven with God! Come with me and you'll be my pal (you can even call me by my nickname!), your nation's hero, your patron saint's ally, and your God's beloved."

Now that's a mission! The director who can tap into this addic-tion can indeed accomplish miracles. Maybe not the kind that earns a ticket to sainthood or a deed to the province of Aquitaine, but Shakespeare himself begged for a "Muse of Fire" to help him "ascend the brightest heaven of invention" in order to create such miracles that, if they could inspire troops into Harfleur, could inspire audiences into the Globe Theater of his day – and the Shakespeare Festivals of our own. Neither hierarchical authority, nor a big salary, nor top marquee billing can achieve a fraction of the motivation that sheer inspiration can.

Few theatrical ventures are as high reaching as to seek the Group's goal of revolutionizing their nation's theatre. But that does not mean that less-idealistic dramatic enterprises seek only to make money, or fulfill class assignments, or, in the self-mocking phrase of many an artistic director, "put butts in seats." Even in the most squalid TV series or self-serving community theatre project, the artistic staff and the performers all hunger for a mission that binds and directs them. And they usually find one. They may not admit it to outsiders (partly as a hedge against professional ridicule – which is the particular ignominy of TV), but they inevitably develop a mission and act on it. And they act *because* of it as well.

The director who can provide a sense of mission will be able to lead the ensuing collaboration with an aura of authority. It's not only in child's play that we "follow the leader," it happens in adult play (and in adult "plays") as well. But note that we do not exactly follow the leader. We follow the leader's *path*. We follow the leader's *direction*. We follow the leader "unto the breach," as it were. And then we assume and embody the leader's mission within ourselves. We become our own leader.

Great leaders never demand to be followed. Rather, they establish missions that are so enticing that they themselves beg, even demand, to be pursued. A mission organizes individuals around it, drawing everyone to face in the same direction. If the mission is well chosen, its goal becomes a group passion – overriding the multiple individual goals (career advancement, showing off, personal profit) that would otherwise dominate.

Such a mission may be a social goal: "We want this play to show the evil of intolerance," or "... to heighten AIDS awareness," or "... to reform the American prison system." Or it may, more simply, be informative, entertaining, and indulgent: "... to bring the Renaissance to life," "... to exploit cultural nostalgia," "... to vivify the Christmas spirit," "... to ridicule macho extravagance." It can aim the team toward a purely aesthetic innovation: "... to make theatre history," "... to re-invent *commedia dell'arte* for the postmodern world." Or it can offer sheer theatrical exploitation: "... to make the audience laugh their heads off for two hours and cry at the end!"

A truly great mission ("God for Harry, England, and St. George!") brings powerful forces into play. A great mission transcends the momentary motives of everyday living and inspires superhuman effort – and sublime excitement. As playwright George Bernard Shaw wrote, "This is the true joy in life, the being used for a purpose recognized by yourself as a mighty one." A mission – well chosen and crafted, gives a purpose that is individually inspiring at the same time collectively unifying.

So, directors begin the act of collaboration by addressing the question – before they are asked – Why are we here?

What is it we are compelled to do? What is our cause, our calling, our goal? What will drive us through the difficult terrain that lies ahead? What will compensate us for the dangers we will pass?

All this must flow from preparation (the "prep") that will lead to the implementation (the plan). But prepping and planning are not the same things.

Prepping and planning

There's one criticism heard about directors far above all others. Everyone reading this book has heard it before. One version of it is "He doesn't know what he wants." The other version is "She doesn't know what she wants." There are no other versions.

The first thing this tells us is how much performers (actors, dancers, designers particularly) feel that they *need* direction – and directing. After all, the opportunity for free improvisation – to move in different directions – is virtually boundless. The number of viable script interpretations, design choices, and possible movement vectors, gestural actions, and vocal deliveries are all but infinite. Unrestricted freedom can lead to artistic anarchy and aesthetic (if not personal) breakdowns. If artistic impulses cannot be harnessed into some sort of framework, integration disappears and catastrophe looms.

There's only one way for directors to avoid this criticism, and that's to *prepare*. To investigate every detail of the script. To investigate the theatre you're working at, the company of artists you and they are assembling, and the resources that will enable you to probe deeper and deeper into everything and everyone. In short: to know what you want.

But *preparing* is not *planning*. Planning is what you will do later, with your design team, your production team, and your cast. Preparation is what you do on your own. It's your homework. It leads you to your starting point, where you have begun to focus on what you want – but haven't yet determined how you'll get there. If you plan everything out before your team assembles, you leave nothing for your co-workers to do except execute your pre-formulated ideas. Unless you are as famous (and well-funded) as Robert Wilson, you'll find this tough sledding. If your team is not personally involved in your mission, what sort of passion or vitality can they lend to your project?

The director prepares

Directorial preparation is easy. All you have to remember is that you must *start it right away,* for there's a lot to do.

Think you can just fly by the seat of your pants? The legendary stage and film director Ingmar Bergman writes, "I read and reread and reread the play. ... The writing and the blocking take me four pages a day, every day except Sundays." This is from a man who directed 62 films and over 170 plays. If Bergman took this amount of time to prepare a production, you can take such time as well.

Directors, and would-be directors, should be preparing productions all the time – productions you have been engaged to direct, of course, but also productions you will *propose* to direct. And you prepare these entirely on your own initiative; not because you have been asked to, but because you are driven to. No one becomes a director simply to make money or to become famous, which is good, because the overwhelming majority of directors do neither of these. Those who become directors are rather spurred by an impulse – an intense and unquenchable impulse – to create theatre. Without such an impulse, you can never convince a producer to back your show, you can never lead a design team to its greatest effort, you can never inspire a cast of actors to exceed anything they have done previously, and you can never forge an intense collaboration of passionate artists.

And if you are not preparing a production, or the nugget of a production proposal right now, you are probably not a director and never going to be one. It may be true that "they also serve who only stand and wait," but that's about those who serve, not those who lead.

So what does that preparation consist of?

Imagining

First of all, assuming you have a play in mind to direct, it consists in *imagining the play as it might appear on stage.*

Again I would like to cite Peter Brook, who calls this initial imagining a "formless hunch." Brook, who has created a vast array of legendary theatrical creations from Broadway musicals to Shakespearean tragedies and comedies to the Sanskrit *Mahabharata*, asserts that "the director must have from the start what I have called a 'formless hunch', that is to say, a certain powerful yet shadowy intuition that indicates the basic shape, the source from which the play is calling to him." This could not be said better.

The first play I prepared, when I was sixteen and in high school (and had only seen four or five plays in my life), was *Oedipus Rex*. I had seen the Penguin book of Sophocles' Theban plays at a friend's house and read the first one, not even knowing it was written before I was born (2400 years before, as I later found out). It was so compelling I wanted everybody to see it right away, and so decided to stage it right then and there. Well, I'm afraid I didn't manage to do that until ten years later, but my 'formless hunch' was there from the beginning. Another ten years after that, I was in casual luncheon conversation with the artistic director of a professional theatre company when he asked me, out of the blue, if there was any play I'd like to direct at that moment. I immediately said: "Yes, *Hamlet*," and went on to give him a ten-minute summary of why I thought that was the precise play audiences needed to see at that particular place and time. As it turns out, he asked me to direct *Macbeth* instead, but the fact that my preparation simply flowed out of me was the only reason I got the job.

Researching

After the formless hunch, the second step of preparation is research: reading, studying, perhaps traveling, listening to music, looking at pictures, and often just looking around you.

Just what do you study? Obviously the play, or the work that is to be turned into a play, is the most important. Why should the play be done? Why *must* it be done? For whom is it to be done? Who would want to see it? Who *should* see it? Why would they want to/need to see it?

What is it like? What are its greatest strengths? Whom would it make laugh? Whom would it make cry? Whom would it make think? Whom would it make *re*think? And *why* would it make him/her/them rethink?

I will take it for granted that it makes *you* laugh, or cry, or think, or all of the above, or else you wouldn't be craving to stage it. But how will other people respond? The audience? The actors? The press and blog reviewers? The answers to these questions will not determine whether or not you will propose or stage it, but *how* and *where* you might propose or stage it. In a big theatre or a small one? An urban experimental venue or a civic light opera house? And your research is your first step in finding these answers.

You should understand that research isn't only for college students. Professionals do it more than you may realize. Prior to choreographing her Broadway production of *Show Boat*, Susan Stroman went down to the levee at Natchez, interviewed the historian at Chicago's Palmer House, and read as much as she could about the play and the era, looking at pictures and seeing films. "A lot of people think that choreography is just doing steps when in fact the steps are the very last thing that you do. The research I do is quite extensive because when you find that one particular piece of information, it's like finding gold," she says. When she discovered that black people had invented the Charleston, she felt as if a "wash of riches" had fallen over her. "That's what is going to propel you through the number. In order for the choreography to enrich the story or the music, the lyrics, it's that research that you do."

Your preparation may include other sorts of research. The playwright's life story and the chronology of his or her writings is, for many directors, a useful beginning point. Studies of the theatre in the playwright's era, and of the key social and political issues at play in that era, even if not referenced in the play, can be enormously helpful.

Preparing a dramaturgical analysis of the play's structure, and making a breakdown that lists the scenes and the characters appearing in each one, will give you a firmer understanding of the flow of the play's action. Making the breakdown on a spreadsheet will be even better, since in addition to listing the scenes and characters, you can also enter the number of lines each character speaks in each scene, and, by a simple formula, determine the total number of lines each character speaks as well as the total number of lines in each scene. Such a chart will prove extremely helpful in all sorts of ways later on: casting the play, figuring out which actors could possibly play multiple characters, estimating the length of time characters are offstage and could make costume changes, and, since you can see at a glance approximately how long each scene is, developing the preliminary rehearsal schedules. Sample charts, with procedures as to how to make the appropriate spreadsheet formulae, are in the Appendix.

A critical and literary analysis of the play's history, language, political relevance, and deeper themes can also prove revelatory. But research extends to more than reading. It may include looking at paintings you feel might be relevant, listening to music that might lead you into a world that might be that of your production, and watching films and documentaries that might provide new insights. It can include looking at real-life environments that resemble what might become the play's setting, traveling to places mentioned in the play or potentially relevant to its action, and, indeed, anything that you feel might be of use in helping you create "the world of the play" as you are beginning to see, hear, and feel it in your imagination.

Collaborations between directors and dramaturgs

But research into the text of the play is not something that the director needs always do alone. In major theatre companies, the director may be assisted in the research – as well as in choosing or preparing a translation or an adaptation and evaluating how the play is coming along in design meetings and rehearsals – by collaborating with a *dramaturg* during the preparation stage and afterwards.

The dramaturg (sometimes spelled *dramaturge*) is a relative newcomer to American theatre. The position was invented, more or less, by the eighteenth-century German playwright/director Gotthold Lessing – hence the word's German spelling. Dramaturgs have occupied stable positions in the English and American theatre for nearly half a century now, but their roles have been varied. Basically, the dramaturg is the theatre company's chief adviser on matters concerning the play's text; specifically its dramatic structure, its use of language and linguistic tropes, its historical, political and cultural setting, and the precise meanings of its individual lines and references. The dramaturg is also typically conversant with the current critical analyses of the play, as well as its stage history, and may have useful notions as to its relevance to contemporary culture. Thus the dramaturg is in a good position to collaborate with the director in analyzing and interpreting the play, choosing the best translation if one is required, helping find the best lines to cut if cuts are desired, and by watching the rehearsals closely, to advise the director if his or her interpretations of the script are actually coming across.

But who initiates this collaboration: the director or the dramaturg? The only answer is that either may do so, although in most cases the director will take the lead – mainly because the director's primary responsibility is to lead, and to lead everybody: the designers, the cast, and, yes, the dramaturg. Let's look at an example.

Example: Twelfth Night

A director is engaged to direct Shakespeare's *Twelfth Night: or What You Will.* This play is classed as a comedy in its first publication (the 1623 First Folio), and it certainly has some of the funniest characters and funniest scenes in the Shakespearean repertoire. But it also has a darker side: the heroine, Viola, comes onto the mythical island of Illyria believing her beloved twin brother has just died in a shipwreck, and the melancholia that sweeps over her from time to time contrasts strongly with the hilarity of the farcical scenes. And since Shakespeare was the father of twins himself, a son who died at age 11 with his twin sister surviving, the poet himself may well have been grieving for her tragic situation at the time he was writing this play, possibly that same year. There are other serious themes too: the punishment and humili-ation that Malvolio receives seems unusually severe for his offenses (mainly stuffiness and pride); Sir Toby's drunkenness becomes con-siderably less amusing as the play goes on; and the unrequited love that Antonio repeatedly asserts for Sebastian, and that Duke Orsino feels for Viola (believing she is a male named Cesario), and that Olivia strongly feels for Cesario (not knowing that "he" is the female Viola) makes the play a wild cacophony of homo/hetero sexuality. So what is the dominant tone that the director should take in producing this play – Poignant? Erotic? Comic? Fantasy Island? And what are the play's main theme and the inner meaning of its odd subtitle, "What You Will," possibly a pun on its author's name? Since virtually *every line* of the play could have a bearing on these issues, conversations between the director (presumably a master of stagecraft) and drama-turg (a master of dramatic literature) could prove immensely helpful prior to putting things in motion (such as scenery construction or the actors' line memorizations) that cannot be easily or arbitrarily changed in the midst of rehearsals.

So it would be important, in this production, for the director to be able to start the ball rolling by saying to the dramaturg something like, "I really would like to emphasize the comedy of this play," or "I am really hoping to focus this play on Viola's confusion after she loses her brother," to initiate these discussions. Such openings can then be followed with "So, if you're comfortable with that, how can we work together on this?" And if the dramaturg and director are indeed comfortable, and the director is open to the dramaturg's responses, ideas will start flying across the table in both directions.

There's nothing, however, to prevent a director at the first meeting with a dramaturg from saying something on the order of, "You know this play better than I do, what's your take on it?" Or, "This play is done all the time; what can we do that's different?" Many dramaturgs spend their lives sitting on brilliant ideas that they never have a chance to see executed: Why shouldn't a director explore some of them?

After the initial conversations, the dramaturg and director may become more of a team, shooting questions back and forth and making observations to each other before and after design meetings and rehearsals. During subsequent rehearsals, the dramaturg can then become the "in-house critic" of the show, seeking to anticipate which scenes, characters, and lines aren't coming across as fully as they might, and advising the director about potential shortcomings-in-process – at least when asked by the director to do so.

The dramaturg may also prepare a "dramaturg's book" for the company, with essays, pictures, and other materials that members of the company may find useful, and leave it in a convenient place for designers or actors to glance through or even study between their shop and onstage worktime. And the director may call upon the dramaturg to give a talk to the cast on specific areas in which he or she is particularly expert – the play's historical background and/ or its political implications in its own era, perhaps – or to invite cast members to seek out the dramaturg to answer new questions that may arise about the meaning or best interpretation of certain words or phrases in cases where the director may not have time, or feel sufficiently expert, to do so.

But except when the director specifies otherwise, the dramaturg should never *direct* the actors or the designers. The dramaturg is not the director nor, unless so titled, the co-director. While he or she may suggest *to the director* how an actor might play a certain line, or how a designer might revise a certain prop, the dramaturg must not – unless specifically requested by the director – directly give that suggestion to the actor or designer. To do so would be to introduce a dangerous note of dissonance, since the dramaturg and the director can never speak with exactly the same voice, and the actor or designer spoken to would be in the uncomfortable position of having to choose which of the two voices to follow. Worse, he or she would then have to decide which voice to seek out when the next such question arose! No, dramaturgs are far more effective at reaching cast members and artistic staff members by *working through the director* than by working as the director's surrogate.

Dramaturgs play many other roles during the course of a production's development. They may, when a new play is involved, work with the playwright on possible revisions. They often work with producers on developing materials for the theatre program, writing essays and historical background notes or charts to help the audience better appreciate the show and its larger social context. They may work with audiences by giving preshow lectures or moderating talkbacks after the curtain call. In the course of a theatre season, dramaturgs may aid in selecting plays for production, in reading and evaluating new manuscripts that may be offered the company for possible premieres, in soliciting and commissioning such plays, in selecting and commissioning translations of plays that have been chosen for production, and, in general, in seeking to match the 2500 year-old global dramatic repertoire to the skills of the company, the interests of its producers and directors, and the tastes of its theatre audience.

How essential is the dramaturg to the director, however? It depends. Some directors prefer not to have a dramaturg at all; they wish to be their own dramaturgs. Other directors welcome them heartily, particularly if they are plunging into a work, such as a Shakespearean history play, that is well out of the range of anything they have ever worked on – or even studied – previously. For most directors, it depends on the production, on the script, on the time frame, and on the particular dramaturg. Finally, the collaboration between dramaturg and director depends on the two persons involved, and their mutual regard for each other. The successful collaboration of the two requires a near-complete consonance between them as to the main thrust (mission) of the production, because if the dramaturg cannot get behind the initial 'formless hunch' of the director, and behind the emerging ethos of the production, it is probably best for the director to assume the dramaturgical role him- or herself.

Collaboration among directors, playwrights and/or translators

In other cases, particularly with new plays, directors may actually be able to collaborate with the playwright; in others, where the play was written in a foreign language, they may be able to collaborate with the translator, or even make their own translations.

Such collaborations are different than any other in theatre, for the Dramatists Guild contract – the Guild being as close as independent playwrights come to having a union – specifies that the playwright has "artistic integrity," which, the contract explains, means that "No one (e.g., directors, actors, dramaturgs) can make changes, alterations, and/or omissions to your script –including the text, title, and stage directions – without your consent."

So the playwright has final authority on everything that is said on stage, and even everything that is, if written in the playwright's stage directions, done on stage.* And this is often the case with dead playwrights – and some (the Samuel Beckett estate in particular) will go to court if they must in order to enforce it!

But directors (and dramaturgs) often collaborate with playwrights. Speaking about his Tony-winning 1994 *Love! Valour! Compassion!*, playwright Terrence McNally reports that "plays are truly a collaboration," and that "it was [director] Joe Mantello's idea to have the house there to ground the play. Joe quite rightly knew what my instinct was, but I didn't know how to do it." Match-ups like these have often produced legendary results. Elia Kazan, who collaborated with all the playwrights he worked with, believed that "a writer for the stage must face the fact that the making of a play is, finally, a collaborative venture, and plays have rarely achieved success without being in some manner raised above their manuscript level by the brilliant gifts of actors, directors [and] designers." Kazan's collaborations with Tennessee Williams were particularly notable, with Kazan prodding the famed author to revise his scenes, reshape his plots, and redefine his characters. Their relationship, consequently, was often tense; Williams describing it as "highly explosive," and resenting Kazan's "forcing him" to revise *Cat on a Hot Tin Roof* so as to bring Big Daddy

---

*This is not, however, true in film, where the screenwriter sells his or her script outright and thereafter has absolutely no control how, or even if, it is used in the actual filming.

back in the last act.* Nonetheless, revised as Kazan suggested, *Cat* won the Pulitzer Prize.

It should not be surprising that such collaborations should at times be difficult. The playwright has usually developed the play independently, wholly outside of the theatre (unless it had been commissioned by the company), and he or she may not be familiar – or appreciative – of the theatre's collaborative nature. Some playwrights – Edward Albee is a famous example – simply refuse to collaborate. "I dislike the term 'collaboration,'" Albee explains. "No one collaborates with me on a play, because I am not writing the play with them." And that is certainly the playwright's right. After all, the highest goal of the dramatist is to create a script that is unique, original, startling, personal, important, and perhaps even world changing. And that's why the playwright has joined the Dramatist's Guild: to try to assure that, when the play finally appears before the public, his or her unique and important vision has been realized. Why bring in a "co-author?"

But while the collaboration between the playwright and director or producer may be a tender one, it should not be avoided for that reason. The "play" and the "production" are not the same thing, and few great plays come from the dramatist's pen or keyboard in what will become their final form. Lines can read well on the page but sound dismal on the stage. Speeches the playwright believes eloquent and convincing may prove, when enacted, tedious and bewildering. Neil Simon, the most commercially successful American playwright of all time, is famous for revising his scripts endlessly when they are in rehearsal, often coming up with whole new scenes overnight to improve his text as the production begins to take shape. "Playwriting is rewriting" is in fact a familiar axiom of playwriting workshops, and it is noteworthy that the first volume of Simon's autobiography is entitled *Rewrites.*

Sensitive questions, reactions, and suggestions may therefore be usefully traded back and forth between director and playwright, and the aid of a dramaturg or literary director, when one is on board for the project at the preparatory stages, may prove immensely helpful as well – particularly as long as everyone understands that all

---

* When it came time to publish the stage version, Williams included his original third act, in the appendix, as an alternate to the one Kazan requested, giving future directors a choice of which ending to present.

participants are only interested in one thing, as Rule Number One makes clear: *a great production.*

Simon is not the only experienced playwright to accept the involvement of trusted directors and dramaturgs, and other collaborators as well – those who can ask the right questions and make the right suggestions – but the involvement must be collaborative, not a battle of authority. Both legally (as per the Dramatists Guild contract) and practically (as providing for a successful result), collaboration with a playwright is best when it is a two-way street – or three-way intersection – of give and take, questions and suggestions, as is when playwright Lynn Nottage, who had already won almost every drama award except for the Pulitzer prize for her *Intimate Apparel,* had her play *Ruined* accepted by the Manhattan Theatre Club (MTC) for its New York premiere. Though it had opened previously in Chicago, Nottage agreed to subject it to a final development with MTC's Director of Artistic Development and veteran dramaturg Jerry Patch, who had worked previously with Nottage on her *Crumbs from the Table of Joy* in Utah and *Intimate Relations* in California. With *Ruined,* Patch explains that "I just asked questions... such as 'this is what I'm getting – is it what *you* want?' and at points suggesting, 'This may be too long.' Lynn took it from there – and the play went all the way." Indeed, it did: *Ruined* won the 2009 Pulitzer.

Since the playwright has the protection of the Dramatist's Guild contract, it is certainly helpful if he or she is open to collaboration. While Albee, with his three Pulitzer Prizes and two Tony Awards (one for Lifetime Achievement), certainly has no need to bow to anybody in order to get his new scripts produced, most playwrights are well advised to participate in the back-and-forth collaborations by which plays are usually brought to their final form. And most plays will be greatly improved by such a process. So the playwright's initiative might be to address the director or producers boldly with specific questions, such as, "Is this character's motivation clear to you?" "Is this scene too hurried? Or is it too long?" "Have I given you enough to work with here?"

And in the beginnings of the rehearsal stage the playwright may, if the director approves, question the cast as well: "Are there any lines you're having trouble with?" "Do you feel confident giving this speech?" "Are you unclear as to why you are saying this?" and so forth. Simply providing such questions and listening (and responding) to their answers will probably make the cast more confident in their roles, more committed to the play and its playwright, and very much more assured that they are in the right place at the right time.

And sometimes the director is herself or himself the playwright, or the adapter of a work no longer under copyright. In such cases the collaboration is not with a playwright but can rather be opened up to a much wider group of collaborators. Mary Zimmerman, longtime member of the Lookingglass Theatre of Chicago and winner of the 2002 Tony and Drama Desk Awards for her direction of *Metamorphoses* (which she had adapted from Ovid's classic poem), describes her favored working method this way: "I cast a company without knowing for the most part who will play what, or what parts the show will actually contain. This is possible because I am often adapting a text, or body of work that is vastly larger than any evening of theater could contain, so I'm always making choices as to what parts of that text I'm going to use. Since I don't do that until I have my company, I can tailor the text to the company, to the venue, to the design, to what happens in the world while we are rehearsing."

But we're jumping a bit ahead of our story. Now we return to the most important role for the director in the preparation phase: Conceptualizing.

Conceptualizing

As preparation moves through these steps (and remember, they're not steps in the sense of precisely sequenced observations, but more often simultaneous imaginings, a synesthesia of mental impressions, memories, ideas, and even of colors, sounds, and smells), the director will inevitably begin to conceptualize a production.

Production "concepts" – a term dropping out of fashion at present but still spoken of with awe in some quarters – is an abbreviated description of a production motif grafted onto a play. Peter Brook's "white box *Midsummer's Nights Dream*" and Joseph Papp's "naked *Hamlet*" in the 1960s, and Ariane Mnouchkine's "kabuki *Richard II*" in the 1980s, were only three of the thousands of stage productions that were widely known for their tight focus on a single concept that defined the direction of those plays in recent decades. Some directors – Robert Wilson and Richard Foreman have been mentioned previously – are known for their "high-concept" productions, and these directors conceptualize early, often conflating the roles of scenic,

costume, and/or lighting and sound designer into their own directing roles. Persons signing on to a Wilson or Foreman project, consequently, expect the production's concept will be defined long before
they are engaged with it.

More common today is for directors to arrive at a modest conceptualization that posits a directional arrow rather than a comprehen-
sive picture, as, for example, to conceive a general production style
they simply term "dark" or "giddy" or "forceful" or "whimsical." This
narrows the scope of the adventure without fully focusing it, and is at
least a first step prior to expanding the collaboration beyond the roles
of director and producer.

And why should this narrowing of conceptualization be undertaken at this time? Because the director's primary goal (to create a
great production) and the producing entity's (to advance the long-
term goals of the theatre company) are not always in synch. The con-
troversial production that creates a great commotion in the national
press but alienates the subscribers of the local theatre that produces
it can, simultaneously, be a career highpoint for the director and a
financial disaster for the producer. So both parties must collaborate
carefully to make sure their joint work comes out a win-win and not
win-lose (or, worse, lose-lose) proposition.

And therefore early conceptualizing by the director should be
done in consultation with the production's producer – and preferably
before the final contract between them is signed! In one instance, a
theatre company engaged a notable director to stage its upcoming
production of Shakespeare's *The Tempest,* which they had conceived
as a matinee comedy to contrast with the bleakness of their otherwise
tragedy-heavy summer season, but then had to painfully negotiate
their way out of the contract when they discovered that the director
planned to conceptualize the production as a postcolonial attack on
the occupation of native cultures by European civilizations. There
was nothing wrong with the director's conceptualization – it was in
fact well within the mainstream of *Tempest* conceptualizations during that decade – but it was not in keeping with the producers' desire
for that particular slot in the season. In such a case it would have
been far better had the producers extended their offer with words
like "We'd like to invite you to direct our *Tempest* this summer, which
we plan to present as a light-hearted matinee production for families
of all ages," so that the director could have decided whether or not
to accept the offer with its specified conceptual tone. Alternatively,

if the invitation had been offered (as it apparently was in that case) without any such spoken or written qualification, the director might have thought to respond by saying, "Yes, I'd love to direct it, as long as I can do so as a post-colonial response to the European exploitation of native peoples," in which case the theatre could have simply withdrawn its invitation with no bad feelings on either side.

When the director realizes that a concept is taking shape in his or her mind, therefore, it should be discussed as soon as possible with the producers to make sure there's room for such a concept in the producer's imagination – or in the institution's (normally the theatre company's) stated mission. Not only does this prevent the crossed swords of the *Tempest* tempest, but it will also help the producer and the director assess the individual qualifications of the new artists – designers and actors – that are to be added to the production team, since the candidates in each group will include many with fine credentials in bouncy Elizabethan comedy along with others who have a special interest in socio-political-aesthetic commentary on current cultural issues. Full disclosure between director and producer at an early stage of production is the best way of assuring a coherent production approach for clearly focused – if still only generally detailed – conceptualizations.

Translations and adaptations

If the play was originally written in a foreign language, one of the director's first tasks is to find – or create – an appropriate *translation*. Early conceptualization will help the director select from among alternatives – or commission a new one – but almost always the producing entity will want to be involved in this search as well.

Translations are critical ingredients of the production of foreign plays, and they powerfully shape the play that the audience sees, as well as hears. Translations can differ drastically: in their wit, pace, emotive force, gravity, sensuality, profundity, profanity, and contemporaneity. They may also differ as to period: some strive to retain the original author's setting and context, some are updates in time and relocations in country or region, and some turn verse into prose or formal speech into a local vernacular. So the choice of text is critical, and a mistaken choice in the preparation period cannot be easily corrected after rehearsals begin and lines have been memorized.

In selecting a translation, therefore, a director and dramaturg will often read comparable scenes from the competitive texts aloud to each other, or with other actor friends, prior to making a final decision and starting rehearsals.

Translations under copyright must legally be treated the same way as plays and cannot be revised or combined with other translations without the translator's (or, if the playwright has died, the playwright's estate, or the publisher's) permission. But often the director may collaborate directly with the translator to make desired changes if the reason is appropriate. In a production of Molière's *The School for Wives* I directed in Utah, I selected Ranjit Bolt's British translation, but since it included a few British slang expressions ("clever-clogses," "sodding"), I sought his permission to Americanize some of the language. He agreed, and after emailing back and forth some options we agreed to change, for example:

> "Well, here's a thing:
> The slut can wrangle like a bluestocking."

to

> "Well, this is cute:
> The slut can wrangle like a prostitute."

Conversely, in Susanna Morrow's 2009 Texas production of my translation of Molière's *The Misanthrope,* which was set in contemporary Beverly Hills rather than its own time, we agreed to update:

> "What's with this medieval *idée fixe*?
> Good lord, Alceste, it's 1666!"

with

> "What's with this neo-medieval line?
> Good lord, Alceste, it's now 2009!"

Adaptations of translations are easier to arrange than adaptations of modern plays in the audience's own language, since translations are already adaptations of the original. But adapting a play in its own language – that is, changing the words of a play to change its meaning and make it more "relevant," or perhaps simply to accommodate an actor who has trouble memorizing or speaking the line correctly, is not only illegal if the play is under copyright, but generally cheating the playwright – and probably the audience as well. If Tony Kushner's play asks a character to say "Abbreviated fezlike pillboxy attenuated yarmulkite millinarisms," that's what Mr. Kushner wants the audience to hear, and to simplify that language (or let the actor paraphrase it) is to seriously undermine the character that Kushner has written and the play the audience will be seeing.

Mere *cutting* of classic texts, however, since they are now in the public domain, has now become relatively common. Most directors today cut the texts of long classics before putting them into rehearsal. Sometimes, they are required to do so by their producers; at least one Shakespeare festival, for example, mandates a 2,500 line limit to keep their running times shorter than the "three hours between our after-supper and bed-time" that Theseus describes as the appropriate duration of a play in *A Midsummer Night's Dream*. But exactly *which* words are cut and which retained in Shakespeare's 4042-line *Hamlet* will have a major impact on the story the play tells and the way it tells it, so just *how* it is cut will prove critical to the play's meaning and dramatic power in production.* Still, cutting is increasingly popular today, even with modern plays; the standard "serious Broadway drama" of fifty years ago was three acts and three hours long; now it's much more like two acts and two hours, and older plays often receive some trimming, though only after having received appropriate permission.

The number of characters – and hence actors – in plays is also subject to cutting, either as part of the producer's or director's desire to have a shorter running time, or to reduce the production costs, or simply to give the play a tighter focus. Theatergoers are now used to eight-character *Othello*s and *Winter's Tales*, therefore, with or without actors doubling and tripling in roles, with narrators often filling in the gaps caused by deleted dialogue. England's Royal Shakespeare Company may have precipitated this movement by touring to over a hundred colleges in America and the U.K. in recent decades an "ACTER" program in which five company actors would create mini-productions of Shakespeare's plays, playing all the roles of the cut-down versions they had prepared of those texts.

Other adaptations (of plays in the public domain, where copyright does not exist or has expired) may indeed *add* text to existing plays. *Timon of Athens* is one of Shakespeare's shorter plays, but the surviving text was almost certainly printed from an unfinished manuscript,

---

*Hamlet himself advocates cutting a play that the Players are about to present, telling them "It shall to the barber's, with your beard."

and most directors (including your author) seek to make or have a dramaturg prepare an adaptation that "finishes" the play by tying up loose ends in the plot, clarifying relationships among the characters, and simplifying the play's strange conclusion. Early conceptualization is of great help in making these decisions as well.

Some directors adapt plays into different works altogether. Engaged to direct Shakespeare's *Two Gentlemen of Verona* for the New York Shakespeare Festival, director Mel Shapiro decided the Bard's early comedy would be better as a musical, so, with playwright John Guare, he revised the text and co-wrote lyrics, and with new music by Galt McDermott their show proved a great success, transferring to Broadway where it won Tony Awards for "Best Musical" and "Best Book." With a completely different slant, director/playwright/theorist Charles Marowitz decided that his production of Shakespeare's *Taming of the Shrew* should forcefully emphasize the brutal dehumanizing of Katherine by a male-dominated world, so he eliminated from his production of the play all scenes from the original not pertaining to this theme and added wholly new scenes set in the present day. Re-titled simply *Shrew*, Marowitz's bold adaptation ended with Kate, having been pinned to a table by her father and brutally sodomized by Petruchio, rising to utter her famous request for wives to place their hands "below your husband's foot" in a ghastly, psychotic stupor. Since Shakespeare's plays are in the public domain, adventurous directors are free to make any adaptations they wish, and many do – although if the audience is not appropriately alerted in advance (as they were by Marowitz's re-titling), there may be trouble at the box office when purists discover they are not seeing what they thought they were paying for.

Engaging the artistic team

As the concept begins to emerge, and is shared between director and producers, the artistic team is beginning to be put together. This is basically the producers' role, but the director ordinarily has a hand in it – making nominations, suggestions, and recommendations when invited to do so, and in some cases being given a primary role in the selection process.

The key members of the artistic team (called the Artistic Staff in most theatre programs) includes, along with the directors (including music directors and choreographers), the designers, and the production stage manager. Theatre production heads follow, and then the production staffs that will turn the designs into actual scenery, costumes, and timed and focused sound and light cues.

Of course, the key ingredient to selecting such personnel is the skill, talent, and experience of each member, but one question that will be asked about every fresh applicant for such positions will always be the old one: "How is he/she to work with?" And sometimes the entire list of references on each applicant's list will be contacted to find the answer(s). For in an era when top-down authoritarian management has ceded ground to superb collaborative ability, the recommendation of "oh, she's great to work with!" has become a topmost qualification for professional employment. It may not – and should never – wholly trump talent, honesty, or responsibility, but it is right up with these other gold standards.

So in addition to their research on the play, directors should research their potential "playmates" – particularly the designers – so as to help guide the selection process and, afterward, the ensuing collaboration. What should you look for? Aside from "how are they to work with," you will want to see how well they might respond to the conceptual direction you plan to follow. Some designers have strong political bents, some historical, and some aesthetic; some designers prioritize radical innovation, others splendor and grandiosity, others, perhaps, physical and psychological realism. Look up the resumes of those being considered for the posts that you don't yet know, and do a web search looking for images or recordings or videos of their recent productions. If you find things that excite you, particularly in light of what you are directing, these can become not only reasons to recommend them, but wonderful reference points you can bring up in your upcoming collaborative conversations, so that instead of your first comment to a designer being "Here's my idea for the show," you might be able to say something like, "I loved the intense color palette you used in your Chicago design for *All My Sons*; could you expand somewhat on that for our project?" If this is truly where you want to head, this approach will give the designer an initial buy-in to your concept even before the work begins; the collaboration starts with joint ownership between the two of you rather than you simply telling the designer what you want. And, of course, the designers will be looking at what they can find out about *your* past productions too, and may be proceeding in the same fashion themselves.

Your research may discover useful specialties among your designers that you would otherwise know nothing about – a deep understanding of Chinese Opera, say, or the inner workings of the East German secret police – which could prove extraordinarily exciting if these linked up with your existing thoughts or stimulated new ones. By finding such reciprocal interests, even by accident, you could blend your and your colleagues' high-level visions into a truly revolutionary production.

Indeed, everything that you can find out about your colleagues-to-be can guide you in your search for new aesthetic visions – and toward what might become a newly shared aesthetic, or shared socio-political or philosophical position, that could propel this upcoming work gracefully and rapidly toward a theatrical discovery. You may even create an artistic partnership that will last for many productions – and years – to come.

No matter what you may find in these searches, *the better you know your co-workers' achievements from the outset,* the broader you can probe in your investigations, the faster you can arrive at mutual understandings, and the deeper those understandings may go.

Using your preparation

Your preparation is something you will have in your pocket from the moment you begin meeting your colleagues. It will enable you to answer questions quickly and convincingly. But, surprisingly, this doesn't mean that you must lead off with it. Your preparation is not your plan; it's just your starting point. Actor Danny Aiello tells of director Robert Altman's directorial style on the first day on the set for his film *Prêt à Porter*: "There we were, thirty actors, egos running rampant, and Bob is controlling this monstrosity. First thing he says is, 'I want to start off by telling you all I don't know what the [expletive] I'm doing.' What does that do but relax you? Of course it's not true. He never makes himself seem smarter than you, but my feeling is also that he is smarter than everybody."

The moral: Preparation is something to *do,* not something you broadcast to show how smart you are.

For "knowing what you want" doesn't mean knowing every move that everyone must make on opening night. Premature planning will drastically limit your options and prevent your opportunity to discover the magic your actors could – absent your preconceived directions – create in rehearsal. Peter Brook needs to have his 'formless hunch,' and he also does a great deal of "imaginary" planning, as we have seen, but this is not to be put into use but simply to ready himself for the collaborative work that will follow:

> There is a great temptation for a director to prepare his staging before the first day of rehearsal. This is quite natural and I always do it myself. I make hundreds of sketches of the scenery and the movements. But I do this merely as an exercise…. It is a good preparation – but if I were to ask the actors to apply the sketches that I did three days or three months earlier, I would kill everything that can come to life at the moment of the rehearsal. One needs to do the preparation in order to discard it, to build in order to demolish.

This is "preparation" at its best: *pre*-paration, derived from the Latin *pre-parere*: "before peeling."

But soon it will be time to move to the peeling itself, and getting to the meat under the skin. And this begins with gathering the planning team: usually a mix of designers, the director, and the specialty directors (choreographers, music directors, speech and text directors, and the like), and many others in a series of planning sessions.

From this time on, the director is working with real people – not just texts, charts, resumes, and ideas.

Assignments and Exercises

Here are some assignments and exercises pertinent to the preparation stage that will prove useful for persons to learn and polish their skills as directors, producers, dramaturgs, and playwrights. Some you can do on your own; others are group exercises.

On Your Own

I. **Cut a script**. Download a Shakespearean play from a free website and cut it to 2500 lines, retaining what you think is crucial to the story you want to tell and the themes and messages you most wish to convey.

---

2. **Graph a script**. Create a spreadsheet identifying the scenes in the play you've cut in exercise I, listing the characters appearing in each scene and the number of lines each character speaks in each scene, as discussed above and as exemplified in the Appendix. Total the lines in each scene, the lines spoken by each character, and the total lines in the play.

3. **Multiple-cast the script.** Create a second spreadsheet for the play that reduces the number of actors the production will require by having actors play multiple roles. What roles could effectively be multi-cast? Is there time to allow the necessary costume changes? Do you need to have costume changes? (And are you aware that in a great many contemporary productions, actors do not change costumes or makeup when playing multiple roles – but simply "change roles" through physical and vocal shifts?)

4. **Choose a translation.** Take your laptop to a good library and pull down all the translations you can find of a popular play by Ibsen, Chekhov, or Molière. Write out the first ten lines of each translation and compare them. How would you describe each? What sort of production would each generate? How would you rank them if you were to direct the play? Why have you ranked them in this order?

Group Exercises

I. **Conceptualize a play.** This can be done on your own, but it's more fun to do as a group exercise with five to ten people in a directing class or workshop. The group chooses a classic play, perhaps Greek or Shakespearean, and writes down the names of several eras (e.g., the Gay Nineties,* Roaring Twenties, Great Depression, World War II, Silent Generation, Hippie, Postmodern) and drops them in a hat, and in another hat drops the names of various theatrical styles (kabuki, melodramatic, commedia, operatic, naturalistic). Then each person blindly selects an era from one hat and a style from another. A week later, each presents to the group his or her concept of a production of the play in the context of the era or style they had drawn – illustrating their concept with text samples, music clips, and visual images.

---

*The 1890s in America – the adjective has nothing to do with the contemporary meaning of "gay."

2. **Create a "Directorial Haiku."** I created this exercise – which has nothing to do with Japanese *haiku* except its concise aesthetic integration – in the 1970s, when I had a class that included graduate directing students and both graduate and undergraduate actors and designers. Each director is assigned six or seven "cast members" and given two weeks to prepare and present a ten-minute "performance" using all members. The classroom should have basic theatre lighting and sound equipment available, but the group can bring in any other form of sound media, live or recorded, and non-theatre lighting (candles, flashlights, lasers, portable floodlights), together with whatever they can find for costumes, props and other décor. There are only three other requirements for the presentation: (1) no strictly dramatic material – such as playtexts or adaptations of playtexts – may be used, (2) no cast member can be asked to memorize more than 100 words, and (3) directors must avoid the easy out of parody. The exercises are not graded, and their only stipulated goals are that each piece should (1) have a clear beginning and end, (2) be "fun to watch" for its duration, and (3) get more rather than less interesting as it goes along. Participants take to this exercise with great élan, staging news stories, poems, their own dreams, and exotic fantasies. Inevitably, fundamental principles of theatre silently emerge, including builds, reversals, climaxes, denouements, emotional engagements, and truly original ideas – often in ways that surprise not only the audiences but the performers. The "directors" may rotate so that, ideally, everyone in the group will have a chance to direct his or her own "haiku." Many will remember them years, even decades, later.

4

The Planning Stage

Planning begins with a team of planners: but just who constitutes the team? And how does it come into being?

Gathering the team

The team depends, at the outset, on whether the production is produced on one of three fundamental models: the institutional theatre, the single-production model, or the "regional theatre" model that is somewhere between the two.

The *institutional theatre* model pertains to those companies where the theatre team is mainly comprised of employees – generally permanent and year-round – of a well-funded public or private organization. Such institutional theatres include the great bulk of national- or city-subsidized theatres in Europe, such as the French Comédie Française, the German Berliner Ensemble, the Russian Moscow Art Theatre, the English Royal National Theatre, and the sometimes multiple national theatres of Japan, Portugal, Greece, Hungary, Romania, Costa Rica, and many other countries. Indeed, the vast majority of important European and Asian theatre activity is produced in such institutional theatres that maintain permanent staffs of directors, designers, actors, and other theatre artists. Moreover, despite the connotation the word "institutional" implies in some quarters, many of these theatres – such as the Berlin Volksbühne, the National Theatre of Cluj (Romania), and the Royal

National Theatre of England – are internationally known for their radical and innovative stagings. There are also privately maintained institutional theatres, such as the Kabuki-za theatre in Tokyo, owned by Shochiku, Japan's leading film production company. And there are university theatres, virtually all of which fall under the institutional category.

In institutional theatres, the majority of the artistic staff (directors, designers, actors) and virtually all of the production staff (technicians, dramaturgs, business and publicity offices) are already on hand when the individual production director is selected. Gathering the team in these cases may mean simply going down the hall and knocking on a few doors. With its theatre spaces ordinarily in the same buildings (or at least the same city) as its offices, shops and rehearsal halls, as well as close by the normal workplaces (offices, studios) and home-base residences of its theatre artists, institutional theatre productions easily facilitate close, frequent, and easily arranged face-to-face collaborations among all members of an artistic team.

The *single-production model*, by contrast, is almost entirely the opposite. In this model, each production must assemble its own team independently, from top to bottom. The single-production motif is the basic pattern of America's Broadway and most off-Broadway theatre, almost all films, and most small, independent stage productions, including what are popularly known as "Equity-waiver" and "showcase theatre" productions in Los Angeles and New York, respectively.* To initiate such a production, a self-designated producer (more commonly today a group of producers acting as a team), having raised sufficient funds to set a show in motion, will then engage each individual participant – from directors to performers to ushers – that will become part of the production company. In such cases, the "gathering" of such a team – which may be composed of artists living in different cities or even countries – may for a long time be more virtual than face-to-face, via webconferencing, emails, attachments, and phone calls substituting for conversations

---

*The official names of these production formats are "Los Angeles 99-Seat Theatre Plan" and the New York "Showcase Code." Both are independent productions in those cities (only), which, while they may engage professional actors, are excused from paying regular union salaries, which actors "waive" in return for the opportunity to perform. Certain restrictions apply.

over coffee and donuts. And when actual meetings are arranged, they likely will be on a one-to-one basis rather than a group gathering, at least in the early weeks or months.

Yet while such personal and collective collaborations may be harder to arrange, the single-production model has some strong compensating artistic advantages. Artists can be engaged because of their specific match with the particular project, rather than because they are simply "the designer down the hall," and working with new artists outside one's own periphery of local colleagues can lead to unexpected artistic growth – and professional development – throughout the individually selected team.

The *American regional theatre model,* as we may call it, is a middle-ground model. It is clearly the norm for the great majority of American professional theatre companies outside of New York – and even of some within that city. For while regional theatres are technically institutional, and many were founded on the model of European institutional theatres like those mentioned above, virtually none is today funded sufficiently to maintain a large, resident, permanent company of directors, designers, and, most importantly, actors on yearlong paid contracts. Those which come closest are certain summer theatres and Shakespeare festivals that offer seasonal contracts to artists who work in multiple productions, played either in stock or in rotating repertory for months at a time, such as the Oregon Shakespeare Festival, which produces twelve plays over eight months a year. Others are theatres directly linked to conservatories or universities, such as the American Conservatory Theatre in San Francisco, the American Repertory Theatre (with Harvard University and the Moscow Art Theatre), and Trinity Repertory Company (with Brown University), in which a number of professional artists double as conservatory teachers during the spans of their yearlong contracts.

But for most American regional theatres, often including those above, the "company" is a mixture of a few permanent members, usually including the artistic, producing and/or managing directors, and core business, artistic and production staffs, supplemented by single-production hires for each individual production, which often include the play's director, many of its designers and most if not all of its cast. English regional theatres – such as the Bristol Old Vic, the Chichester Festival, the Manchester Royal Exchange – are much the same, maintaining only small permanent staffs, casting most if not all their seasons on a show-by-show basis, and mixing their own productions with weeklong tours of other regional troupes.

This middle-ground regional model has some advantages as well as some disadvantages vis-à-vis both the institutional and the single-production models, of course. Since they don't have a year-round, salaried company of one or two hundred persons, they are certainly more economical than the government-funded national theatres in Europe, and can be far more flexible in whom they hire. But except where they are located in a major theatre city such as New York or Chicago, they do not have a huge local pool of talent to draw upon, which means that they must recruit artists nationally, provide them housing and transportation if they live more than fifty miles away (an Equity rule), and know that they are not going to be easily available for auditions, callbacks, or face-to-face meetings during the weeks and months of preparation and planning.

In the pages that follow, we will use the regional theatre model as the default pattern, but with the understanding that while the circumstances may be different in the various models, the fundamental principles of collaboration and leadership are essentially the same in all of these varied structures.

Directors and designers

Collaborations involving directors and designers during the critical planning stage are unique for two reasons. First, they are intermittent: usually no more than a few face-to-face meetings that may be days, weeks, or even months apart – and sometimes there are no physical meetings at all. And second, because they require two separate levels of collaborations: director with the designers and the designers with each other. And these don't always happen at the same time or in the same place.

And at both collaborative levels, the balance between collaboration and leadership is crucial, and concentrated. Award-winning Chicago (and Broadway) director Mary Zimmerman speaks of "the intense work between my designers and me which happens before rehearsals...that collaboration is absolutely critical to everything I do. It is a long, groping process." "We are brought in first, which is something I think we all love," says scenic designer Daniel Ostling, who works with Zimmerman often. "It is great to be involved at the shaping of the script; right away she brings us in and we all read whatever text exists and then we start researching and brainstorming.... It goes against everything I learned in grad school about 'read the play, support the action,' but with Mary you can't do that. All of us are...making design choices that are about the integration of the play and not imposed on it."

Directors and designers, in most cases, are individuals who head their respective areas, and the degree in which each may legitimately feel a sense of "artistic ownership" of their area can be delicate. Aesthetic partnering must therefore be carefully, and mutually, nurtured between them.

When the collaboration and leadership are great, the results can be *really* great. Don Holder, lighting designer of the phenomenally successful 2008 revival of *South Pacific* at Lincoln Center, explained this to me: "We had a director [Bartlett Sher] and a set designer [Michael Yeargan] who were incredibly sensitive to lighting, and understood how space needs to be designed in order to accept light and be lightable. And beyond the design there was an atmosphere of trust from the director – as well as a very clear point of view. He trusted us, he let us bring our work to the table, he let us put our choices out there. It was one of the most thrilling, satisfying experiences I've had in the theatre, not only because of the results, but also of the process. That theatre! That staff! That director! Those designers! Those performers! That play! – It was *heavenly*!"

And the results were heavenly as well: individual Tony Awards for the production, the director, and for *all four* designers – scenic, costume, lights, and sound – for the first time in New York theatre history.

Sound designer Vince Olivieri explains that there are two sorts of directors he has worked with: the "dictator-directors" who simply "hand down decisions from above," and the "invitational directors" who set a course but then invite each member of the design team to "come up with independent ideas, from which the director can then make selections that make them cohere." Like most (but not all), designers, Olivieri has a preference for the "inviters," feeling that the dictators either "have self-confidence issues" or, specifying a certain prominent example, are simply "so fierce and demanding that they turn me off." With the dictator type, he explains, "I'm simply not challenged creatively and while I try to support her fully, I know I'm not going to do my best work. I certainly wouldn't choose to work with her again. Hey, none of us are doing this to get rich."

Olivieri represents the majority of his fellow artists when he says, "I like to have a director who initiates a clear idea of where we want to go but then extends an invitation to explore how we get there."

Lighting designer Jaymi Smith expands on this idea, eagerly supporting a collaborative director, but also one who is not afraid to promote ideas and shape the process forcefully. "I like directors who want me to be part of the conversation, who want me to help develop the story with them, but who also will push me and extend my vision." Scene designer Jo Winiarski doesn't want her directors to be patsies, but also doesn't want collaboration to simply mean accepting whatever comes across the table. "I'm always disappointed when I walk in with my model and the director simply says, 'That's great.' I can only generate so much myself. A tough director makes me a better designer!"

Most designers will try to work with either sort of director, of course. To stay in business, they have to. As scenic designer Luke Cantarella tells me, "I've worked with both sorts, the prescriptive director and the loosey-goosey one, and I try to respond to whichever kind they are. I have tools for dealing with each, and how to give each the best steps to working with me." A lighting designer, Tom Ruzika, likewise explains, "I can handle a wide range of directors. With some, such as Broadway director Arthur Seidleman, we read each other's minds so well and have such a knowledgeable trust that we usually need to talk for only about three minutes! This is wonderful." He goes on to say, however, "But I can handle both sides. With the occasional screamers, who demand everything, and all at once – well, I work OK with them too."

Obviously, both sides have their advantages and drawbacks, and finding the middle ground is crucial. The great director Peter Brook gives a lifetime overview to this issue in his book, *The Shifting Point*. Brook first says there are directors who use "actors, designers, musicians, etc. as his servants," and then there is "the director who makes himself the servant, becoming the coordinator of a group ... [and] limiting himself to suggestions, criticisms and encouragement." Brook finds the first style "sad and clumsy" and the second, though "well-meaning," an "unsatisfactory alternative." So what does he propose?

> I think one must split the word "direct" down the middle. Half of directing is, of course, being a director, which means taking charge, making decisions, saying "yes" and saying "no," having the final say. The other half of directing is *maintaining the right direction*. Here, the director becomes guide, he's at the helm, he has to have studied the maps and

he has to know whether he's heading north or south. He searches all the time, but not haphazardly.

Almost all agree with Brook that the *balance* of leadership and authority is the ideal solution. And the primary goal of the director-designer collaboration is a matter of creating that balance *throughout the design process from beginning to end*. This maximizes the artistic potential of your colleagues; screaming at them does the opposite. And while apologizing afterwards for your outbursts may assuage hurt feelings, it won't erase lost aesthetic opportunities. Mike Nichols, you may remember, had to reform his behavior after being told it was "too late" for apologies. But there's no need to go overboard in self-abasement either. As English director Katie Mitchell says, "always apologize if you make an error, ... but keep the apology simple and brief – then move on."

So how does this balance best come about?

Trust and respect

The words that come up all the time in talking with designers are *trust* and *respect*.

- *Trust* in the sense that each artist trusts his or her colleagues to have the commitment to do their best; the skills, time, and energy to deliver on the ideas they bring into discussions; the integrity to accept blame when they are at fault; and the grace to be generous in acknowledging the achievements of others.
- *Respect* in the sense that each artist honors each colleague's opportunity to propose fresh ideas, alternate directions, and objective differences of opinion without fear of scorn or ridicule. Respect for the knowledge, talent, training, experience, skill, and integrity of each colleague, except where events indicate otherwise, in which cases they will raise the issues directly, honestly, confidentially, and seeking both sides of the issue.

Establishing a relationship based on these principles is essential in professional productions, where all artists are contracted on the basis of either their proven skill and experience, or having such extraordinary potential as qualifies them to be raised to professional ranks.

But these goals are wise, too, in academic situations where some of the team (often the director) may be faculty and/or professional thea-tre artists and others may be graduate or undergraduate students – in which cases the disparity of training, skill, and experience between artistic team members indicates the desirability of mentoring during the process. Even here, however, the mentoring should be *in the direc-tion of professional training*, in which *every* artist, professional or ama-teur, should be treated with respect, and this respect, at least initially, must include a degree of trust that the less-experienced student *will commit his or her best effort, ideas, resourcefulness, time, and energy* to the project – unless and until events clearly indicate that a more disci-plinary approach (or expulsion from the program) is necessary.

Designer–director collaborations: design meetings

Designers and directors collaborate in a series of communications, perhaps first in one-on-one introductions, and then in consolidated *design meetings*, either in person or online or, as is most usual these days, a combination of both.

The actual design meetings – where director, producers, and designers are all in one place at the same time are traditional and still considered ideal, but they are becoming more rare in regional profes-sional theatre these days. This is because the artists comprising their teams are, for the most part, hired on single-production contracts and may live in different places around the country, traveling from job to job. When I was planning a production of Molière's *School for Wives* I was to direct at the 2008 Utah Shakespearean Festival, for example, I was in California, the scenic designer was in New Jersey, the lighting designer was in New York, the sound designer was in Florida, the cos-tume designer and executive producer were on opposite ends of the state of Utah, the two coproducers were, respectively, in Illinois and Wisconsin and the stage manager was running a show on a cruise ship in the middle of the Atlantic Ocean. And many of us had never previously met! Obviously, our initial design "meetings" were not meetings at all, but telephone calls, faxes, and emails with multiple attachments, but we *got to know each other* as well as our production through these technical devices.

Institutional theatres with a core of resident directors and design-ers are more likely to have face-to-face design meetings: a first one, which is largely introductory, where the director will provide his or her basic notion of where the production should head, and where the designers will then voice their own initial thoughts and concerns, which will be followed by several successive meetings to go over the designs in each area as they are being developed, and to make collective aesthetic judgments as to how they will or won't coalesce with each other and with the theatre's schedule and its available budget.

Regardless of the number of meetings, however, or whatever form they take, face-to-face or virtual, it is essential that the director and the design team are *working together from the beginning*. Nor is this collaboration merely a two-way exchange between each designer and the director: the designers must also collaborate – and collaborate *effectively* – with each other as well, so that the resulting production will have a shared and integrated style. The goal is to create a production that adds up to "something" and not just "some things." No great theatre production has been merely an olio of random objects, visions, actions, sounds, and moments, no matter how sublime these may have seemed in and of themselves. Just as people must work together, elements of a play production must work together. Scenery and costumes are invisible without lighting to illuminate them. Sound cues can drown out actors' voices and video projections can upstage their actions. The various scenic, costume, and lighting color palettes, seen together for the first time in dress rehearsals, can blend or clash, define or confuse, elucidate the action or muddy the waters. Although these elements will have been developed by different artists, in conjunction they will appear to the audience – and the press reviewers – as the collective creation of the artistic team. So the team should be unified in its creation.

That doesn't mean the production must be pleasing, of course. The theatre has many possible goals. "Bizarre!" "Confusing!" "Garish!" "Trash!" "Disgraceful!" are epithets aimed at plays now considered masterpieces – Beckett's *Waiting for Godot* and Ibsen's *Ghosts* are just two examples. But since the audience will receive a collective impact from what is put on stage, the artistic team's goal is for that impact to be derived collectively. There are always happy accidents in play productions, but they are happiest when they are grounded in the willed, creative syntheses of artists that generate them.

Having everyone equally "on board" at the beginning of these discussions helps create that artistic synergy that makes the product better than the sum of its parts. It also gives each principal artist a deep sense of participation in the project, and of his or her "ownership" of the theatrical event, having been there, as it were, "since the beginning." No single person actually owns the production, of course – with the possible exception of the producer (and that in the financial sense only) – but each artist should have a feeling that he or she owns a partial role in its creation, as well as its execution.

This also means that the designers must know from the outset that they have a measure of artistic independence. That, indeed, is what collaboration really comes down to. For the collaboration among directors and designers – as with everyone else in the theatre – is not merely among artists but among people: proud, sensitive, intellectual, feeling human beings. Professional artists are of course trained to give "one hundred percent" of their artistic skills and ability in every engagement, but the "hundred and ten percent" that every great production requires only comes about if these people have a *personal stake* in going that extra mile, and can look forward to a sense of *ownership* of its eventual result.

And so it is the job of every member of the artistic team to seek that 110% not only from themselves, but from everyone else on their team.

This has not always been easy, of course. Looking back over her long career, scenic designer (of more than 200 productions) and stage director Pamela Howard writes, "Sadly, the ideal of collaboration is not always realized. The director and the scenographer often have a different perception of their relationship. A director [may] speak with admiration about…how wonderful it is to work with a person so creative, amenable and flexible, however when scenographers get together they reveal the opposite, and the talk is of being used as servants. Because they are put on separate career paths, directors and scenographers are polarized from the start." Because of the long-time work of Howard (now Professor Emeritus at the University of Arts London) and others, however, this polarization has been greatly diminished over the decades – and it is a goal of this book to diminish it further in the decades to come.

The main areas of theatre design

The primary or "big four" designers – meaning those in scenery, costumes, lighting, and sound – appear in this book immediately after directors because, in both professional and academic productions, they almost always comprise the second tier of collaborators (after the producers and directors) that engage artistically in the artistic production planning. If the director is hired a year in advance of opening night, the primary designers are often hired within the following month, and planning may begin mere days after that.

Why are these four design areas considered "primary?" Because other designers generally work under their supervision; property designers, for example, are usually subject to the authority of the scenic designer; wig and hair designers are normally overseen by the costume designer; projection designers may be under either the scenic or lighting designer or both; and Foley artists (who create live, not recorded, sound effects) are under the sound designer.

Another mark of these four areas is that they are the only categories, at the time of writing, in which designers are eligible for Broadway's Tony Awards. Designers should be grateful there are four: when your author was in graduate school there were only two – in scenery and costumes, which had been so anointed at the Tony Awards creation in 1947. Lighting designers joined this select group only in 1970 and sound designers as recently as 2008. (The Tony category of "Stage Technician," created in 1948, silently disappeared fifteen years later – the awardees in that category were often called "chief electrician" or "sound man" but were what today would probably be called, respectively, their production's lighting and sound designer.)

Is there a hierarchy within the design team? Politically: no. Historically: yes.

There is a historic ranking of designers, which Tony-winning costume designer William Ivey Long lists as "sets, costumes, lighting, sound." Many designers argue that such a ranking – a hierarchy within a hierarchy – no longer exists, or no longer should exist; Long, however, finds it reasonable and accepts it. "The set designer creates the world"; he says, "the costume designer peoples the world; the lighting designer tells you where to look, in addition to time and atmosphere; and the sound designer controls what your ears hear. In that order." Is this harmful to those not at the top rank? Long doesn't think so: "I do not mind being number two," he says. "I respect the tradition; I respect the creation of the world as the first step."

Yet while directors often think first of a production's scenic elements, this is by no means universal. The actual priorities of a given production, as they are initially prioritized by the producers and directors, are dependent not merely on the director's preferences but on the nature of the production to be mounted – for which the producing entity may plan, budget, and even hire designers with a firm notion that areas other than scenery would be given the dominant focus. Costumes are often prioritized, for example, in the outdoor productions of the Utah Shakespearean Festival; since the festival's tiring house (the wall behind the outdoor stage in a traditional Shakespearean theatre) includes permanent pillars, doors, balconies, and a "slipstage" that can move in and out soundlessly, much of the scenic investiture is already in place – regardless of what the scene designer may wish to add (or cover over) – while the number of costumes designed for a traditionally staged Shakespearean history play (152 in the festival's 1995 *Henry VIII,* for example) can easily dominate the visual picture the production creates, as well as consume the bulk of the production budget!

Other, more experimental productions – particularly in black-box theatres with limited offstage space or scenery-flying capability – may prioritize lighting and sound, since locale changes can be represented instantly, less expensively, and with smaller stage crews with these design options prioritized. New technological innovations, indeed, have greatly intensified the role of lighting and sound design in recent decades, with the extraordinary additions of electronically controlled moving lights and color-shifts, greatly enhanced image-projection technologies, and a revolution in sound recording and editing that has turned what used to be called "sound effects" into a full-scale "sound design" that can underscore an entire production in the same way it has been doing in film for several decades. Scenery too has profited from new opportunities provided by computer-controlled scene shifting, which now has a flexibility and magnitude previously unimaginable – and is capable of creating a fluidly kinetic scenography that has overturned the traditionally sedate techniques of pre-1950s design into a vastly expanded contemporary palette, often comparable to the visually spectacular rock concerts, postmodern Cirque du Soleil extravaganzas, and the ultra-extravagant 2008 Beijing Olympic ceremonies that we see elsewhere in today's entertainment world.

But the largest design innovations that have come in the twenty-first century, and those most pertinent to this book, are not in technologies but in aesthetics. While the theatre from ancient times to the early twentieth century had almost uniformly heralded the designer's ability to create a visual context that was considered "cor-rect" and "appropriate" for the play (and perhaps "beautiful" as well), the current age has witnessed an accelerating demand – by now vir-tually a mandate – for designs, both aural and visual, that are not aimed so much at being "correct" but rather for being unique, origi-nal, surprising, meaningful, and often shocking. Today, the "appro-priateness" that was once so highly prized now appears, to all but a few purists in the field of opera, as simply a failure of the directors' and designers' imaginations.

The modern has given way, in other words, to the postmodern. Audiences that in Shakespeare's time came to "hear" a play (as thusly proposed both by *Hamlet's* Polonius and *Midsummer Night's Dream's* Theseus) now come to the theatre mainly to "see" one.

And so all design areas, from those handed down from ancient times to those freshly invented in the lifetime of living artists, have erupted into an increasingly escalating level of abstraction, fragmen-tation, planned disturbances, text deconstructions, and the bold use of new and found materials.

This is not limited to theatre, of course. The general category of design has become a powerful art in its own right, and you may be surprised to hear that the number of working professional artists in the American labor force calling themselves "designers," as reported in the 2008 report by the U.S. Bureau of Labor Statistics, totaled more than 800,000 individuals, more than four times the number of actors, directors, and producers combined.

Therefore, even though theatre designers' names are rarely famil-iar to the general public, the leading professionals in these fields are widely known and respected within the theatre community, and their specific accomplishments – as well as any purported failures – are often given high priority in published reviews of productions they design. Designers are, in short, a giant force to be reckoned with in any artistic collaboration – and nowhere more so than in the theatre.

The design statement

The biggest single upshot of this growth in the design contribution, without question, is the notion that the designer does not merely lend "support" to the production, he or she makes – or collaborates in the making of – a "statement" about the work. Indeed, the possibility, or even the duty, of each designer "making a statement" has become so ingrained in today's theatrical culture that it may shock young designers to realize there was ever a time when such an idea was unheard of. Yet today's senior directors, trained in "old school" notions and unaware of this new design ethic, often face challenges when collaborating with today's "statement-aggressive" young American designers in all areas.

Both the technological and – more crucially – the aesthetic changes in design culture have indeed made for a true paradigm shift, which has raised theatrical designers from the level of supporting players to co-creators and even co-stars. Some, perhaps since the great Czech designer Josef Svoboda (1920–2002) who popularized the term "scenography" instead of merely "scenic design," have indeed been considered the true stars of their productions, as have several American director-designers including Robert Wilson, Julie Taymor, and Richard Foreman, the Canadian *auteur* Robert LePage, Romanian director/choreographer/designer Mihai Maniutiu, and the Italian *enfant terrible* Romeo Castellucci.

Now seen as independent artists, today's theatrical designers often seek to create designs that comment upon, more than simply support, the plays with which they engage: notions that would have been unthinkable a half-century ago, and virtually mutinous in the centuries of Shakespeare and Molière.

But if the designer makes a statement, do the four principal designers make four statements? And does the director make a fifth statement – or a first? These are the questions addressed here.

Leadership: the director with the designers

Even with the rise of the designer in the theatre universe and the rise of collaboration in the theatre's working process, the director is still expected to provide substantial leadership.

Broadway scenic designer Robin Wagner (*The Producers, City of Angels*) explains, "The first step of the collaboration is to get from the director the style of the show ... whether or not it's going to be realistic or naturalistic or high style or whatever." "I need someone to steer the ship," says lighting designer Jaymi Smith. "I like the director to take the lead," says lighting designer Tom Ruzika. "I want a director that will push me," says scene designer Jo Winiarski. "I want a director that will push me" echoes costume designer Holly Durbin, employing the identical words in a separate interview. These are all longtime professional designers who believe *very deeply* in collaboration, but also continue to insist that they require leadership from the director.

Having a leader in the forefront also can make the experience more enjoyable. Gabriel Berry, a veteran costume designer, says, "If you feel you know better and start telling the director what to do, it becomes less of a collaboration, and the fun goes away."

It is entirely natural that designers (and everyone else on the team) will expect leadership from the director, who, after all, is engaged to "direct" the work. And directing requires the assumption of leadership that has been discussed throughout this book. But leadership is not a one-way street, and costume designer Janet Swenson chooses excellent words to describe what she needs from a director – and what she doesn't: "I love a director who, while firmly keeping everyone focused on the final goal, allows the members of the team to dream dreams and add their voices to the song."

So this is the balance that the director ideally makes between authority and giving designers (and others) their say – and allowing them to "add to the song." Or, as would be generally said today, to have a sense of ownership of a production for which they will be making massive contributions of their own personal imagination – as well as their talent, training, energy, time, and profound commitment.

How then do you strike this balance in this planning, where directors and designers first meet and collaborate? We will proceed with some specific suggestions for both groups. We will also divide the timeline into two parts: *Conversations*, which are largely (but not always) one-on-one, introductory and personal, and *Meetings*, which are multiparty and work-centered. Either may be face-to-face or virtual.

Initial conversations: introductions

Each director-designer conversation should begin with some sort of introduction – even if the two persons have worked together before.

And it is indeed right from the beginning that a letter, email, or phone call of introduction from director to each designer can set the tone for creating a welcoming atmosphere and a collaborative tone, whether the individuals know each other or not.

A sample first line in an email with a stranger: "Hi, Joan, I'm [your name here] and am delighted to know we're going to be working with each other on *The Threepenny Opera* this summer," is always a good start. Or a sample first line to a previous collaborator: "Hi, Janet, I'm delighted to be able to work with you again!"

In either case, a sample second line: "I've got a ton of ideas floating around in my head for this show, so I'd like to know when would be a convenient time to get together/get in touch to thrash about some possible starting points."

The opening line makes clear you're looking forward to working with the designer in question; the second shows that you are already considering a variety of options, but are wide open to new ones, and far from foreclosing alternatives.

Except, of course, where you *have* made decisions, firm or tentative, in which case you should make that clear in your third line. As, for example: "I should let you know that the producers and I are already keen on using the Marc Blitzstein translation, because of its political directness and the jazziness and muscularity of its rhymes, but if you have any alternate suggestions I'll be happy to take a look."

Or, if you have made a firm decision on the translation, you should be upfront but not heavy-handed by saying something like, "I should let you know that the producers and I have decided to use the Marc Blitzstein translation of this play, because of its jazziness and muscularity, but all other decisions are wide open at this point." This lets the designer know that such decisions that have been made have been pre-approved by the producers (who in fact may have prompted or even mandated them) and that you and they have a solid *reason* for making that choice.

In either event, you are establishing your *willingness and capability to lead the project* – but also that you remain equally *open to welcoming a vast array of contributions* from all members of the design team.

You may have made other decisions too, which were significant in your deciding to accept the assignment of directing this particular play. Or maybe you are a producer-director and know quite firmly what you intend in certain areas, in which case such decisions should certainly be mentioned in your letter of introduction, though your language can still remain welcoming rather than dictatorial; for example: "The producers and I are hoping to emphasize the depth of the characters' longings more than the more typical Brechtian alienation, and see if we can tap into the sense of personal anguish of lost loves in the unsettled era between the two world wars that seems much like our own time." Or "I know this play has often been done in Victorian dress, as the era in which it is set, but I am planning on setting it in the time of its writing as I think the European jazz-age hairstyles and costumes will make a thrilling parallel with the excesses of today's fashion." The language in these sample sentences – which includes the director's reasons for making these decisions rather than just baldly stating them – will help guide your colleague to the "same page" that Hal Prince speaks of bringing your entire team toward, since you have not, in your careful language, squelched any further discussions your teammates may wish to initiate.

Sometimes, a single design idea can spur an entire concept. Director/choreographer Susan Stroman cites one example from her own work: "The design team can sometimes give you the key to an entire show. For example, in *Contact,* I merely told costume designer William Ivey Long that I envisioned a girl in a yellow dress. Nothing more than that. It was William who came back to me with the absolute right color yellow and the absolute right style."

So the director's letter (or phone call or email) of introduction is not merely a social nicety. It is a baby step that starts the artistic collaboration. It's also a *personal* contact that makes clear you are eager to be working with the human being within the design professional. (And it won't hurt if somewhere in your email you remark, as we noted in the section on researching your collaborators, how much you liked a previous production of the designer's that you have seen, or seen pictures of – if of course you really did.)

And it's a step that invites a designer to respond in kind, and *this becomes the designer's opportunity* to take one or two baby steps of his or her own. Below, for example, are excerpts from introductory emails between the director (myself) and the scenic designer (Jo Winiarski, whom I had not previously met) for the 2008 production of Molière's *School of Wives* at the Utah Shakespearean Festival (USF) in Cedar City:

> from me:
>
> Sept 26, 2007
>
> Dear Jo,
>
> I'm so pleased to be working with you on School of Wives next year at the USF!

I won't load you down with any material until you're ready – I know you're in the thick of opening three shows for the Fall season, so I'll await word from you when you're ready to tackle M. Molière. I'm in fact coming up to Cedar City in a couple of weeks to see the Fall shows and I look forward to getting acquainted with your work.

The "material" I've begun to prepare, I should make clear, is at this point just a series of questions and discussion topics. While I've settled with the artistic directors on a translation (the new one by Ranjit Bolt) and the period (1662 – the date of its writing), I'm otherwise open to anything. But I do have some starting points I'd like to share...

Well, for now it's back to our current work...

Robert

And from Jo:

Sept 27, 2007

Dear Robert,

I have started researching 17th century French architecture and have an idea that I think relates to your French theater of the period. I should have a rough sketch to you by the end of next week – as a place to start a conversation.

One thought I did have is that I would love for the set to be very saturated in color – fuchsia-chartreuse-gold. This is the strongest thought I have immediately – and it is unlike anything I have ever done in Utah...

My very best,

Jo

In this exchange, I as the director narrowed down the scope of collaboration on only two fronts – the choice of translation and historical period – making clear that everything else was on the table, and that my next communication would only be to frame questions, discussion topics and introduce a couple of additional "starting points." In responding, Jo as the scene designer implicitly accepted the period choice and signaled her own primary design interest – regarding color – while giving a reason for this choice. This proved a perfect set of introductory "baby steps" to start narrowing the field down for more specific conversations that would follow.

The initial director-designer collaboration at this stage may be more than just a few letters or emails – it may be a series of discussions that go on for weeks or months. Nor need it be straight-to-the-point planning. Hal Prince describes his initial conversations with scene designer Boris Aronson on the 1966 world premiere of the musical *Cabaret* as lengthy and wide-ranging: "We talked for three months, rarely of things visual, mostly of the characters, false motivations, interpersonal behavior, people in different countries, ethnic peculiarities, emotional expression as affected by national or ethnic considerations. Of course, he collected thousands of photographs, but he never observed the predictable: never the leg of a table, the shape of a lamppost, the ironwork on the hotel balcony rail. Rather, he would call my attention to the expression of the shoppers on the street, to the quality of light in a room, the emotional content in the architecture of a section of the city…. When Boris talks, I hear and see things I neither heard nor saw before." Clearly, this is an ideal collaboration – the meeting and melding of two very different minds leading to a synthesis that is greater than the sum of its parts. The show played 1165 performances, won Tony Awards for Prince and Aronson (along with Best Musical and five others) and changed musical theatre history. Those shoppers on the street would have a lot to be proud of, if they only knew.

Group conversations

At some point, usually after such one-on-one introductory conversations, broader, multiparty conversations will ensue, either face-to-face, over coffee or lunch perhaps, or electronically (virtually), employing videoconferences, conference calls, group emails with attachments, or extended, where necessary, to the occasional FedEx delivery.

The earlier such group conversations take place, the better. Gordon Perlman, who largely invented computerized lighting for the original production of *A Chorus Line*, remarks that, "In any collaboration, the sooner people are brought together on any project, that's always the way to eliminate problems when you walk into the theatre."

As with the Prince-Aronson conversations, however, the initial steps in these conversations need not be about scenic dimensions or lighting wattages. Ordinarily, the collaborative work begins with the director's expression – conveyed to the entire team (and here's where a mass email, if a face-to-face team meeting is not possible – is useful) of his or her first thoughts as to the *mission* and initial *conception* of the production as described in the previous chapter. What does the director hope the production will *do* – rather than what it should *look like* or *sound like?* Jo Winiarski says, "I hope that the first conversation is *not* about scenery at all. I don't think I would do a show where the scenery is simply dictated."

If the first conversation is not about scenery (or costumes, or lighting, or sound), then what *is* it about? For most, it is about ideas: a tone, a style, a concept, a series of drifting images. Winiarski gives the example of director Dan Safer's first comment about the set as he saw it for a *Bus Stop* production he was directing: "This needs to be a diner where dreams can be realized." The simple, almost metaphysical comment opened up a completely new world of imagination for the designer.

Susan Stroman gives useful guidelines as to what else this initial directorial expression should contain: a signal of leadership. The director, Stroman says "has to make sure from the beginning that everybody is on the same page. What is the idea that you want to present? Do you want to present an entertainment? A serious morality tale? Something that pulls at the heartstrings? That teaches a lesson? The director has to make sure that the whole team knows exactly what the point is and why they are working on the project…. Why are we doing this *for the audience*."

What else do the designers hope to receive from a director? Here is a list that Utah Shakespearean Festival veteran costume designer Janet Swenson wants from the directors she works with – and which any director aspiring to lead an effective collaboration might well keep in mind:

- Careful and thorough **preparation**. The director gives the team its starting point – a reason to read and study and research and contribute.
- **Guidance**; a clear vision; a goal. A common destination – and the director is ultimately the one who should provide it.
- **Sharing** of ideas, no matter how diverse – the give-and-take with the entire creative team that leads to a final vision.
- **Perceptiveness**: the director must be willing to really look, really listen and fully understand how all parts can work together and complement each other.
- Thoughtful, informed **responses** to designers' questions. While many questions can be answered with a quick "yes" or "no," there are others that need to be given more than cursory consideration.

- **Joy** in the process. I love working with directors who get as much pleasure in the creative process as I do!

Directors who pay attention to these suggestions are virtually certain to get the greatest energy and commitment from the designers they work with. Yet nothing here should suggest that directors should cease "directing" the design elements of the production. As Broadway director George C. Wolfe says, "Collaboration does not mean surrender." Rather, he continues, "Collaboration consists of going forth with your strongest passion and your strongest idea and meeting someone, or any number of people, with their strongest idea. And then, something new emerges, something hopefully better."

Designers and designers

The collaborative relationships forged among the designers, each with each other, can be absolutely crucial to the final result, yet these collective processes are often ignored by the director – as well as by many in the design team. This is a mistake. In surveying today's designers about their recent collaborations, nothing came up as frequently as poor organization and communication *within* the design team.

Of course it is ideal to start a design process by gathering everyone as soon as possible, and at the same time and same place, but this rarely happens today – particularly in the single-production model where designers are often geographically distant and not all hired at the same time; moreover one might be ready to start work while another is in the midst of technical rehearsals for another show.

But a welcoming email from the director to the *entire team* can at least create the sense that ideas are welcome from the start – if indeed they are. And so the director can exercise some initial control over this, and the designers can follow suit by shooting off at least a quick, if necessarily brief, response.

A lighting designer points out the obvious snag if this is not followed: "Some directors involve the entire team from the start. Others I've worked for, however, go to the scenic designer first and only share afterwards. But if I get the scene design when it's already finished, I'm simply not part of the creative process! I'd prefer that we could all brainstorm about the play and think about its possibilities before committing to any finished plan. But then that's me!"

No, it's not just her; almost every designer feels this way. Another lighting designer reports that much of the time "I'm simply hired to come in and light the show" as the set is not only already designed, it's already been built. "I don't have any ownership, even though we're said to have collaborated together. Of course there are always different levels of personal investment, but I don't want not to be invested at all!" Nor should the director or the other designers: if the lighting designer is not invested, can they really think he or she is going to give the 110%?

It's not always scene designers, of course, but since they "create the world" as William Ivey Long says above, and are at the top of the "informal" or historical hierarchy, they very often get a jumpstart on the process. A veteran costume designer lists this as the major recurring problem throughout her entire career. "I've worked on a huge number of projects where the first time I meet the other designers in person is tech rehearsals. Most of the time the scenic designer is hired well before the costume designer; by the time I come along, the set is designed or well under way. And since they've started earlier, they've often been amazingly uncooperative. One opera designer said to me, 'My set model was done months ago – Just design your clothes to go on my set.' Many haven't even sent me photos of their set models or even returned phone calls or emails, explaining they've already moved onto another project or aren't in their studios where they can access their files. I've had to track down the tech directors to look at set models, the scenic painters to see what color the set really will be, and the props people and set decorators to find out what the upholstery looks like! On a recent production, the set designer changed the paint color after my costumes were built without telling me – so at dress rehearsal I was mortified to find my costumes blended right into the walls. My leading lady's costumes had to be re-dyed for opening night!" These are indeed problems that need addressing. Designers do come into the process at different times and in different ways: often for budgetary reasons. Lighting and sound designers are often hired late in the process, showing up for the first time at the designer run-through (a rehearsal where the cast runs through the entire show, so the designers can see the staging as it has thus far developed), and are therefore relegated to doing the bulk of their work from then to – and through – the technical and dress rehearsals that follow. And the newer technologies of projections, moving lights and videography are often brought into the process – along with their own designers – later than that, which if not carefully pre-planned can throw the schedule and the artistic "look" of a show into utter chaos.

And since, as one scenic designer says, "a great lighting designer is a scene designer's best friend, and a bad one is a scene designer's nightmare," and, as most directors today want sound design integrated far earlier in the process, it is incumbent upon all to plan the *timing* of the collaborative integration skillfully to allow for the healthy development of a brilliantly created production. Production Managers are, in theatres that have them, specifically charged with coordinating the timing of the introduction of such design and technical elements during the production process, but the director should be fully aware of how and when these elements are stitched together to form the fabric of the final product.

Of course, it is ideal in the single-production-model to have all the designers and the director come together, in person and collectively, long before rehearsals begin. Costume designer Holly Poe Durbin loves those directors who "cajole, whine or browbeat producers into paying for group meetings early in the process." Lacking that, however, ideas, designs, concerns, and feedback can be exchanged throughout the team by electronic means with (literally) lightning speed, and at any time of day or night, and there is simply no excuse for not doing so – except when someone simply doesn't want to. So your "noncooperation," if that's what you exhibit, becomes a documented part of your record; this may be fine, if you're a superstar in your field, but it's not so great if you're trying to build a professional career – or reach the high standard of theatrical art that Bartlett Sher and his four designers did winning their individual (but yet collective) Tony Awards for *South Pacific*.

There are some designer-to-designer relationships that are particularly critical. Scenery and lighting have already been mentioned, since the appearance, and particularly the color, of scenery is entirely subject to what light falls on it. Scenery and costumes need special conversations because where there are walls or a cyclorama (as in most proscenium settings), costume colors should clearly "pop out" in contrast to them – unless having them blend in is an intentional part of the production's concept. Sound and lighting design must be in especially close rapport with each other, first because lighting instruments and sound speakers can get in each other's way, and second, because their cues are normally timed to coincide with each other – as well as with the scene shifts and indications of time's passing. "We're collectively focused on the rhythm, the beat, the movement; so we must work out the beats together," says sound designer Vince Olivieri about this process, who finds it essential to sit next to the lighting designer during technical rehearsals so they can build their cues together.* Sound coordination with scenic and costume designers is also important, of course, particularly with regard to the placement of visible loudspeakers on the set and to body mics in the actor's hair, wig, or costume.

And of course sound designers must collaborate with composers and music directors. For *The Hurt Locker,* for example, Kathryn Bigelow reports that she "wanted to sort of blur the distinction between sound design and score, and I presented this as an idea to both the sound designer and the composers and they both loved that ... They thought that it would be a really interesting creative space in which to work. For instance, [Sound Designer] Paul Ottosson gave the composers many of his sound design tracks ... like the sounds of helicopters or F-14s flying overhead ... so many of these beautiful textures that he had .... So the composers were able to actually utilize the components of the sound design and begin to weave together subtly rhythmic and sonic textures that melded beautifully with the design. And it was really ... that kind of cohesive collaboration right from the beginning." Bigelow became first woman ever to win the Academy Award in Directing for her work on this film.

Often the specific needs in collaboration follow no general pattern but depend on the specific production. Where a production is using sound and lights to tell much of the story (as for crucial battle or fantasy scenes that are heard but not seen), the sound and lighting designers should be part of the design collaborations from the earliest possible time. But even when these special cases are not anticipated, the earlier all designers can get together, the more options can be imagined and explored early enough to begin experimenting with actually employing them. "I like the blank slate, where everyone comes to the table at the same time and in the same space. I want to be creative, not reactive; I want to dance with the scenic designer," says lighting designer Jaymi Smith.

---

*Olivieri is admittedly one of the few sound designers who works this way, but directors who have worked with him, and I am one, find the integration achieved by this method astounding.

But of course these are often ideal circumstances. There is often friction among design teams, partly because of the presumed hierarchy among them, partly from the difference in timing (who gets hired first, who gets consulted first, who gets a design approved first), along with differences in geography both before the team assembles (who lives where) and after they do (whose shop is where). Unlike the acting ensemble that works together in the rehearsal hall on a daily if not hourly basis (see next chapter), the "design ensemble" generally builds their product (scenery, costumes, cues) in separate studios and shops, sometimes even in separate cities, and they – and, more importantly, their collective creations – do not ordinarily appear together in one place until the period of "load-in" just before tech and dress rehearsals begin, at which scenery, lighting, costumes, and sound are all put together in the theatre for the first time.

Yet it is the integration of the design *ensemble,* not simply the assemblage of design components, that truly defines the theatrical masterpiece, and when a reviewer reports having left the theatre "whistling the scenery," the scenic designer, as well as the director, should not be pleased but embarrassed. Broadway director Susan Stroman reports that one of her first shows "was a disastrous experience…I don't think all the departments were working on the same show. The collaboration was not as strong as it should have been."

In sum, it is chiefly the responsibility of the designers – and overseeing them, the director – to assure the successful "working together" of all those who plan and create the design elements – with each other and with the actors and other artists who come on board in the production stage. Designers should consult freely with each other but not – unless specifically and openly asked by the producers or director to do so – assume a hierarchical authority over each other. The collaboration must be a willing and continual effort of director and designers alike, with their integration with the acting and staging as the ultimate goal of the entire production team.

Directors and producers

Finally, we might identify one more level of collaboration at the planning level, which is between the director and the producer, or perhaps we should say the director and the chief accountant, because these collaborations have to do with reconsiderations of established budgets.

Most productions go into planning with an estimated budget already in mind, based upon the cast size, expected number of costumes and the complexity of the other design elements. But of course this budget is usually subject to further negotiation.

During the planning process, every decision has budgetary implications. Whether or not to add a costume, a prop, an actor, a mechanical lift for a climactic entrance through a trap door, follow-spots (and follow-spot operators), or fifty more hours of overtime labor in the wig room – all of these will add to the cost of the production. And as brilliant as these additions may appear when they arise in the planning meetings, the producer may have to be asked to bump up the budget estimate if they are to be actually realized on the stage. So here the director, speaking for the team, must seek to renegotiate the show's budget with the producer. (If there are senior designers working on the show, with institutional ties to the producer, they too may be useful in this negotiation.)

Needless to say, the director's or designers' hands will be stronger if the new ideas come not just from themselves but from the entire artistic team. And of course their case is stronger if something already in the budget can be given up, or acquired more cheaply, to compensate for the added expense of the newer elements. And it's *far* stronger if the idea is truly brilliant – that is, if it augurs for a much more exciting and successful production, and perhaps even a larger ticket sale to pay for the new costs.

But directors and artistic team members should bear in mind that there is almost *always* more money available, or that can be made available – under most circumstances, and no director should shy away from making respectful and well-studied requests – unless, of course, this route has been specifically and irreversibly prohibited.

Exercises

Here are some exercises that have been used effectively to help theatre practitioners polish their skills in communication and collaboration during the planning stage. Unlike the exercises in the previous – preparation stage – chapter, these are all for groups.

1. **Bake cookies**. My colleague Cliff Faulkner uses this exercise in the first weeks of his class in collaboration for graduate theatre directors and designers. The class is divided into groups of four or five students from each of the directing and design areas, and assigned to make and serve a batch of cookies. Nothing to it, it would seem – but the results are revelatory. Meetings must be held, a kitchen found, a recipe voted on, ingredients acquired, a schedule created, a labor allocation determined, a budget established and assessed, phone numbers and email addresses obtained and circulated, delivery arrangements for the final batch decided, and a final accounting made and costs equally divided among the members. Wow! And all that just to bake a batch of cookies! At the following class, each team of cookie-bakers distributes its product and reports on what each encountered and learned from the others.

2. **Walk in another's shoes**. This is adapted from another Faulkner exercise. Each student director and designer in his collaboration class prepares a report on the two or three things he or she thinks a student artist in *another* area finds most challenging in the collaborative process: a costume designer, for example, reports what she thinks directors worry most about; the director might report on what pet peeves a sound designer lives with, the lighting designer might second-guess the scenic designer's major concerns. Then each student in the "other" area ranks the reporting student's comment from one to five on how correct his or her report is, also pointing out what the report may have omitted. Thus each student "walks in the shoes" of someone in another discipline, and learns how much he or she *doesn't* know – and needs to learn – about how people in that discipline might feel.

3. **Plan a show.** This one is easy – because it's hard. A group leader (the teacher if in a class situation) acts as a producer and assigns a "team" of a director and three or four designers, giving them a hypothetical production to stage, such as "a two-hour *Hamlet* set in the American Civil War, limited to a cast of nine actors and to be performed in the campus's black-box theatre." The director has two days to initiate introductory emails, and two weeks to come in with his or her team and a fully realized written concept, together with a staging plan and a sampling of costume renderings, scenic drawings, sound clips, and lighting ideas – and, in an appendix, copies of all written communications between the team members.

5

The Production Stage

And now everything – and almost everyone – involved in mounting the production comes together, at one place and at one time.

The team is multiplied fourfold, eightfold, maybe twentyfold, because by now the actors and the stage managers and the carpenters and electricians and seamstresses have arrived.

They are, of course, not all strangers to the team. For the most part, the actors have been auditioned and cast and the stage managers and technicians appointed in the previous weeks or even months. Some have already started work. The lead stage manager (usually titled the production stage manager or PSM) has possibly attended one or more design meetings and probably contacted the director during the production's planning phase to develop the rehearsal procedures and initial schedules that will be put into effect. Technicians have consulted production heads to review the designs and order necessary supplies, tools, and equipment. Now, as the acting company meets in the rehearsal hall and the building of sets, props, and costumes begin in the theatre's shops, hearts begin to race. The air of excitement is obvious. The production, until now merely words and images on paper, three-dimension models, sound clips, and computer screens, actually begins to breathe.

Actors and directors

The most intense collaborations in the theatre are between directors and actors – as moderated and overseen by the stage managers.

This is mainly because of the sheer amount of time that directors and actors spend in each others' presence, intermixing and interacting with each other for hours on end, six days a week. But it is also because of the intellectual and emotional intensity of those interactions as the play's conflicts, love stories, passionate debates, and epic adventures come to life in the minds and bodies of actors and directors alike.

Therefore, while we have referred to directors and actors separately in the previous chapters, it is now time to consider them in concert. How can actors best collaborate with directors? And why should they? And how can directors best lead this collaboration without destroying it?

The actor's schizophrenia

One might forgive actors a bit of schizophrenia. On the one hand, they all but dominate the stage. Historically, they were the first artists of the theatre; improvising their texts before there were playwrights and staging their moves before there were directors. These ancient thespians probably designed and made their costumes as well. Why should they need a director?

Moreover, they are the celebrities of the theatre. In almost all cases, they are the only theatrical workers the audience actually sees and hears and the only ones who receive the audience's applause. They are generally the primary targets of critics' praise and brickbats. If they become the "stars" of their profession they become world-famous in a way that few directors and virtually no other practitioners achieve. They make the most money, land the sexiest housemates, tout their achievements on the best talk shows, and segue into the niftiest second-career jobs you can imagine (President of the United States and Governor of California for starters). When actors are on top, they're on the top of the top.

But when they're on the bottom, they're the lowest of the low. There's no question about this. Workaday actors (as opposed to stars) are generally the last hired, least consulted, and most exposed members of a theatrical or film production company. They are herded from dressing room to rehearsal hall to costume shop to photo-shoot and then back to the dressing room – with little to say about their scheduling or comfort or next assignment. TV directors rarely even know the names of the day-players (actors hired for a single day) in their shows, and their directions are more often than not given to them not in person but via an assistant director or even a "floor manager." They are put on hold for hours at a time without explanation; they are stripped, corseted, clothed, high-heeled, bewigged, and grease-painted at the discretion of dozens of anonymous, and occasionally all-thumbed, technicians. And this is all to become fresh meat for the sharpest tongued journalists alive, whose scathing comments may extend over their talent, looks, age, personality, sex appeal (or lack of same), and presumed sexual proclivities.

It is little wonder that actors, torn between such contrary depictions of their profession, may struggle with ontological insecurities or identity crises. That acting is itself the art of *creating* an identity – a stage character – only emphasizes the seriousness of their problems.

All this means that actors cannot afford to see themselves so far up nor so far down life's ladder as to be outside the parameters of ordinary humanity. They, like all professionals, must develop healthy self-images and vigorous but balanced egos. Workaday actors – meaning those who seek to make some or all of their living performing in plays and films – cannot expect to become superstars; the odds against that are akin to being hit by an errant asteroid. But they should not expect to become victims, either. Actors are *workers*; and, necessarily, coworkers in the theatre's artistic and commercial engagement. They must position themselves accordingly.

And so the next sections of this book are addressed directly to actors, and particularly to those persons who want to become actors. Some of these precepts may seem harsh, but the world will prove all the harsher to those who haven't yet reckoned with them.

The actor's attitude

Attitude is, most basically, the way we face – or confront – the world.

The word has taken on a negative connotation in recent years, as in the expression, "We don't need any attitude around here." But the word's denotation is actually neutral; it refers only to positioning. In aeronautics, a rocket ship's attitude is its angle of orientation to the ground – an angle of descent, say. Come in from outer space one degree too head-on and you crash-land; come in one degree too flat, however, and you skip back off into the atmosphere.

And so, in acting, we should more properly say that the actor's attitude is his or her angle of orientation to the play and the production. In both theatre and aviation, only the perfect attitude will leave you aiming high and flying fast – but landing gently.

But bad attitudes will have you plummeting to earth like a rock or sailing off into the great unknown. It's exceedingly well known in the theatre that having a reputation for a "bad attitude" will destroy the career hopes of even the most talented below-star-level performer.

Such reputations spread through the theatre and film colonies like viral videos. Jeff Greenberg, the veteran casting director of *Cheers*, *Frasier*, and *Ugly Betty* makes it quite simple: "I want to hire wonderful people to take to a set filled with wonderful people. I don't want an inkling of an 'attitude.' There are enough people out there that if there's someone we feel might be troublesome, we just don't...go down that road."

A "ruinous" attitude

But what exactly *is* that "attitude" that Greenberg doesn't want an inkling of?

Almost everyone knows the obvious traits of a truly *ruinous* attitude: it's showing up late, showing up drunk, not showing up at all, not knowing your lines, upstaging other actors, talking off set within hearing (and therefore disturbing) distance, drinking coffee in costume, goofing off when no one else is, and a whole host of sins for which directors and stage managers have chided actors since the time (no doubt) of Aeschylus.

In a professional situation, any one of these sins may stop you from being rehired for your next job – and any two of them are likely to get you fired off the set you're already working on.

I'm not going to spend any more time talking about a ruinous attitude, since you wouldn't be reading this book if you thought you could get away with anything this horrendous. But there's a lot more yet to say on this topic.

A bad attitude

There are far more subtle examples of attitude malfeasance that, if not ruinous, will stall if not completely stop your professional career. You may not have noticed these, so pay attention.

The merely "bad" attitude includes displaying an archly raised eyebrow, a wrinkled nose, a studied puzzlement, a weary glance toward another actor, and any such behavior that tells everyone who sees it that you think your time is being wasted, or your talent is being ignored, or the director (or floor manager, or costume fitter) has no idea of what he or she is doing or talking about.

Understand that even such silent expressions of your irritation, which of course do nothing whatever to advance your artistry, are potentially catastrophic to your future. Niccolò Machiavelli, in his 1513 essay *The Prince*, introduced the extraordinary maxim that "men should be flattered or annihilated." As we approach the 500th anniversary of this remark, we note that nothing in the intervening centuries has disproved an iota of it. The apparent cruelty (and sexism – it also applies to women) aside, the aphorism only means that you really only have two choices when confronted with disagreeable people: get along with them or get rid of them. Well, you can't get rid of them, so you're going to have to get along with them. But what you must *never* do is to *insinuate your disapproval* of them. That is the world's worst lose-lose option. All it will do is make them even more disagreeable, and then they'll get rid of *you* – eventually, if not immediately. There is absolutely no room, in an adult collaboration, for whining, sneering, rolling your eyeballs, or expressing your boredom, skepticism, or irritation by the use of such sophomoric showing off of your vaunted superiority. Absolutely nobody wants to work with someone who gives him or her less than full-hearted support, and nobody will ever work *again* with such a person, if they can find a way not to do so.

Understand that you won't find this confirmed by watching film stars chat with the TV talk show hosts. They will only emphasize how loose, chummy, outrageous, freewheeling, and free-spirited they are when they work. That's because they're appearing on television to let the world know they are Big Stars Who Can Do What They Want. This is their image, and they're burnishing it. And if they really are stars, they pretty much *can* do what they want – at least up to a point. But unless you're a star, you can't. There are two ways of destroying your career fast: trying to behave like a star before you are one, and believing that what a star says on a TV show is a guidepost for becoming a star yourself. The overriding principle is that pride, ego, and cynicism defeat more acting careers than bad technique, dopey readings, and leaky sibilants put together.

Here are some even more subtle examples of what could be considered bad actor-attitudes:

- casting aspersions on fellow artists
- showing up even thirty seconds late and not apologizing at the first opportunity – and with a very persuasive explanation
- seeking special favors or privileges from the theatre staff
- calling in sick on anything other than an urgent occasion
- giving unsolicited acting notes to fellow cast members
- asking too many questions of the director
- not knowing your lines

You may have done some of these in your high school or college or community theatres, and it may be that no one corrected you for doing so. But know that any *one* of these behaviors can put you on the producer's "don't hire next time" list if you employ them in professional situations. And you will never know why the phone has stopped ringing.

Holding disparate views

But does "flatter or annihilate" mean you must smile in compliance at everything you're told or asked to do? Or that you have to totally sacrifice your personal vision, goals, ideas and artistic responses in favor of some idiot director? No, not at all. Working successfully within a *collaborative framework* means both much less than mild acquiescence to everything thrown at you – and also much more.

Honesty is not contradictory to collaboration – it is essential to it. Kenny Leon, director of the 2004 Tony Award-winning *A Raisin in the Sun*, writes about his work with Sean Combs who played Walter Lee Younger: "He's a perfectionist and that goes with my personality because I'm a perfectionist. He likes the truth and I always give him the truth and he gives me the truth. We're working toward the same thing." You do *not* need cave into falsifying your views or even to silently agreeing with whatever comes your way. But you *do* need to know where, when, and how to draw lines between your views and those of others.

Disparate views are commonplace in the theatre, as they are in all multi-individual artistic creations. Actor Edward Norton has wisely noted that "Harmony on the set is way overrated," and understands that, in rehearsals, "conflict is a very essential thing." But this doesn't mean that deliberate disharmony – pushing other people around – is some sort of goal. Norton concludes his remark by saying, "but if the reasons everyone is pushing each other have to do with *a group desire to make things as good as possible*, that's a *great* thing!"

The starting point

So a good collaborative attitude must be your starting point. This means that Rule Number One, as identified earlier in this book, becomes the actor's Role Number One, with that role being the production as a whole rather than just his or her own part. As Peter Brook says, "The actor must never forget that *the play is greater than himself.* If he thinks he can grasp the play, he will cut it down to his own size. If, however, he respects its mystery – and consequently that of the character he is playing – as being always just beyond his grasp, he will recognize that his 'feelings' are a very treacherous guide. He will see that a sympathetic but rigorous director can help him to distinguish between intuitions that lead to truth and feelings that are self indulgent."

America's first great acting company – the Group Theatre, which set the tone for the century of great actors that followed – was created on that very foundation. As the great actress, acting teacher, and Group co-founder Stella Adler said about those early years, "The actors who were interested from the beginning in the formation of such a group were those who accepted the theatre's *overall concept –* and consequently knew [their] place in relation to it, especially as it pertained to the actor's ego. The very nature of ensemble demanded this understanding."

This requires a constantly good attitude. It comes from what Norton called a "group desire" and what Stella Adler (and Harold Clurman, Lee Strasberg, Elia Kazan, Clifford Odets, and the other members) called a Group Theatre. Take away the capitals and know that the people you work with comprise a "group theatre" like that one. And that you're in good company – as well as a good company.

This focus leads to the positive charge you can to bring to your acting ensemble so that they can bring it to the audience. And for an actor, as was said in this book's introduction, being seen in a fabulously received *production,* even if in a minor role, is far more important for your future prospects than whatever you might be able to achieve in a mediocre one: more people will see it, more people will love it, and more people will remember it. And therefore more people will see remember *you* for having been in it, certainly more than will see and remember actors – even the stars – in a failed play, movie, or sitcom. And among your new admirers will be most of the agents, directors, producers, and casting people in the business. That is why being in a long-running and critically successful production is the best single step toward getting your next – and possibly better – role. So make the brilliance of the *production,* not just your role in it, your greatest concern.

It is not easy to make this transition from self-interest to ensemble-interest, though. In your younger school days you were largely expected to work on your own: to do *your* homework, get A's in *your* exams, and get *yourself* into college. Whatever higher education you may have experienced, this self-propulsion has probably been much of the same order. Learning to throw your professional lot in with strangers – sometimes dozens and sometimes *hundreds* of strangers – is for many theatre artists a new experience when and if they enter the professional arena. And being judged not primarily on your own merits, but rather on the merits of the project you happen to have landed in, is for most at this point in their lives a radically new experience.

But what must be overcome is the *self-centered* attitude you brought with you from high school. You must work away from the egocentrism (seeing yourself as the center of everything) that privileges *your* problems and *your* personal and career goals over those of your collaborators and outside of the mission of the project. "Acting is not a competition," says Michael Caine, the British stage manager who became a great stage and film actor, in his fine book, *Acting in Film*. "Almost without exception, actors help each other," Caine reports, adding that "in [this] business, the list of people whose careers suddenly ground to a halt is the same as the list of actors who tried to make enemies or pull tricks."

A good attitude, then, is one that leaves egotism and self-centeredness behind, and lends all its force to the collective enterprise.

But how do you do that without sacrificing your individual gifts? How do you get in the hit show and make certain you also deliver a hit performance? On a larger scale, how do you integrate your individuality – and your individual views – into the collectivity of the enterprise? For this is the actor's problem more than any other theatre artist's – because while all the theatre's contributing artists must collaborate, the actors will form a "living collective" within the production's overall collective. They exercise their art as a group, interacting with each other *during the production* and not just in meetings and activities during the weeks leading up to opening night. They form the production's *permanent ensemble*.

In that ensemble, actors must blend their individual goals into Edward Norton's "*group* desire to make things as good as possible," and must merge their multiple paths toward the production's single-minded mission. They become the manifold tributaries that ease their way into a single but mighty river.

So, how do you play your role as a tributary of the river rather than a barrier? How do you add to the river's flow rather than just dam it up?

Tone of voice

The first technique begins by realizing that disparate views are not – at the outset – disagreements. They begin as simply disparate views. So you should treat them as such. Consider the difference between saying, as an actor playing Hamlet, to a director who has just asked you to play a line a certain way,

> "I disagree, Jim. I think that Hamlet here is saying such and such…"

from asking,

> "Jim, do you think it could be possible that Hamlet here is saying such and such?"

In both cases, disparate views are being placed squarely on the table, but the first utterance – a statement – starts a battle in which there will either be a winner and a loser, or perhaps an unresolved antagonism. The second utterance, however, which is a question rather than a statement, merely starts an inquiry, one that will in all likelihood lead to a quick mutual agreement.

It is *tone* (of your voice, your attitude, your physical expression) that is crucial here. You can hardly say, "I disagree, Jim" without a bit of smirking: wrinkling your nose, raising an eyebrow, cocking your head, or subtly dropping your final inflection in mock despair. But with the second utterance, delivered with a cheerful tone, a broad and genuine smile, and a rising and hopeful inflection, you will induce – and perhaps even seduce – a positive response. Guess which of these will be the most effective "tones" to strengthen, rather than dam up, the river you're cruising down? Guess which is the best at getting you *what you want*?

Indeed, merely starting your comment with the word "I" is to privilege yourself, and thereby your personal viewpoint. Whereas starting with "Do *you*..." privileges your collaborator, whose opinion you are soliciting, and the *topic* (the production) that is your mutual goal. And with this question you're discussing the production and its mission, not just yourself and your role. In either case you are raising the issue, but in the second version your inquiry will be welcomed and appreciated, while in the first it might become a live hand grenade – particularly if presented at an inopportune moment, and certainly if it is done publicly, in front of the cast – who will read it as a challenge to the director's authority, ideas, or leadership.

The overall point, simple enough, is to present yourself in a manner that's *collaborative rather than confrontational*. All directors will, from time to time, give a blocking note or request that an actor will not feel comfortable executing. The issue is how to deal with it. The actor who, given such a direction, turns and asks,

> "And exactly why should I do that?"

even if speaking in an apparently friendly manner, is clearly taking a confrontational stance, stopping the rehearsal and publicly challenging the director. Suppose, instead, the actor were to go ahead and execute the action as directed but, at the next break (and if he still feels as he did), take the director aside and ask,

> "Jim, what do you think is the best reason Hamlet would make that cross?"

The identical question is posed, but as part of a conversation rather than a challenge. "Why should I do that?" openly signals disdain – not just for the direction but also the director, implying that the director does not understand the actor's basic need to motivate his or her character's moves from within, and flinging down the gauntlet of Stanislavsky and suchlike acting gurus. The all-but-inevitable debate that will follow, in addition to taking up a large block of rehearsal time, will segue quickly from the specific blocking move to fundamental issues of acting theory, and whatever emerges will be, at best, a grudging compromise rather than a flowing river.

Whereas "What do you think is the best reason Hamlet might do that?" does not dispute anything at all. It only seeks guidance; indeed, by asking why Hamlet would make that cross instead of why *you* should, you are asking the director to respond about the character in the play rather than about you the actor. And what do you know – the director might in fact have a darn good idea why Hamlet would do it! And if he or she doesn't, you'll probably get an "OK, how do *you* think you should respond?" So in either case you have won the battle without losing the war – or your next job.

The same applies to any of the new and original ideas you might wish to introduce into your part of the production. "What would you think if I explored Hamlet's fear of his father?" "Suppose Hamlet jumps off the platform when he says this line?" "How about if I try to make Ophelia laugh here?" "Could Hamlet tear off his shirt when he leaps into the grave?" "What would you think if I yanked off my shoes when I approach the arras?" Phrasing them as questions rather than decisions does not weaken their chances of acceptance – it probably strengthens them.

Of course directors must make the same sorts of accommodations when they speak to actors as well. We'll be discussing these shortly.

But understand now that, for actors, such simple changes in wording, tones of voice, and facial expressions create the collaborative attitude that will allow you not merely to express disparate views and goals from those around you but to give them the greatest chance of acceptance and incorporation into the performance. Learning to use these regularly will earn you a reputation for "good attitude" without any sacrifice of your individuality or potential for greatness.

A *great* attitude

But I'm going to move beyond discussing a good attitude in order to speak about a *great* attitude.

For while a good attitude will, all things being equal, keep an actor from getting fired, or getting placed on a "do not rehire" list, it's the *great* attitude that will actually get an actor work even when things are *not* equal.

And indeed, the great attitude can make that work (when you get it) better than you could ever imagine. It can make collaborations fly and productions soar. "Theatre poetry is made when a group of people works together, and the divine fire, because of their interrelationship, touches them all," says the acclaimed late English director, Don Taylor.

And on the more mundane level, it can also get you your next job. As Broadway star Brian Stokes Mitchell says, "A great attitude will also help you get hired *again*. If you are a team player, you make the show look good. If the show looks good, the actor looks good. And the casting director looks good. And the producer looks good. And these are the people who do the hiring!"

A truly great attitude starts with an exuberant spirit of mutual generosity and a massive commitment to the success of the project in which you are engaged. The adjectives "exuberant" and "massive" are not hyperboles. They are realities. Developing a great attitude is a proactive process, not a passive one. It's a creative process too, indeed, every bit as creative as acting is.

A great attitude means nothing less than being *continuously enthusiastic, infectious, forthright, positive, giving, and helpful.* Moreover, you must do all this *believably* backstage – just as you must *act* believably when you are on the stage itself.

Of course, this should apply to everybody in the theatre, and indeed it often does. But it applies most especially to actors: Why? It's because actors, most of the time, are the only workers in the theatre who are *seen* as an ensemble – a collective within the collective. Unlike the director or designers, the actors are *seen* working together and, during the curtain call, will be applauded together as a group. Thus the actors must be seen to blend together seamlessly while onstage. Even if their individual characterizations are wildly different, they must all "seem to be in the same play" if the play is to become a critical success.

In fact, at many times actors act characters who themselves act as a collective, such as members of a Greek chorus, or the Hot Box Girls in *Guys and Dolls,* or as the Nubian slaves fanning Cleopatra in Shakespeare's play or Joseph Mankiewicz's movie. In such cases the individual actor may have no room whatever for creative individuality, and the proactive positivism we are talking about may be particularly hard to summon up on a day-to-day basis. But these are *exactly the sorts of roles in which actors often begin their professional careers,* and the chorus girl that surges into starring roles – think Shirley MacLaine, Shelley Winters, or Ruby Keeler – is almost always the one who has enchanted producers, stage managers, and cast members alike with her unstoppable and infectious enthusiasm.

Such a great attitude, however, does not simply mean pasting a smile on your face from the moment you hit the rehearsal hall. It means being *aggressively* helpful: genuinely enthusiastic, infectious, forthright, positive, and giving. These are not the actions of timid people, or even of simply "nice" people.

But what should you be aggressively helping? You must first be aggressively helping the *project,* and only afterwards your own role in it.

So having a great attitude – a *terrific* attitude – is nothing less than a prime professional responsibility. It's not something you simply hope will show up; it is something you must bring to the theatre with you on the first hour on the job, and every hour thereafter.

An eager subordination

Like it or not: Unless he or she is a bankable star (one whose fame is such the play or film can be financed solely because he or she is in it), an actor in theatre or film occupies what can only be termed a subordinate position. This is simply a professional reality; the journeyman actor does not have the final authority over his or her casting, staging, costumes, lines to be spoken, or lines that are cut. And when conflicts arise which are truly irresolvable, it is a virtual certainty that the actor rather than the director will suffer the inevitable consequence.

But a good actor will accept this situation, and a great actor will accept it eagerly. As Michael Caine explains, "There are good directors and bad directors; you learn something from both. From a bad director you can learn the art of self-preservation – how to give and sustain a performance all from within, [which] ... is just part of being a professional. For better or for worse ... you're married to that director. Either you learn to love him, or you fake it.... [Actors] who succeed listen to the director and immediately translate what he says into their performances. They take his direction straight into their bloodstreams." So the great actor (and Caine is one) transfuses the director's request into his own blood, letting it pulse through his body and give his character life. This is a not a reluctant but an eager subordination, because it is not bowing to the director but to the collective mission that everyone undertakes together. And if you're going to do that anyway, why don't you do it eagerly? You have nothing to lose, and everything to gain.

The distinguished actor Donald Sutherland similarly writes that while his "best work comes in relation with other actors," his relationship with the director is "the key to it all." Sutherland describes this relationship as "sexual – I'm his concubine." But, Sutherland concludes, this relationship (metaphorical, of course) is limited to the duration of the artistic project. "Once the movie is over … the relationship is over."

Subordination in these senses is not permanent. It does not mean self-oppression or self-humiliation. It does not mean lowering your self-esteem. And if you are able to consider it subordination not to the director but to the *production* – Role Number One – it can liberate the character you are playing. It can provide you with a channel to commit your deepest (and sometimes darkest) energies to that character's behavior, and a rock-solid foundation for the actions your character will perform. It can be the key to your most intense creativity.

A tactful *in*subordination

But of course there are times you may decide *not* to subordinate yourself. Disparate opinions cannot always be reconciled by tone alone, and expressing open, frank disagreement may prove unavoidable. There is nothing necessarily wrong or hurtful about this, and keeping your strongly dissenting views under wraps can destroy company morale – and your own enthusiasm – in insidious ways. But disagreement, no matter how frank, need not be expressed disagreeably. Not subordinating yourself, in other words, is not the same thing as being insubordinate. Expressing a contrary view – specifically actor to director in this case – is always an option, but for maximum benefit it should be done in the greatest privacy, and with the greatest tact and the greatest specificity, and with the absolute minimum of disruption to the work process. Breaking these down a bit:

Privacy prevents you from polarizing the issue or being seen as creating factionalism. It also makes clear that you are presenting your *own* view rather than that of other cast members, and thus are challenging one of the director's directives rather than the director's right to direct. It therefore initiates only the consideration of an issue, not the threat of a cast mutiny.

The most agreeable way of initiating such a disagreement is during a momentary break or at the end of a rehearsal, at which point you invite the director out for a drink, or a coffee, or just a private talk, while identifying the general subject so as to clearly limit the area of discussion. "Hey, Janet, can we get together for a few minutes after rehearsal to talk about scene three?" Almost any director would be willing to respond favorably to such an invitation. Indeed, most directors, sensing disparate views lying beneath the surface, may make that suggestion themselves. I certainly have.

Tact is a conversational and self-presentational style that allows you to "disagree agreeably." To negotiate tactfully, for example, you might demonstrate at the outset of the meeting that you at least understand the other person's point of view. Understanding that view does not mean accepting it, but it allows your counterpart (the director, say) to move directly to the specific topic of disagreement without re-explaining his or her positions and motives that have led up to it. A tactful negotiator will then proceed to emphasize what both sides have in common, which is the primacy of the *project* you both are working on, and to which you *both* are subordinate.

Specificity is how you can then isolate the problem that has brought you to this point of negotiation. If your tactful approach has taken areas of misunderstanding off the table ("we both clearly understand where the other is coming from") and eliminated differences in rank or personality between the negotiators ("since we're both in this together"), then specificity will be the single issue of the particular direction remaining on the table.

And finding your way to an *absolute minimum disruption of the work period* gives you the freedom to consider options as you approach a solution in a relatively relaxed manner – rather than racing against a fixed schedule while other actors are standing around waiting for the rehearsal to resume. In all the performing arts, time is quite literally money, and money is always in short supply.

And so, as an actor, you *can* tactfully challenge a direction, honestly and forthrightly, as long as you don't publicly challenge the director's right to direct. And if you do *that*, better prepare for the consequences.

Actors collaborate with actors

So far, we've been talking about how actors collaborate with directors, who are a step up on the hierarchical scale. But how do they collaborate with other actors who are, technically at least, on the same plane?

Christine Ebersole gives an ideal answer when she writes about co-starring with Mary Louise Wilson in the Broadway production of *Grey Gardens* with words actors should surely pay attention to: "She's so hilariously funny, she's so utterly authentic and honest, there's not a phony bone in her body. It's sort of like the ultimate tennis game; when you lob the ball you know it's going to come back. There's this tremendous feeling of safety, and feeling that safety on the stage, you are able to soar." For that's the nature of the *best* stage acting: a full, authentic, and open interaction with your fellow-actors that gives you a "tremendous feeling of safety" and allows you to "soar." Such interaction doesn't occur automatically, and it can altogether disappear when actors compete – either for attention or stage time or their interpretation of a given scene. *Characters* battle with each other onstage all the time – that's what dramatic conflict is all about: characters trying to win different goals and fulfill different intentions. But when the *actors* are trying to upstage or draw attention from each other, their professional rivalry will defeat rather than enhance the human drama in which they are playing. Indeed, to battle an opposing character should be a mutual thrill for the actors playing both opponents. Boldly played character confrontations make acting one of the most exciting of all performance arts. Actress Meryl Streep made this clear to Kevin Kline when, before they began shooting a scene where Kline was to toss her about in *Sophie's Choice*, she told him, "Don't be afraid to hurt me, you won't. And do whatever you want; go wherever you want with it, I'll go with you. I love to be surprised." The beating she took was actually *fun*.

For collaboration, while it is certainly hard work, should also be fun. Indeed, while this book is titled "working together" for actors it could also be called "playing together." Being thrilled while "playing" a character onstage is a plus for the play and a plus for the player. TV director James Burrows (*Cheers, Frasier*) considered his most successful directorial attribute was simply to "bringing the sense of camaraderie that the actors are capable of transferring – how they are with one another and what they feel about one another – to the screen." Actors flourish when they can make their own playfulness and mutual rapport integral to their performances. It makes them feel safe with each other as actors even when their characters are at each other's throats.

One thing that actors should never do, however, is to coach or critique a fellow actor's performance – either during the rehearsal period or in performance – unless the fellow actor requests it. While there may be an unstated social ranking among the cast – some are veterans and others beginners, some play leading roles and others are walk-ons, some are paid millions and others receive a pittance – *all* actors in a production must be able to look the other actors in the eye and see the *character* they are addressing (e.g., the Earl of Northumberland), not the *actor* who, perhaps, just told you your performance sucked.

If *asked*, however, actors may help each other out enormously. I'll give you an example from my own life. When I was in graduate school, I was in the acting company of the Williamstown Theatre Festival in Massachusetts. It was a great experience as I was acting with actors I had seen or would soon be seeing on Broadway – Frank Langella, Rex Robbins, Louis Zorich, and Sheppard Strudwick. At the end of the season, however, the company produced its first-ever musical and I found myself cast in a mid-sized singing role. Trouble was, I was not a singer, and the first rehearsals were a nightmare as I struggled to find my pitches. My efforts to get help from the musical director went nowhere; afraid to make me more nervous than I already was, he only said, "don't worry, it'll be fine." Finally, I approached one of the veteran Broadway music-theatre actors who had been brought in to play one of the leads and was in a quartet with me. I put it to him directly: "I'm flat, aren't I?" To which, to my everlasting gratitude, he simply replied "Yup!" – and worked with me until I became a passable singer. It was great actor-to-actor collaboration and the number received encores each night of our run. So while you mustn't go around instructing your fellow actors, you can certainly ask them to instruct you!

But most actor-to-actor collaboration has nothing to do with instructing or coaching but simply with doing what you can, *simply with your acting,* to make the persons on stage with you give the very *best performances* of their lives. This means, from as soon as you can in the early rehearsals right through closing night, to *interact fully, authentically, and powerfully with the actors playing those characters* your character speaks to, listens to, argues with, falls in love with, and tries to induce, seduce, inspire, threaten, or drive insane during the course of the play. This does not mean show-off histrionics in the rehearsal hall so as to let the world know what a great actor you are – it means trying intently to "get under the skin" of the actor playing the character that you're engaging, to *make him or her a better actor.* In other words, give your fellow actor lots to work with. If your character is supposed to frighten another actor's character, then try to *really frighten that actor.* If your character wants another character to fall in love with you, then try to *make the actor playing that character fall in love with you.* This level of deep, emotional, non-self-serving, mutual penetration between two actors is what makes *both of them* give great performances. The most important possible level of collaboration is to make your fellow actor think that *you really mean it* when you threaten, or induce, or seduce him or her.

And don't worry. Your partners *know* that you're acting. They will only bless you for your intensity, for it will make their acting better as well. And that in turn will make *your* acting better. So bowl them over. "Don't be afraid to hurt me, you won't," said Ms. Streep. Though she was talking about physical pain at the time, Streep was really referring to emotional and psychological pain, which in that play were immense, worthy of the Oscar she received for experiencing – and performing – them.

So *really* attack your acting partner psychologically. Make her wet her pants! (She won't, but you can still try.) *Really* seduce your partner. Make him get an erection! (He won't, but it's your authentic effort to that end that can make you a great actor.) By *really trying* to achieve your goal (your objective, intention, task – Stanislavsky's term was *zadacha*) is what makes a passable actor a good one, and *really trying to achieve it by getting under the skin of another actor* can make a good actor a great one. Try to really "get what you want from the other actor," says playwright David Mamet in his book about acting, and this is the strongest possible way for actors to collaborate with each other to the benefit of all. Just know how to pull out of it when you leave the stage. At that point you remember that acting is play, is playing. It's Ebersole's "ultimate tennis game."

Actors collaborate in simpler and less intensive ways, of course. One is simply offering to "run lines" outside of rehearsals with other actors. Some won't take you up on it – that's of course their choice and you shouldn't challenge it. But just running lines – even after you think you know them – can prove immensely useful in surprising ways. It can certainly give you greater confidence in speaking them on stage, and that greater confidence can let you improvise your *behavior* while saying the lines, and burrow deeper into the mind of the character you're speaking them to. Your acting will become less self-conscious, more natural, and more individually creative. Here's where collaboration with others will, paradoxically, help bring out your individuality – "the real you." And since you're only "running lines" and not rehearsing your scene, you needn't perform them as staged but run them in wildly different improvised situations: while jogging, doing pushups, playing imaginary basketball, or washing dishes, for example. Just don't talk about them: then you'll start directing each other. The point of running lines in this sort of manner is to *reach your fellow actor through your lines and behavior during the scene,* not by pre-arranging it, doing postmortems, or stepping outside the scene to make comments on it. In that way you run lines *as character-to-character* rather than actor-to-actor. Running lines this way will not, as you might think, make the scene stale; it will only let it get deeper into your blood.

Actors collaborate with designers

In the professional American theatre, actors rarely participate in design meetings and designers rarely spend much time in rehearsals, at least until tech. But this should not be construed as an ideal situation. European theatre companies have often developed stunning productions with intensive co-participation from actors, designers, technicians, and directors throughout the planning and rehearsing stages. Bertolt Brecht's Berliner Ensemble provided splendid examples in the immediate post–World War II period, and Ariane Mnouchkine's Théâtre du Soleil does so in the present day. Indeed, Mnouchkine's *Les Éphémères,* which dazzled American reviewers and audiences in its 2009 New York appearance, was in large measure designed by its actors, who collected and contributed from their own homes most of the furniture and props that dominated the various "chariots" on which the play was performed. Actors also served as the chariot's "horses" that wheeled them on and off the stage, and as silent choruses responding to the dramatic actions being performed amongst them. Many American ensemble companies, as those mentioned in the first section of this book, also employ broadly collaborative actor-designer-director-stagehand relationships in which Brecht and Mnouchkine have pioneered.

But even in the conventional single-play production model, actors and designers may collaborate in a variety of ways. Nowhere is this more the case than with sound and costume designers, since sound design must be integrated with the actors' voices, often augmenting or enhancing them, while the costumes must be donned, doffed, and worn by them. Sound designer Vince Olivieri is an exceptionally collaborative theatre artist who seeks assignments where he can attend virtually all of the rehearsals, designing, timing, and integrating his sound cues in concert with the actors as soon as the play gets on its feet in the rehearsal hall. He also likes to bring the actors into his sound studio to experiment with a variety of possibilities that either they or he have come up with. By the time the production opens, Olivieri has created an exquisitely modulated design that has been refined many times over, usually with stunning results. And multiple Tony-winning costume designer William Ivey Long points out that "the costume designer is in fact the one person – after the director and choreographer – who deals with the actual corporeal body of the performer." Long explains his process with performers as developing a mutual confidence: "I try to develop a trust and a bond of support between myself and the actor. I ask how the rehearsals are going, what specifics in movement and action the actor requires – 'How high do you lift your arms?'… [so as] to stay connected with what is going on in the process of making the play come alive." Veteran costume designer Holy Durban emails cast members selected renderings of their costumes after they've been approved – yet before rehearsals begin – so the actors can begin to sense what is in store for them, and pose questions and/or provide feedback to Ms. Durbin ahead of time. Scenery and lighting designers will also find that circulating with the cast, asking questions and sensing their reactions to the objects and lighting that surround them as the show nears its technical rehearsals, can pay great dividends. Are the door handles easy to grasp while the actor carries the required props? Do the windows swing widely enough so that the actors can see through them what they need to? How safe do they feel on the set? Does the grand staircase need a railing? No matter how much better the stairway might look without one, if the actress wearing high heels and a long gown grimaces on her way down, her "grand descent" won't look as grand as either the designer or director had hoped. It is far better to discover this in the rehearsal period – when a railing can be added or the high heels replaced – than at the final dress rehearsal when it may be too late to make sufficient adjustments.

And it is a well-known adage that "the lighting designer is the actor's best friend." Lighting designer Lonnie Alcaraz actually gives classes to actors on "how to find your light on stage," and actors who find time to chat with him during tech rehearsal breaks may get hints at which moments a slight turn of their heads or a half-step forward may pump up the lumens (and hence luminosity) that brighten their faces during the climax of their big speech.

Naturally, all such collaborations between designer and actor should be done with at least the implicit blessing of the director, who oversees all aspects of the production and should not be blind-sided by blocking changes that deliberately subvert the existing staging – but directors who encourage their casts and designers to speak freely with each other will rarely encounter serious problems by doing so. If, however, a designer and actor collectively wish to propose a change in a design – say in a costume or a prop – they should be free, outside of rehearsal hours, to ask the director to consider it.

Directors collaborate with actors

Thus far in this chapter we have been talking about how actors can collaborate – and behave – with both directors and with other actors. But what are the ways in which directors can best work with actors? And why should they?

First, the director should be comfortable in wearing the mantle of artistic leadership. Hired (generally) before the actors, and almost always involved in casting them, the director enters the rehearsal hall with an assumption of authority. If this assumption is squandered, the production may be in trouble. "Stage fright" is not only something that occurs on the stage: it is also present in the rehearsal hall, and the excitement of the cast at the first rehearsal has elements of terror as well. One wants someone at the helm from the get-go, and the director must fill that role with apparent (if not actual) confidence.

Second, the director is the one person involved in the production who must at all times be cognizant of the "ticking clock" – the amount of rehearsal time before the play's opening. For during rehearsals, every discussion initiated, question posed, compliment offered, complaint registered, coffee or toilet break taken, and "let's talk this over" proposed will represent exactly those minutes that will be lost forever – since unlike football games, the rehearsal clock doesn't stop when someone goes out of bounds.

So in rehearsals the director must assume final responsibility for both artistic leadership and time management – which, however, are often in direct conflict. Artistic leadership inevitably involves reflection, questioning, nurturing, and thoughtful discussion at certain times, but such "times" are also what the director is charged not to waste. Nor does the stage manager's monitoring of the schedule (see next chapter), or the producer's occasional monitoring of rehearsals (see Chapter 3) relieve the director of making the key decisions as to when to cut off the discussions and get back to "work."

But of course everything that happens in the hall is "work," and each director must create his or her directorial style, one that will maintain sensitive artistic leadership and vigilant stopwatch efficiency in balance.

A directorial style

All directors have – and develop – their own rehearsal styles, both for productions in general and for different types of production in particular, and nothing in this book suggests that they do not nor should not.

Rehearsal collaborations between directors and actors are qualitatively different than others in the theatre production, for while emotions can certainly run high in all professional interactions in theatre, they are at the very heart of the *content* of the acting rehearsals. For the close encounters of actors exactly mirrors those of the characters they play: they are as much or more physical as aesthetic, as much or more psychological as intellectual, and as much or more emotional and sensual as life itself. When characters rage at each other, the actors playing them rage at each other; when characters fall in love, the actors playing them fall in love; when characters are sexually aroused, the actors probably are as well – at least during the time they are acting. Acting involves real tears, gasps, racing hearts, perspiration, and elevated blood pressure – and that's all *in addition* to the routine psychophysiological changes that occur when a person in *any* job faces professional pressures. Shakespeare's Hamlet calls the art of acting "monstrous" for just these reasons, and the director may often feel that he or she is leading a pack of wild animals.

This means that very successful directorial style must sensitively balance the desire to be collaborative, approachable, encouraging, protective, receptive, and sharing, on the one hand, with the clear responsibility to be persuasive, authoritative, decisive, and sometimes driving on the other. "Use all gently," Hamlet says to the Players, but then adds the caution to "Be not too tame, neither." Hamlet is talking about acting, not directing, but he is directing the Players as he speaks it, and, as elsewhere in the play, he is also directing himself.

Finding that balance – between flattery and annihilation, between directing "gently" but at the same time being "not too tame," is hardly easy. Peter Brook describes advice given to him at a young age by an opera director: "Flatter! Flatter all the time, flatter shamelessly, never ask yourself if you are overdoing it, because that's not possible, go on flattering." But the same director also told him to learn "when to shout, when to threaten – in fact all the repertoire of roles an opera director has to play." Brook decided, however, that both of these were extreme; "Fortunately, these lessons were only of use in the hysterical opera world," he declared. "Ever since, I have found that in the rest of theatre, no violent or aggressive tactics have the remotest chance of producing any good result. On the rare occasions when I have lost my temper, or bullied, or reduced an actor to tears, I have deeply regretted it…. In my experience, tension and friction in rehearsal help no one – only calm, quiet, and great confidence can bring about the slightest glimmer of creativity."

The great Swedish stage and film director Ingmar Bergman came to the same conclusions. Bergman had quite a temper in his early days, admitting that in those times he "threw chairs as easily as tantrums." By the later years of his career, however, Bergman began to realize that reaching a shared consensus with his casts got him better results than did intimidating them, and his tantrums turned to friendly overtures, as, later in life, he would routinely hang out by the stage door a half-hour before rehearsals "in case the cast wants to fraternize." Bergman became a director who respected his actors, listening seriously to what they had to say about their roles. "If I listen to them, they not only listen to themselves, they also listen to each other," he explained. And his eventual directorial style grew to become inductive, drawing out the actor's performance through encouragement rather than force. "It's a good idea to have the actor feel good about the blocking, the thinking, the rhythm. Then we will make a common creation," he declared, urging the actors to see their characters' goals through their own eyes and not through his. "To force an actor to do something is silly," he explained. "You can convince him, you can talk to him.... [But] then, five days after the opening, he starts to change, and then suddenly there are ten actors who start to change and there is no rhythm anymore. There is no performance anymore." So when speaking to the cast Bergman neither lectured them nor even discussed their roles; rather he simply tried "to say the precise word," and see how the actor would react – physically and psychologically. "I know before he knows if his body-mind accepts or doesn't accept what I want," he explained. And, as his actor-son reported, "when father is displeased with an actor, he merely looks away, but when he's pleased, he's shouting, screaming, laughing, 'Good!' like a cheerleader!" Thus, Bergman's directorial style essentially changed during his extraordinary, sixty-plus year career, from tyrannizing to encouraging and from throwing chairs to leading cheers. And his favorite actors, including Max von Sydow, Bibi Andersson, and Liv Ullmann, became his informal "repertory company" with whom he worked regularly for the last decades of his life.

But is encouraging always the whole story? No. Although he abjures any trace of threat or "aggressive tactics," Brook's "great confidence" still radiates a fearsome authority. And even in his later rehearsals, Bergman admitted he would raise his voice for the "occasional well planned 'pedagogic outburst," if he had to.

And so "be not too tame!"

A directorial voice

The director's use of language is an important aspect of establishing close collaboration – and communication. It is immediately helpful for directors to rid themselves of possessive pronoun "my" – as in "my actors." They're not *your* actors and you don't own them. They're the *production's* actors, just as you are the production's director. Whatever your individual ranks, each of you "belongs" to the production, not to any single person. This is not a matter of role-reversal; it's simply the adoption of a non-possessive working vocabulary. So directors should refer not to "my actors" but "our actors," and to "our cast" rather than "my cast."

And how about finding positive language targeted to your goals and the production's mission, rather than negative language that simply rebukes what you feel are the actor's shortcomings? Your major task in directing actors is to bring each one of them to his or her highest level of achievement, and to synergize their performance into a masterpiece, but merely saying "this is terrible," while it may stop them from repeating things you don't like, will do little to help them achieve what you're looking for. Celebrated English director Katie Mitchell spent years learning, as she explains, "how to give the actors freedom rather than trying to control them." Mitchell wisely advises young directors to avoid making merely judgmental assessments. "Remove the words 'good,' 'bad,' 'right' and 'wrong' from the rehearsal room vocabulary," she says. "They are value judgments that may position you inappropriately in relationship to the actor – as parent or moral arbiter. Replace them with words like 'clear' and 'unclear,' 'specific' and 'unspecific,' 'focused' or 'blurred.' Establish a culture in which the highest praise an actor can receive is: 'That was very clear.' "

Such language modifications will help to level the collective "playing" field, particularly at the start of the rehearsal phase, and allow the players to play *with* you and not just *for* you. It will initiate, through its generous and yielding tone, a truly *participatory* collaboration without in any way diminishing your authority to exercise the necessary directorial leadership. This takes practice to learn, however; it is not something you can simply learn "by the book." "Directing is tone," says film director Jason Reitman (*Juno, Up in the Air*). "And tone is the hardest thing to explain to someone. It's like how you know you're in love with somebody."

For you must remember, if you are a director, that you are not merely directing an "actor," you are directing a person: a perceptive, sensate, emotional human being. And as acclaimed Irish director Garry Hynes says, "When you work with an actor you forge a personal relationship with them. And all personal relationships evolve and change ... [as do] all human relations."

The ultimate goal

For what is the ultimate goal of directing actors – and human beings? To induce their *full participation* – body and mind – in the enactment of the production, so that the seam between actor and character disappears, the actors' and their characters' goals are the same, and the actors don't just perform their roles, they enter them, they inhabit them, they *are* them. And when this happens, their speeches will not emerge as lines memorized from a preexisting script but as words that *they themselves have decided to say at this place and time.* Those words will appear to have been initiated – and indeed *have* initiated – in their brains, not just their mouths, nor even from the playwright's pen, and certainly not because they are rigidly doing what the director told them to.

This is perhaps the actor's single most important goal in creating a convincing performance, whether on the live stage or before the camera, and whether in Shakespeare, musical comedy, opera, theatre of the absurd, or modern American realism. When it takes place, when the actors' efforts are poured entirely into winning their characters' quests, rather than just demonstrating their histrionic skills, true "theatre magic" can occur.

And to achieve this, the director must create a process that *turns the play over* to the actors. For although the director is the unchallenged leader in the rehearsal's first day, the actors will become its leaders when the lights rise on the first performance. Indeed, at that moment the director is nowhere near the stage; probably somewhere in the back row or, as many a Broadway legend tells us, in the toilet of the next door bar, throwing up as they await the next morning's newspaper reviews.

But in order for the actors to possess their roles by opening night, the director must turn those roles over to them at some point during the rehearsal process. By then, those roles must belong to those who now inhabit them, not those who first created their outline. But if the actors are to own their roles, the director must *disown* them. As the distinguished English director Deborah Warner puts it, "The actor's ownership of the material has to be total for a good piece of theatre to be made…. When the director's ownership of the material is greater than the actor's, it becomes an act of academia… or simply an act of bad theatre. One has to empower the actors *totally*."

Other directorial goals

There are many rehearsal goals for the director. The acting mechanics – line and blocking memorization, for example – must be developed on a firm schedule, since a single actor who remains "on book" (rehearsing script-in-hand) while the others are off cannot fully interact with colleagues on stage, cannot sustain eye contact with them, cannot respond to their body language, cannot gesture fully or unselfconsciously because of the unwanted baggage (the dreaded script) he or she still carries in hand. The acting must be fully integrated with the scenery which is yet to be installed and with costumes yet to be donned. The plotlines must be made to be clear, the characters consistent, and the jokes funny, before any of these dramaturgical necessities can be tested by actual audiences who experience them for the first time. The play's action must develop a strong momentum, so that the play gets more rather than less interesting as it proceeds. All these are crucial directorial goals during the rehearsal period.

And so the director, while not appearing overly judgmental, must still make judgments on all these issues and decisions as to how to achieve them – at least daily at the beginning phase, hourly in the middle, and at minute-by-minute or even faster intervals by the time of technical rehearsals. For while the director gives over the roles to the actors, he or she is, at the same time, taking up the reigns of the production – and making the vital decisions that will shape its every second. And as film director Ridley Scott says, "The biggest part of directing is being able to make decisions." And the rehearsal period is when those decisions must come faster and faster, and be executed with greater and greater precision.

Rehearsals begin

We've discussed some general considerations about directorial leadership and company collaborations within the multi-week and sometimes multi-month rehearsal process, but now we will look at the rehearsal period's four fundamental phases, particularly as they apply to directors and actors. These are the *establishing, reading, staging*, and *finalizing* phases. These are not of equal time lengths – the first two may take place in the first day, and the last one in the final week – but they actually have equal or near-equal importance.

The *establishing* phase centers on a *first company meeting*, which normally takes place on the first day of rehearsal. Though brief, this meeting is critical. Beginning with a general welcome, introductions, and important announcements, the director will, with the designers, publicly introduce the basic mission of the production as it has evolved through the planning sessions. Depending on the director, the play, and the schedule, this phase may be measured in minutes, hours, days, or even weeks. But regardless of its duration, it will shape everything that takes place afterward.

The *reading* phase usually starts with a first reading of the play, aloud, with the actors seated with their scripts around a table, and may continue through one or more days of *table work*: continued readings around the table frequently interrupted with discussions and questions that investigate the play's actions, language, characters, and deeper meanings.

In the *staging* phase, which normally occupies the largest portion of rehearsal time, the director and actors work through the play's physical staging, along with its moment-to-moment character interactions and subtexts, the performative styles of the production, and everything else that may come under the basic rubric of "acting" and "directing." This phase is where collaboration comes into full play, filled as it is with broad and subtle movements, physical as well as psychological interactions, and stage experiments and improvisations, all punctuated by questions and discussions. Here the communication between actors and directors is almost always a two-way street.

In the *finalizing* phase, the director readies the play for its opening performance. In this period, normally beginning a few days prior to technical rehearsals, the director again largely assumes the leadership role, but must now remain acutely sensitive to the ownership of their roles that the actors have attained during the preceding phases.

Let's look at these four phases in the order they occur.

The Establishing Phase

This phase of the rehearsal process – which mainly involves the director, the actors and the stage managers – while it begins with a first company meeting, is, perhaps ideally, preceded by the director's initiation of some sort of welcome, in person or by email or phone call, to actors he or she has never met. As with an email something such as this one:

> Dear Lucile,
>
> I've very much enjoyed looking over your photo-resume and other materials sent me by the casting director, and delighted to know that you'll be playing Georgette in the USF production of *School for Wives* that I'm directing this summer! I certainly look forward to our getting together next month at our first rehearsal.
>
> Please let me know if you have any questions about the role or the production at this time, OK?
>
> until we meet, then,
> my best wishes,
> Robert

Among other things, such a letter of introduction says something very important: "I am not an ogre." You will be surprised how many actors may otherwise be worrying that you might be.

It also invites the actor to pose any questions he or she might wish to ask before rehearsals begin, which will create a collaborative environment right at the outset. And it will assure the actor that she will feel warmly welcomed into the ensemble by its director when rehearsals do begin.

The introductory email establishes a firm starting point to the working rapport between director and actors, establishing a bond of trust and respect, rather than one of fear and trembling. Trust and respect are the same items discussed when speaking of directors and designers in the previous chapter, and they apply even more strongly in this case since directors and actors work side-by-side, day by day, and sometimes tear by tear. And if the director can express trust and respect toward the cast, the cast will begin their work with trust and respect for the director, which will get everybody off to a fine beginning. If such values are maintained and built upon, they will lead to bold and buoyant collaborative work *from the very outset*. And with this sort of friendly introduction, actors can be assured that the director has "bought into" their being cast in their roles (even if the director had nothing to do with casting them), and that the jubilation they felt when they were cast has not been misplaced. Collectively, this can inspire the cast to begin their rehearsals with a welcome – and welcomed – confidence.

And since every director wants the actors to perform "convincingly," how better to begin rehearsals than by giving them a platform of self-confidence upon which they may eventually be able to stand, unaided, as a potent dramatic character?

There's one more person the director should "meet" – at least virtually – prior to the start of rehearsals, and that is the production stage manager (PSM). The PSM and his or her assistants (ASMs) work closer with the director than anyone. They will implement many of the director's decisions, such as posting and distributing the rehearsal schedules the director creates, and they will manage many of the details – such as monitoring the precise union-required rehearsal breaks, enforcing the Occupational Safety and Health Administration (OSHA) and local fire department safety regulations, and administering the policies of the theatre facility – that the unions, governments and producers require. Basically, the director directs and the stage managers manage *what* the director directs, and together they accomplish what no one could do alone. So early communications between them – which can be initiated by either – are extremely helpful to get a jumpstart on the first company meeting. At minimum, the director and PSM should collectively develop a "schedule of scheduling" together – working out not only the schedule of the first day of rehearsals, but just how and when the scheduling should proceed, and how the director plans to conduct the rehearsals once they are under way.

Following these introductory discussions, or cyber-communications, the stage is set for the first company meeting. This is "where it all starts," as far as the actors are concerned, and "Where it all starts *coming together*" as the director and producers know only too well. For this is the word made flesh.

The first company meeting

There's a bit of magic in the first company meeting, where actors and the director-stage management team first meet each other in an ensemble. And whether the company becomes a true ensemble, or fragments into a group of single individuals or even warring cliques, depends a great deal on the tone of that meeting.

The director and stage managers should arrive well ahead of time to set up the room, sharpen their pencils (metaphorical – i.e. digital – and otherwise), arrange the materials that are to be distributed and, most importantly, to *be there to greet the cast members,* particularly those they have not previously met, as soon as they arrive. And then to introduce them to *at least one or two other members* who have already arrived – so that *no one* in the company will feel like a total stranger when the meeting actually begins and all but the director and stage manager will, for a certain time, fall silent.

Indeed, there is one thing every director should probably do that has probably never been mentioned in any book or manual: this is to *learn the names of the cast members before the first rehearsal.* Simple? Sure, but while it may be relatively easy with a small cast, some directors (particularly older ones, I'm afraid) may find it challenging with a large one, many of whom they are meeting for the first time. But the actors always know the director's name, so why shouldn't the director know the actors'? Knowing their names as they first walk into the rehearsal room creates a reciprocal recognition that sets the collaboration off on a close to equal footing, and makes all the actors, particularly company newcomers, feel secure and appreciated rather than worried and estranged.

And if this proves simply impossible for the first meeting, it should certainly happen by the first rehearsal. In a Shakespeare festival production of *Coriolanus* some years ago, the director, in his first production with this company, began blocking the play before he had learned the names of the dozen-plus actors who played the "Roman citizens" who, though unnamed, have many lines and strong individual presences in several scenes. So the director identified them by number, calling out directions such as "Number two cross left!" "Number twelve, sit on the ground!" "Number six, turn your back on number four!" He probably felt that by doing this he was streamlining the process and saving everyone some time, but the actors playing the citizens felt terribly marginalized and – though they should have known better – they never reached the performance levels of which they were certainly capable. Not surprisingly, the director was never rehired. Even worse are the television directors who invariably refer to the day-players (those paid by the day, and ordinarily for one day only) by their character's name – or sometimes by their appearance as in "Hey, redhead," or "Hey, you on the green stool!" Television actors have been known to quit the business entirely because of the humiliation of being perpetually anonymous on the sets where they were working.

So if you are not the sort of director who can remember names from the moment you hear them (and I certainly am not), it's a good idea to get out their headshot photos before that first meeting and study them until you feel you can greet each actor by name at the door – no matter how small the part he or she plays. Or, if you don't have such photos, take some yourself at the first meeting and memorize them before the next rehearsal. The rewards, I can assure you, will be substantial.

The director arriving ahead of time for that meeting also sets a good example for the rest of the team. "If the director can do it, we can do it," is its unspoken message. There is also a tradition in the theatre that "on time" means ten minutes *ahead* of schedule, which assures that by the official start time you will not only be in the hall but also relaxed, warmed up, and ready to work. Actors who arrive at the last moment, huffing and puffing, are not off to a good start for that day – or for this career.

Once the meeting begins – which should be on the very first second of the clock after the scheduled time, unless the director is willing to live with late arrivals throughout the rehearsal periods – the director will publicly greet the company *as a company*. Even just a few words at this point can suffice for such remarks: but they should be well-chosen, and convey in tone as well as content the excitement of finally beginning this phase of the process, the thrill in gathering such an ensemble of artists, and the expectation that this production will be a special experience with high aspirations. The tone should be positive, infectious, inspirational – but not rambling or giddy. Most important, it should be inclusive of everyone in the room – not focusing on any one person nor highlighting the director. That the director is giving these initial welcoming words, even if they last only thirty seconds, makes clear where the production's leadership resides.

This brief welcome then segues to the introductions – of actors, designers and stage managers, and all others who are in the room. Before they hear more fully from the director, they should get to know one another.

Introducing the company

Ordinarily the director will first introduce the designers, specialist directors (e.g., choreographers, fight directors), and dramaturgs with whom he or she has been working together directly during the planning stage.

It's normal then to introduce the actors, or have the actors introduce themselves – which is not a bad idea since the actors' job is to
speak up anyway and they might like to get used to speaking in this
particular public.

But the most important introduction, though it might come at
this point rather than earlier, is of the PSM – the Production Stage
Manager. I think it is important for the director to make this introduction, because the PSM and his or her team really is going to run
the rehearsals, at least their technical aspects, and the director's
introduction can make clear that the director and the PSM work as a
team. We'll have a much fuller discussion about the stage managers
and their roles in the following chapter, which will make clear why
this is so important.

Once everyone has been suitably introduced, the director should
turn the last part of the introductory phase – the "distributions
and announcements" – to the stage manager, who is best qualified
to handle these matters. Such distributions will possibly include,
among other things, final script copies, contact sheets with phone
numbers and email addresses of company members, overall schedules for the entire production period and specific schedules for the
first day or days of rehearsals, printouts of theatre and company
policies, emergency information about safety, local police and hos-
pitals (often printed, along with stage management phone numbers, on company ID cards), and maps showing the location of the
various shops, offices fitting rooms, rehearsal halls, and other places
company members might need to find in a hurry. The announcements are generally about company protocols, safety issues, union
policies, general information about where to find the callboards and
such matters, and explanations of the current union rules govern-
ing rehearsals. The PSM will also conduct an election among Actors
Equity members for the "Equity Deputy" who will represent the acting company in any dispute about union rules.

And now this meeting segues into its most important, even critical,
operation: Defining the production's mission.

Defining the mission

Once the introductions are completed, the director again takes the
floor, and begins to shape the mission of production as it has been

developed during the planning stage. This may begin in any number of ways: with a theatre game, an exercise, a group song, a picture show, a recounting of a personal experience, a discussion of a current political issue, and so on.

However, usually it is going to be a talk. Some companies even insist on this, finding it essential to get everybody "on the same page" on day one. Sometimes the talk can be a full-on speech; the distinguished British director Trevor Nunn, when he was Artistic Director of the Royal Shakespeare Company, would begin rehearsals with a two-hour lecture on the historical and political environment in which the play was to be set. Other talks might be no more than fifteen seconds: "This is the funniest play Molière ever wrote, and we want the audience to laugh like hell, OK? Let's get started." Whatever it is, an introductory talk should inspire a communal focus that will remain with each actor for the ensuing weeks or months of rehearsal and performance.

What is inspiring about the two above examples? Nunn's two-hour lectures would galvanize the company by the sheer intensity of the work that he had obviously put into its preparation, and by the compelling vision – theatrical in its own right – that he could plant in each actor's mind. And the second director's "talk" could arouse the company's excitement in trying to create one of the greatest laugh-fests of their lifetimes, together with the little "OK?" tag that would give each actor at least the opportunity to say "No, it's not OK with me, I want to explore this play's deeper issues of x, y, and z." But by *not* taking the bait of raising an objection to proposed mission – and who would dare to? – each actor has, by the process of cognitive dissonance, implicitly bought into it.*

The most common goal of the talk, whatever its length, is to establish the production's basic mission – its thrust, concept, and overall goal in reaching the anticipated public. But although the director gives the talk, and the director probably initiated its mission, by this time it is no longer solely the director's mission. It has become the *collective*

---

*The principle of cognitive dissonance explains our unconscious tendency to "believe in" what we find ourselves saying or doing, even when such actions were initiated at someone else's request. Thus debaters come to believe in the arguments they are assigned to present, lawyers in their clients' cases, and actors in the roles in which they are cast – and in the directions they are given to perform.

mission of the entire team. Other members of the team have already
signed onto it, certainly the producers, who have accepted and perhaps encouraged it during the preparation stage, and the designers,
whose ideas and designs have already been incorporated into it during the planning stage. And by now the dramaturg, producers, and
even those principal actors whose casting involved discussions with
the director have probably also made contributions to this mission.
The director's presentation of the mission, therefore, will normally
include a presentation of some of these contributions: certainly the
design models and renderings if available, and samples of the music
and sound, which would desirably be presented by the designers
themselves, who could talk about the intended uses and significance
of their designs, thereby bonding the collaboration more closely on a
broad personal level.

And to further the interests of creating a collaborative environment, these presentations would desirably replace the word "I" by
the word "we" wherever possible, so that regardless of whether it's
the director or designer speaking, sentences begin with "We have
decided that..." or "We want the music to be...." Because at this point
it is only the idea that counts; how it may have come into being is of no
importance whatever. In fact, by this point most collaborators don't
even remember who came up with it. What is essential, though, is
that everyone on the planning team has signed onto these decisions.
They are now team goals and the entire team is behind them. If seeds
of discord show up in this first meeting, even under the surface, they
will probably sprout to second-guessing later on, and perhaps even
debate and/or accusations after that – especially when turning back
is no longer an option. If there is a sense of unity in the planners,
however, and if it is infectiously communicated to the cast, *everybody*
will be at one in working to realize the production's mission and its
goals.

The mission need not, of course, be called that. Most directors
have other terms for it. Arthur Miller, who watched Elia Kazan stage
his *All My Sons, Death of a Salesman,* and *After the Fall*, was amazed
at Kazan's directorial process with the actors, which he attributed to
Kazan's creation of a "center point." Miller recalls that, "Kazan, with
his marvelous wiles, [was always] tripping the latches of the secret
little doors that lead into the different personalities of each actor....
He does not 'direct,' he creates a center point and then goes to each
actor and creates the desire to move toward it. And there they all

meet, but for different reasons, and seem to have arrived there by themselves."

Probably no one has more clearly stated than Miller this paramount gift of a truly great director, which is to let *the mission of the production itself* – as you have identified and framed it during your preparation and planning and presentation during the meeting – evoke the performances of the actors. The production's goals, which may initially emanate from something like Brook's "formless hunch," will then be focused by the attraction of Kazan's "center point," called by whatever name one wishes. In which case, the director's primary actions in rehearsal are not to bully the actors into following his or her concept, but to *create their collective desire to move* toward that point. One director calls this "lowering the ground in front of the actors" so their progress will seem to be downhill, not uphill, and so they will feel drawn toward the goals ahead of them, rather than pushed toward them from behind by their director. Through such processes, the actors will make the roles their own naturally, not by force or persuasion, and will enjoy a well-nurtured sense of "buy-in" for the entire production.

How to inspire the actors to come to the "center point," however, takes as many forms as there are directors. The introductory talk is certainly not the only way and in many cases may not be the best way. Many directors begin rehearsals with exercises unrelated to the script, focusing on building relationships between the actors before tackling the text – although even here the exercises might segue to subjects that are fundamental to the play. Other directors begin by provoking group discussions: "OK, well, this play is obviously about people who can't decide what to do with their lives; what do you think is wrong with them? Or is anything wrong with them? Or just some of them?" And so the cast starts talking about the world of Chekhov's *Seagull* or *Three Sisters*. Still other directors begin with improvisations that also may eventually move into the sorts of interactions that the play highlights. This may even prove necessary if the play has not yet been finished. For instance, when the actors met for the first time in Minneapolis to rehearse the world premiere of Tony Kushner's *The Intelligent Homosexual's Guide to Capitalism and Socialism with a Key to the Scriptures* at Minneapolis' Guthrie Theatre in 2009, director Michael Greif and the actors were "nearly panic-stricken when they discovered there was no script to be had. Kushner wrote the play over the next six weeks in a white heat, barely sleeping, handing new pages every day to Greif and the cast.... For most of the process, the actors did not know the arc of their characters because they did not know how the play would end, an experience some found frustrating, others thrilling and liberating."

Most directors, though, move quickly from the introductory talk to a reading of the script.

The reading phase – or not

The traditional first reading of the script begins with everyone – producer, director, dramaturg, cast, stage managers, and others involved in the rehearsals – sitting around a table, scripts on the table and pencils in hand. The director gives the go and the actor with the first speech reads it, then the other actors follow suit when their lines come up. The director may stop from time to time to make comments, and/or to call breaks (at intermissions, say), and after the reading is completed, the director might turn to the cast and say, "Well, what strikes you most about the play?" and a discussion ensues. The vast majority of American theatre productions begin with such a "first reading" rehearsal.

That's not the only way to begin rehearsals, however. Declan Donnellan, founding director of England's Cheek by Jowl Theatre, explains that in his initial rehearsal, "There are no discussions with actors hunched around a table chewing pencils; there are no lectures on history and ideas; there is no imposed concept on the play. Nick [the designer with whom Donnellan customarily works]...does not present a model box on the first day and show costume drawings to a bemused circle of actors who have only just met each other." Nor is there a first reading of the script in a Donnellan production: "We start by doing movement...Often we start with a dance."

Katie Mitchell, another of England's most prominent contemporary directors, similarly finds the "formal read-through...completely terrifying for actors – they either mumble, paralyzed, into their polystyrene cups of coffee, or construct elaborate clichéd performances that are difficult for them to leave behind." And she's talking about veteran professional actors at England's Royal National Theatre! Mitchell and many other directors therefore have actors read the play "around the table" instead of by assigned roles, so that one actor is given the play's first speech, the actor on her left takes the next one, and the following speeches are thereafter read around the table without respect to who is playing which part. This has the advantage of each actor, from the leads to the walk-ons, having an equal share of the reading duties and, therefore, an equal "buy-in" to this first rehearsal, while no actor needs sit silent for three hours simply watching everybody else have a good time reading their parts.

Silviu Purcarete, a brilliant Romanian director who now works worldwide, feels that his most important task in rehearsals is "to keep the text alive"; as such he has adopted a highly improvisational working method: "With actors I work very much on rough improvisations and in rehearsals I provoke some kind of chaos. "Then from this chaos we start to articulate, to build something."

And prize-winning American director Mary Zimmerman, who develops her scripts in rehearsal rather than beginning them with a finished text, employs what may be an even freer method. "Going into rehearsal is a bit of a free fall," she says. "On the first day of rehearsal, we present the designs to the cast. The set itself already has to be pretty fully conceived by this point and there is a complete model for it, but the costumes will be in flux until the very end. There will be basic designs, but when we start we don't even know all of the characters that will appear. And props are conceived, made up and brought in from day to day. Then, we sit in a circle and read stories, or episodes from stories, aloud by passing the actual text around hand to hand, each reading a paragraph. We talk about them. I say what I like about them, why they might end up in the play, or how they are similar to something else and I'm not sure which will end up in the play. Then, I might have some physical improvisations to do such as "How can we make a camel? A boat? Three different ways of sailing? Of flying?" I usually have some ideas in mind that are just fantasies and I want to see if they are physically possible. Generally, these physical images transform as soon as an actual body is try-ing to do them. I might say, "Can you three go off and make up a sequence of gestures you can do together, sitting in chairs, that all have to do with sight?" Zimmerman's method requires, of course, a tremendous range of time and talent to execute (in addition to winning the Tony for directing *Metamorphoses*, she received a Tony nomination for semi-simultaneously writing it!), but most actors find it worth the effort: many have been working with her since their college years.

Collaborative research

We have talked of the director's research during the play's preparation phase, but the director might ask actors to do research as well – and many actors will do so on their own – all of which can be collaboratively shared with the director and fellow-actors. Director Mitchell, for example, asks actors to prepare mini-biographies of their characters' lives, and the history of interactions between their characters – since, as she says, actors "will always have to discuss or answer questions such as: 'When did we meet?', 'How long have we known each other?' and 'When did I last see my uncle?' Then she gathers the actors around a table and has each talk through their character's biography in terms of the other "characters" sitting around them, adjusting the proposed biographies so that they mesh with each other – and the facts of the play and concepts of the production.

Mitchell also suggests the sort of language the director might use if intervening in such a discussion. "Rather than telling the actors that their choice of dates is 'wrong,'" she says, "... you might, for instance, say: 'I'm not entirely convinced that putting the death of Nina's mother so long ago is useful. It might be better to consider putting it a little closer to the action of the play so that your stepmother is newer.' "

A director might also assign, or invite, the actors to research topics in the play that will enrich their performance and offer probing avenues of exploration that might add deep texture and depth to the play or film. Shared either in or out of rehearsal, these can give the entire company an opportunity to enrich the production's initial concept: Director Kathryn Bigelow, for example, depended heavily on actor-initiated research for her film, *Hurt Locker*, where she was pleased to find herself working with what she quickly realized were "very smart, talented, creative actors [who] took it upon themselves to do a lot of the homework." Bigelow details three actors in particular: "Jeremy Renner spent some time with the EOD [Explosive Ordinance Disposal program] at Fort Irwin in California, and ... ended up being incredibly well-versed in the mechanics and logistics and processes of bomb disarmament, as was Anthony Mackie, who spent time in Fort Bragg and Brian Geraghty, who was in country once he got to the Middle East and spent time with some of our EOD technical advisors on location. All three of them, by choice, completely immersed themselves so that they would have the benefit of that understanding." No one can seriously doubt that this research was a strong factor in developing the intense realism of the film, which Roger Ebert praised as "a great film, an intelligent film, a film shot clearly so that we know exactly who everybody is and where they are and what they're doing and why."

Table work

The first read-through of the script is often followed by further readings, in which actors will speak their own characters' lines and begin to probe deeply into the play's language, subtext, references, themes, and meanings. Such readings are known as "table work," as the actors and the director can regularly interrupt the reading to ask questions, discuss points, reread sections in different ways take time for each member of the company to pencil ideas into the margins of their scripts for further research and/or implementation once staging begins. Esteemed American director Anne Bogart is committed to table work: "I spend a lot of time with actors around a table before the staging process begins. We move slowly through the text and related materials in order to study and ask penetrating questions." But table work, she says, "is not about finding answers. The discussions and slow, deep readings are about opening up possibilities and making room for discovery…. We look for clues and hints that can lead to unexpected associations and fruitful directions…. We attempt to enter into the mystery of the material by opening up to the myriad of possible readings that one text can provoke."

Some directors devote as much as half of the rehearsal period to such table work, particularly for plays with complex themes and character relationships. Others are ready to start blocking on day two – if not before the end of day one. The decision as to when to make this transition, for most directors, depends on the nature of the play (its style, complexity, political relevance) as well as the nature of the acting company engaged for it (its collective experience, familiarity with the material, knowledge of each other, and like factors).

But at some point the reading phase will turn into the staging phase, with actors working on their feet instead of sitting in their chairs.

The staging phase

When the actors are up on their feet – able to run, walk, jump, fall to the floor, and slap each other on the back – the director will move toward actually staging the play. Standing, moving, and speaking will now replace sitting, talking, and reading.

There are two basic ways this phase can begin. One is for the director to "block out" the movements of the actors by telling or showing them when, where, and how to move at different moments in the play. The second is for the director to invite the actors to "move where you feel like," whereupon the actors improvise their movements as they rehearse the play. Some directors have strong preferences for one method or the other; some developing reputations as "block and run" directors, others, such as Paul Sills of Chicago's Second City and film director Robert Altman, becoming known as "improvisational directors." It is obvious that the former concentrate on staging first and then focus on the acting afterwards, while improvisational directors begin by letting the acting emerge first and setting the staging to fit it afterwards.

Which is best? There is no single answer to this question, since both methods have led to magnificent – as well as disastrous – productions. The reality is that most directors find a midpoint between these techniques, which are absolute only when written on paper, and most will also vary their methods depending on the play they are directing and with whom and where they're working. Their decision will thus depend on many situations, key among them being the style of the play, the size of the cast, the experience of the actors, the complexity of the production's full-stage actions (e.g., battles, murders, shipwrecks, coronations), and the amount of available rehearsal time, in addition to the director's own, innate preferences.

Improvising rehearsals

Certainly for realistic plays with small casts and few actors onstage at any time, many directors will choose to segue from table reading to "putting the play on its feet" by having the actors continue to read, but improvise movements around the stage – which is furnished with appropriate rehearsal props and furniture – as they do so. These rehearsals will segue into setting the scripts aside once the lines have been memorized, and allowing the staging to evolve naturally from these improvisations, with the director intermittently shaping the result by making suggestions from time to time like, "John, why don't you sit on the sofa here?" or "Ellen, what happens if you put your hand on his shoulder." It is certainly possible, and even common, for a director to stage a play entirely through such a conflation of the actors' instincts, improvisations, experiments, and spontaneous choices, interposed with director-led questions, suggestions, discussions, and, eventually, decisions. This "guided-improvisational" staging method is intensely collaborative, and can create miracles of both subtlety and power when there is sufficient time and imagination to proceed effectively in such manner.

Blocking rehearsals

But there are other situations where straightforward blocking will be virtually necessary. One instance is where features are already designed in the setting where certain actions are to take place, such as a door from the outside at stage left, or a window stage right or a balcony above, each planned for actions that take place during the play. These planning decisions preempt improvising where a character might enter the house, or look out the window or climb over a balcony, since these scenic elements are most likely being built in the shops shortly after rehearsals begin.

Another obvious case is the large-cast production where there are many actors on the stage at the same time. In Shakespeare's *Antony and Cleopatra,* for example, there are thirty-three named characters, and thirty-six scenes in which they appear. Having all these actors "moving wherever they like" during rehearsals of the production's big scenes would make it all but impossible to ready the show for its designer run-through. The sight-line complexities alone would be brutal. Moreover, many of these big scenes were presumably "blocked" by characters in the play! The opening scene of *King Lear,* for example, which portrays a formal abdication ceremony attended by eleven speaking characters and perhaps another dozen or so knights, nobles, and guards, would itself have been "staged" by the king himself, or by a "ceremony director" on the king's staff. So the staging of *King Lear* is actually a staging *of the staging* created by the "real" king's "director." And we can be sure that no real King Lear (indeed, no real king) would permit his daughters, nobles, knights, and guards to simply move about "where they feel like" during his abdication. He would have them "blocked" where everybody could see him – and where they would not "block" anybody's sight lines.

Directing textbooks often devote large sections to whether or not a director should pre-block a play, meaning to work up the blocking on paper before the rehearsal, usually with diagrams and charts. The reasons to answer yes are all about efficiency; the naysayers argue that this is too top-down and inhibits collaboration with the actors being "blocked" from participating in the decisions about their own characters' actions.

The real question, though, is not whether directors should pre-block but *how much* should they pre-block. Because on some occasions, such as the *King Lear*'s opening scene or the full-scale street fighting that begins *Romeo and Juliet,* they almost have to. Not only because the sight lines (what portions of the action the audience on the extreme left and right of the seating area will see and what they won't) are hard to establish effectively without such pre-blocking, but the safety of the actors are at stake.

So most directors – certainly those facing tight rehearsal schedules – will almost always at least pre-block the major starting positions for such large-cast scenes on paper, working out the sight lines, major movement patterns, and focus points on paper (usually on a diagram of the stage floor drawn or printed on the director's script copy), and linking the movements to the appropriate moments in the text, before the actual rehearsal begins.

There are clearly some advantages in such pre-blocking. A large scene such as Lear's abdication, with all its characters and their many comings and goings and physical actions, would require hundreds of individual character moves; trying to decide on these by simply "winging it" on the spot would eat up a huge amount of rehearsal time. But there are pitfalls as well. Since pre-blocking prioritizes physical staging over exploration of human relationships, and elevates the director's role to that of temporary dictator (i.e., "one who dictates" – which is what one does when doling out pre-formulated instructions from a book), the actors may feel creatively stultified, that they are being pushed around like pawns on the director's chessboard. Director Anne Bogart describes a rehearsal she once watched. "The director spent hours telling the actors exactly what to do," she recalled. "The actors learned their blocking from the director. The air in the rehearsal hall felt stale and heavy. No art was happening as far as I could see." To insist on rigidly pre-blocking even large-cast scenes may undermine the basic lessons of this book.

The most common way that directors can work through this problem is by combining both improvisational and pre-blocked staging in the same play, varying the modes within adjacent rehearsal blocks. For example, to stage that first scene of *King Lear* in a single, four-hour call, the director can, after preparing a pre-blocking script, very roughly stage the entire scene in the first hour, but follow that with four individual half-hour rehearsals with Regan and Goneril, then Lear and Cordelia, then Lear and Kent, and finally Edmund, Gloucester, and Kent. These second and third hours of the rehearsal are not devoted to staging, however, but to the acting – with the director concentrating, now in a looser and more improvisational manner, on those characters' interactions with each other during these sub-scenes within the larger one. Then, in the fourth and final hour of the call, all the actors in the scene return to the rehearsal hall to review the entire scene. By the end of the four hours, the basic movement patterns have been roughly staged, all nine principal actors have had at least a half-hour to work with the director and each other on character relationships, and all the actors – including the dozen nonspeaking attendants – will have had a chance to review the entire scene and perhaps learn some, or even most, of their lines. The scene will have been staged and reviewed, the principals will have explored key moments of their parts, and everyone (other than the director) will also have *at least one hour off*, during which they would have been able to study the script, probe its subtext, run lines with each other, or just head out for a cup of coffee and a chat. And this all accomplished done in a single four-hour rehearsal block – which is nice to know when you still have twenty-five other *King Lear* scenes to stage!

Such an integrated rehearsal schedule combines the director's need to get the play on its feet with the actors' needs to develop their subtexts, goals, and tactics within their character relationships. Leadership and collaboration are merged, and everybody can come out with a sense of positive participation in creating the scene.

Probably all directors pre-block certain scenes, at least some of the time. Sometimes they do so in their heads, sometimes on the page, and sometimes just as an exercise to be discarded when the rehearsal actually begins. Bonnie J. Monte, Artistic Director of the New Jersey Shakespeare Festival, creates a "blocking script" for each of her productions, but the nature of that script varies entirely depending on what's involved in each scene. "Sometimes it may take two hours just to block one page, depending on its complexity," she says, "but on other pages, I just write, 'Play around with it,' " so that the result will be something "really organic that the actors and I find together." The blocking script is Monte's preparation and guidance, not her rulebook. "I use it as a guide, a road map." Peter Brook's practice, you might remember (see Chapter 3), is to pre-block the dramatic action well ahead of time – but only "as an exercise" that he will "demolish" before coming into the rehearsal hall. Neither mode is – or even can be – absolute. There must be a level of actor buy-in when a director simply lays out the staging, and a level of leadership when the actors are urged only to move where they feel like. Determining the balance between these is often the director's toughest challenge, but one for which there is no teacher that can match actual hands-on experience.

Certainly, a deferential tone when blocking will prove useful in defusing what might otherwise become overly proprietary directorial language. If, for example, instead of simply telling the actor, "On this line, John, sit on the couch," the director *asks* the actor, "John, why don't you try sitting on the couch here?" the ensuing action – which will almost certainly be exactly the same – will be accepted by the actor as a shared decision rather than simply a command-and-obey decree. And this is not a trick: the actor will have *genuinely* shared in creating the move by "deciding" to "try" what the director has asked – and found his "trial" move to be a good one. The next time John rehearses the scene, he will remember the move not because he was told to do it, but because he, as his character, "decided" to do it. And he will do it convincingly, because it is his move and not the director's.

It is also helpful if such staging requests by the director are coupled with a reason – a motivation if you will – why the character (and not just the actor) is being asked to consider them. "Turn left when you say that" is a pretty meaningless stage direction – it gives the direction only to the actor (Ellen), not to the character (Cordelia). "Face Lear squarely when you say that," is better, since the director is now talking to Cordelia about how she interacts with Lear. And "Why don't you face Lear squarely when you say that?" is even better yet, as the director is now giving Ellen the chance for Cordelia to *decide* to face Lear, so that when character Cordelia does, actress Ellen will "buy into" the action Cordelia takes, as well as the reason she takes it.

And "Why don't you face Lear squarely when you say that, and show him you're not going to give up without a fight!" is an even better way to give such a blocking direction. Such a direction, still phrased as a question, couples the action with not just a motivation but also a target for that motive and an expectation of its eventual success – which will give Cordelia's move a true burst of energy and commitment when the actress executes it.

Director-actor discussions

A great deal of this staging phase is normally spent in discussions, from brief, one-on-ones between the director and a single actor (such as Kazan's going to "each actor"), to open group discussions with the director and the entire cast, and perhaps others – a dramaturg, say – that might follow a run-through of the play.

Whatever their duration, however, these discussions should be genuinely participatory, reasonably open-ended, and clearly (though not necessarily equally) involving of both sides. The point of conducting such discussions is not simply to express viewpoints but to dig into the play with multiple shovels, so that everyone participating feels they are extracting material from the same sources (the play and their research on it), and placing it onto the same pile (the production they are creating together).

On rare occasions such discussions may resemble seminars, and some directors may feel it useful to gather the cast for a formal discussion – sometimes led by a dramaturg or guest scholar – on the background or potentially deeper meanings of the play. Much more commonly, though, discussions arise spontaneously at crucial points during rehearsals, when scenes do not seem to be coming together, or dramatic points seem to be confused or unfocused, or performances are becoming less rather than more convincing as the days go by. Sometimes (and only voluntarily, if the production is being rehearsed under Equity rules), the discussion can spill out beyond the rehearsal call, over a round of drinks at the local pub, perhaps, or in someone's home or apartment.*

---

*For a production I directed of Shakespeare's *Measure for Measure* at the Colorado Shakespeare Festival, I invited the actors playing Angelo and Isabelle out for a beer following rehearsals of the scenes where Angelo tries to convince the would-be nun to sleep with him to spare her brother's execution. Most of their arguments, however, are based on New Testament theology, on which none of us were expert, so I invited a biblical expert to join us. Without those pub-gatherings, those arguments would have been purely superficial.

Wherever they take place, such discussions should allow for mutual, shared input. These need not be analytical: a director or cast member might share a personal experience along the lines of a key event in the script, for example, which may then prompt one or more company members to share similar experiences in their own lives. If such revelations arise without being programmed, and with no one directly asked or prodded to reveal their life stories but simply volunteering to do so because it seems relevant to the task at hand, deeper levels of the play's actions and the characters' motivations will almost surely be conveyed, profoundly enriching the emotional investment of the play's interactions when the scene is next rehearsed.

For this reason, today's directors often use discussions more to pose questions than give answers. "Why do you think you (i.e., your character) would do this?" "Why do you want to marry him?" "What do you see in her?" "Why does she get you so frustrated?" "Where are you going when you leave the house?" "Why are you going there?" and "What makes you so enraged in this speech?"

It's of course easy for a director to jump in with the answers to these questions, but when the *actor* initiates the answer, he or she owns it – and will then play it by instinct rather than by outside direction.

Carefully *focused* questions, rather than commands or instructions, are also a good way to stimulate specific actions that a director may wish to provoke. "How can you make Jane respect you more when you say that?" the director may ask Joe, the actor playing opposite her, which will make Joe work harder to *figure out* how to gain Jane's respect. This gives Joe a task (something to *do*) rather than a result (something to *show*). Then, when Joe unconsciously draws himself up a little taller, deepens his vocal tone, raises his left eyebrow with a sly smile and flexes his muscles, it's the *actor,* not the director, who has created this action, and the actor has done it *instinctively*, not merely on command.

And if "Jane" is the name of the actor rather than that of her character, Joe is figuring out how to gain a *real person's* respect, and is creating his role in real-time and in real-life by interacting with a real person. Joe is then, in Stanislavsky's phrase, "experiencing his role" on stage rather than just imitating it. The point of posing such questions rather than handing down commandments is that the actor – not the director – does the *work* of the character, even when the director may have planted the seed. By herself initiating the action, the actor creates – rather than merely executes – her role, and the actor-director collaborative process has seen its highest reward.

Finally, the actor-director relationship is a give-and-take exchange in which it is never entirely clear who does the giving and who the taking. Each does a bit of each. Director and actor are partners, not competitors. The difference in their "roles" is not one of status but of duties: the director's to prompt and shape, the actor's to execute, create, and convince. And if the mutuality of actors' and director's co-ownership of the parts and the production is freely acknowledged, individual egos become moderated and the competition for status never even arises.

Often this has to do with confidence – on each side. Harold Prince admits that he "had difficulties with the actors" when he directed his first Broadway production, but after staging many shows he began to feel trusted. "I can be as scared on the first day of rehearsal as I was then, but it is different. My record gives them the confidence they need." Such confidence gives Prince security, mainly because he *no longer has to prove that he's the director.* "Today I can go dry .... All I have to do is admit it. Invariably it works to my advantage, giving the relationship the mutuality rehearsing requires." Thus letting the actors help him find the right direction to direct them makes the production even better – because a new "mutuality" of actors and director has created their joint ownership of the performances – and thereby a far stronger ensemble.

For as Prince makes clear, directors don't only direct actors, they also learn from them. In a famous example, director Martin Scorsese had to play a small part in his film *Taxi Driver* when the actor he had cast took ill. Playing a passenger in the back seat of a cab driven by Robert De Niro, Scorsese had the line, "Put the flag down," (i.e., "Stop the meter"). After the first take, and without turning around, De Niro called back to Scorsese: "Hey, Martin, don't just *say* 'Put the flag down.' *Make me* put the flag down!" "And Bobby wan't going to put that flag down until he was convinced that I meant it," Scorsese remembered. "It was the best acting lesson I ever heard."

"On-your-feet" techniques

Discussion and dialogue between directors and actors is not, however, the only way – or even the best way – of sharing artistic impulses in the actor-director collaboration.

Warm-up exercises are fairly universal in rehearsals around the world for preparing both voice and body for the strenuous muscular activity – from the larynx on down – which acting always requires. They also provide opportunities for group rapport and, with certain exercises, the feeling that "we're all making fools of ourselves together." Lying on your back and saying "Huh! Buh-buh-buh, buh-buh-buh, buh-buh-buh!" forty times in a row gets everyone off his or her metaphorical high horse and into the spirit of group play and group playing. Even a quick loosening up and bouncing around can create a lovely transition between the me-first world outside the theatre and the ensemble spirit that prevails within it.

Theatre games and *group exercises,* particularly after the pioneering work of Viola Spolin in the 1960s, can play powerful roles in breaking down barriers among actors and directors, and can release creative energies that can be shared in any theatre company's whole-group collaborative efforts. Many directors – Peter Brook being one of them – have begun productions with entire days or weeks of early rehearsals devoted to such activities.

Improvising the text has long been a staple of collective theatrical creativity, as actors in rehearsal are invited to improvise (create on the spot) wholly new scenes between their respective characters, perhaps in interactions they imagine would or could have taken place before or after the actions portrayed in the play as written. Such improvisations in rehearsal essentially invite the actors to be temporary playwrights and directors, and to say and move as they wish within the general context of the roles they are preparing for the production. Improvisations can be initiated as a group exercise within the rehearsal segment. Or a director can, at a pause in the action, simply say to an actor who just spoke, "Tell him that again in your own words!" and see what happens. Ordinarily the actor will just "let fly" with his or her own feelings, expressions, vocalizations, and behaviors – and afterwards the director and actors can assess with each other what if any of the resulting actions could prove helpful to the performance-to-be when the actual text is brought back into play. (It is wise, however, prior to initiating any such improvisations, to make clear that potentially dangerous actions are out of bounds.)

Personal sharing. Director Cynthia Croot asks cast members to bring in, and share with their fellow performers, art objects that they love and feel illustrate their characters and could stimulate deeper understanding of them among fellow "characters" (i.e., cast members). Katie Mitchell, directing a Greek tragedy (*Iphegenia at Aulis*) for England's National Theatre, asked the actors to recall a situation in their lives when they were deeply afraid, and to reenact it, either on their own or with another actor, in front of the entire company. "In this way," Mitchell reported, "you encourage the actors to think about using very precise physical information from real-life situations to communicate the moments in the action of the play." Post-rehearsal gatherings – voluntary cast parties – which the director may host, can also become occasions in which personal stories may arise and be shared naturally, in chats about the play on which everyone is working. These not only bond actors to each other, they bond them to the situations of the play they are jointly creating.

All of these are time-honored ways for directors to establish a deeper rapport with and among the cast during this phase of the rehearsal process. But now it's time to ready the production for an audience, and most of these techniques will yield to the need to make final decisions.

The finalizing phase: leadership takes the helm

The fifth and last rehearsal phase is finalizing – narrowing the show's focus, clarifying its message, synchronizing its style, building its dramatic momentum, and heightening its final impact. At this point leadership – normally from the director – quite naturally reasserts itself. For while games, improvisations, discussions, and even cast parties can help discover a play's depths, they can also be excuses to avoid them.

After all, talking about the play is easy. Reading lines around a table is also pretty easy. Being blocked or improvising blocking are equally easy. It's *experiencing the role* that is truly difficult. This means putting yourself on the line as the character; committing yourself heart and soul to a mentally or psychologically scary action; knowing that if you do what you need to, you will look ugly or sound ugly or lose all your treasured dignity. All of these acting tasks take great reserves of courage. And to say to the director, "Can we just talk about this?" is often only an excuse for not *doing* it.

I have never liked the phrase, uttered in exasperation by many directors in my earlier years, "Just *do* it!" I have never used this line and never will. But I certainly understand the impulse to do so.

The director has the first and final responsibility of leading the company from the comfort levels of pleasant (even if profound) discussion and elegant (even if intricate) staging to the agonizing discomfort of crisis, climax, conflict, and catastrophe (Aristotle's words) describing the impact of high drama – or to the volcanic eruptions of sublime hilarity that mark farce and comedy and leave the spectators without bladder or tear-duct control. These high points make theatre the passionate and vivid enterprise that it has been for more than 3000 years. Such splendors don't arise mainly through intellectual probings or clever blocking, however, but from the flesh-and-blood acts of performance, whether in the rehearsal hall or on the stage. It is when the actor becomes Lear, stripping off his clothing and saying to the near-naked Edgar, "Thou art the thing itself: Unaccommodated man ... a poor, bare forked animal."

For acting, at its most profound, is a sort of striptease, baring one's inner evil (if playing Iago), inner whore (*Othello's* Bianca), inner masochist or sadist (*Marat/Sade*). And the director often must guide the actors right down to the core of their inner bare forked animal – but also keep them from falling into its fiery pit.

And so there are times, certainly as the rehearsal period is coming to its close, when the answer to "Can we talk about this?" is simply "No we can't." For now it's time to do 'the thing itself.'" Once again, however, knowing just when that time has come is mostly a matter of experience – experience in the theatre and experience in life itself.

For leaderless and/or overextended collaboration is unhealthy in the production's final stage, and even problematic in the immediately previous one. Peter Brook, whose use of games and improvisations was legendary, also cautions against the "many traps that are in what we call theatre games and exercises." Such experiences can also "lead nowhere," he eventually realized. So too are text improvisations. "If you really want to know what boredom is," Brook continues, "watch an improvisation where two or three actors get going and 'do their thing' without being stopped. They inevitably find themselves very rapidly repeating clichés, often with a deadly slowness that lowers the vitality of everyone watching."

Discussions, too, can be a crutch. They can stray to irrelevant areas and take up time that would be better spent addressing relevant ones.

They can be simply one actor's call for more personal attention, or to show off his or her braininess, or expertise in some area not pertinent to the production. For while it seems nice for a director to take the time to answer every question an actor might pose, this would also mean that the director would be taking *everybody else's* time for this private Q&A, while the rehearsal clock is still ticking and the other actors are itching to get back to business. So "too nice" can be just as bad as "too mean."

Leadership, in other words, means acute attention to the importance of Brook's "vitality of everyone watching." And directing means, among other things, directing the schedule, directing the way time is spent.

For "time" becomes a word of greater and greater importance to the director as rehearsal nears its end point, for now almost every discussion must be directed toward bringing that discussion to an end, and replacing it with a decision.

Being nice? Being mean?

So let's put collaboration and leadership back together again. It's crucial to realize that collaboration is not simply about "being nice" and leadership is not simply about "being mean." In real-life we are drawn toward things we find attractive, and we recoil from those that seem unpleasant, and so do characters in plays and so do the actors who play those characters. So both lowering the ground in front of the actor (luring her toward her goal) and raising the stakes for her failure (forcing her to try harder) are complementary, not contradictory directorial techniques. Each, when effectively done, will draw maximum effort, emotion, and intensity out of the actor with whom the director works in creating a theatrical moment.

It's certainly not wise for a director to develop the reputation of being *too* mean – you want to make clear, as mentioned earlier, that you are not an ogre – but it's also not wise for being thought of as too nice. "Be not too tame, neither," we remember Hamlet saying. The fact is that inductions and threats, used at the right time and the right degree, are *each* important ways of shaping behavior. The jockey knows that there is a time to coax the horse and a time to use the whip; the parent of a young child knows there is a time to cuddle and a time to glare; the street detective knows there is a time to play good cop, another to play bad cop. And *both* collaboration and leadership are required to create the sense of trust and respect we have been talking about.

Collaboration creates both as it induces the full cooperation of everyone. And leadership creates it because authority offers a protected environment in which to take chances. "Nice" may be nice, but it is not a directorial goal in itself. Roland Polanski is rarely described as a "nice" director on the set. Stuart Wilson recalls that in *Death and the Maiden* he was "terrifying and strange." But Ben Kingsley, in the same film and without denying Wilson's observation, reported that Polanski provided an "extraordinary level of trust" while directing it. "[He] lavished just the right amount of attention on his players – neither clamping down too hard nor leaving so much leeway you didn't know where you were…. This allowed Sigourney [Weaver] and me to get closer and closer so that we could in turn become more and more violent with each other in our scenes. And that's not a paradox. That's what acting is: the more trust, the deeper you can venture into the abyss."

And here's where leadership blends with collaboration. The shared trust that can be engendered in an intense dramatic production will be not superficial but profound: it will be the trust of comrades in battle. But it requires a profound *commitment to the mission* of the show, and the *dangers of falling behind*. Both are crucial, for you don't get your troops to go "once more unto the breach," as Shakespeare's Henry V realized, unless you're willing to go there yourself and make it clear to everyone around you that you're prepared to shoulder the responsibility, and the brickbats. For nice guys may not necessarily finish last, as legendary baseball coach Leo Durocher opined, but *too* nice guys (and gals) certainly do – particularly in the final phase of rehearsals, when tempers are high and the opening nigh. Directors at that point must be fully prepared to employ vinegar as well as honey, and the stick as well as the carrot. And they must know how and when to use these occasional instruments of (imaginary) torture – for example, Bergman's "pedagogical outburst" – when needed. They must not be too tame.

I'd like to come back to Polanski, because he seems to combine the sheerest extremes of directorial pushing and pulling. Wilson says that it was to the "female stars – especially those from whom he needed to evoke an aura of fragile vulnerability – that Polanski could be the most brutal. Yet the performances he extracted from those actresses have consistently been among their most terrifyingly memorable." And that's not just a man's opinion. Sigourney Weaver summed up Polanski's double nature in almost the same way: "Roman ... wasn't there to make us feel better: 'Grow up, get real, be an adult' was [his] continual subtext .... [But] by the end I think all of us felt this tremendous *loyalty* .... He may be the best actor's director I've ever worked with." And Wilson concluded by explaining this paradox in succinct terms: "he can make you feel more insecure than you ever have felt in your entire life – but then safer, too."

So it's an abyss out there, and you can only fully trust someone who, yes, has your interest at stake, but who is also brave enough to take you unto the breach and confront its dangers with you.

A director directs people

Directors do not direct plays. They direct people.

The play exists on the pages of a manuscript or book. The director aims, focuses, energizes, and oversees the process of converting that text to a stage production, and that production is populated wholly by people – specifically, live actors, numbering as few as one or as many as several hundred.

Obviously, a director should know a lot about the plays he or she directs, and how to get the most out of them. But it is more important that the director know a lot about the *people* he or she directs, and how to get the most out of *them*. Knowing all there is to know about a play, or about its author, or its meaning – and/or having an opinion about all these things (which is really all that "knowing" actually means) – that is the easy part. Knowing about the *people who will be remaking the play with their own live flesh* – that is, the actors who play the play's roles – is the hard part.

Consider Shakespearean plays. The outside observer may imagine that the best director of a Shakespearean play would be a literary scholar who has spent a lifetime studying and lecturing and writing about that play, who has studied all of Shakespeare's plays and poems and the historical facts of Shakespeare's life and times and theatre company, and who has analyzed all the major commentaries upon his plays, and the stage history of those plays over the centuries. Such a person would know, or think they know, "what Shakespeare intended" and could then simply "tell the actors how

to play their roles." But though there are many such English professors in universities around the world who have this confidence, and
a great many who have tried to test their knowledge by directing
one or more of Shakespeare's plays, only a very few have emerged
as superior Shakespearean directors. Why not? There are three reasons, I think.

The first is because scholars can be entirely content to concentrate
on just a single issue in the play they are studying. They can write
whole lectures and even books on the implications of a single speech,
or scene, or single theme of a play. But a successful director must
direct – and bring to vivid theatrical life – *every single moment* of that
play: each line, each character, each issue, and certainly each plot
point. Take a look at the footnotes of an edited text of any Shakespeare
play. Virtually every one will tell you the *meaning* of a word or phrase
that might be unfamiliar to the average reader, but virtually none
will tell you *for what reason* the character decides to say it. Why, for
example, does *Bernardo* ask, "Who's there?" when meeting Francisco
in the opening line of *Hamlet? Francisco* is the guard on duty; *he* is the
one who should make the challenge, not Bernardo who is coming to
replace him! Yet no edition I have ever seen footnotes this line, which
may seem understandable since the words themselves need no explanation, but finding a satisfactory *reason* why Bernardo rather than
Francisco makes the challenge initially will fundamentally shape the
scene, and perhaps even the entire production.*

Second, the director must shape the play's character interactions
so that in combination they prove not just clear but *momentous,* in
order that the play, instead of coming off as simply a series of interesting actions and conversations, builds to a thrilling and emotional
climax – or, if it is a farce or a comedy, to an escalating series of hilari-
ous interactions provoking riots of laughter. The director must not
merely deal with words and ideas but also create a *dramatic event* – a
series of vivid actions which, in sum, make an audience of strangers

---

*The most fundamental job of a guard on duty is to immediately stop and
challenge anyone who approaches, yet Francisco has completely failed to
do this, and Bernardo has witnessed his failure. Since his post is guarding
the King's palace, and his country is already expecting a foreign attack, his
punishment for such a failure in this period would be execution by torture.
So while this short scene may only be exposition for Shakespeare, it is a life-
and-death situation for Francisco.

weep at one moment, laugh at another, hold their breath at a third, and develop dramatic momentum throughout. Rarely does anything in a purely literary seminar address this demand.

But the third and most important reason is that directing Shakespeare, like directing any play, is directing *people*. And this means getting the most out of *them* as well as getting the most out of Mr. Shakespeare's words. Which is a lot more than just telling the actors what you want them to do, and how and when they should do it. For the director is not directing Shakespeare. He or she is directing Joe, Jane, Bill, and Bertha. And they are the ones who have to deliver the goods. As Peter Brook says, "It takes a long while for a director to cease thinking in terms of the result he desires and instead concentrate on discovering the source of energy *in the actor* from which true impulses can arise." But this is the life training to which the director must commit, and few scholars have spent Brook's "long while" in discovering such sources of energy.

Group Exercises

1. **Block a blockbuster.** With a large group of actors holding scripts in hand, block the twenty-one lines in the opening scene of *King Lear*, from Gloucester's "Do you know this gentleman, Edgar?" to Lear's "May be prevented now." Work out the location of each character on the stage at that time (Edmund, Gloucester, Kent, Lear, Albany, Cornwall, Goneril, Regan, Cordelia) as well as the other "followers" (knights and guards) who enter with the king. This scene includes the entrance of the royal train, the handling of a coronet (crown) and map, and the indication of characters who are onstage but who have not yet spoken or been identified. Try to make sure that everyone in the "audience" can see the characters that are important to be seen at every key moment. Discuss afterwards.

2. **Hamlet.** Do the same exercise with the "Mouse-trap" scene in *Hamlet*, Act III scene ii from Hamlet's "This play is the image of a murder done in Vienna..." to the exit of everyone but Hamlet and Horatio. Study the entire scene from the beginning, making sure you can stage everyone in this portion of it, and examine closely just who must be seen seeing whom, and when must they be seen seeing them. Discuss afterwards.

3. **Change of Venue.** Repeat exercises one and/or two but for a different theatrical configuration: for example, if the first was done in a proscenium format, switch to a thrust or in-the-round staging.

4. **Pre-block and Improvise.** The group is divided into two or more subgroups of, say, six people. In each group, two directors will separately stage and direct the same three-person scene from a well-known play, using different casts. One director will be assigned to stage by pre-blocking the scene on paper; the other will work purely from the actor-inspired improvisation. Each subgroup presents its two versions to the full group, after which the group members evaluate the comparative merits of each pair of subgroup scenes, and then the actors and directors evaluate their own experiences in preparing them.

6

The Presenting Stage

The presenting stage takes place *on* the stage. This is the final putting-together of this work of theatrical art that has been in preparation, planning, and rehearsing for many months and often many years.

And the implementation of this final phase is largely in the hands of theatre workers who have often been mentioned but yet not fully discussed in the previous pages: the *stage managers*.

You are probably already aware of the multiple duties of the stage management team during rehearsals: posting the schedules, taping the stage floor with the set dimensions, keeping track of the rehearsal time (both for the rehearsal units and the required breaks), recording the director's blocking, prompting the actors' lines, acquiring and arranging needed rehearsal costumes and props, and in general seeing that the rehearsals are proceeding in concert with what is simultaneously being created in the various shops; making sure, for example, that the actor reaching for the pipe in his jacket pocket is reaching for a pocket that the costume shop is actually building – and that the pocket is large enough to hold the pipe the prop department is purchasing!

The stage managers also provide an important filter for a director by addressing technical concerns, such as the temperature of the rehearsal room or the locations where rehearsal calls are posted. If gripes about such issues, which are rarely the concern of (or under the control of) the director, are left wholly unaddressed, they could simmer – and create morale or even discipline problems.

But the main role of the stage management staff during rehearsals, and in particular of the PSM that leads it, is to serve as the communications hub for the entire theatrical collaboration. The PSM is the primary link between the director, actors, designers, shop heads, and crew chiefs alike, and normally with the producers, publicity staff, box office staff, and house staff as well. The PSM staff must be up-to-the minute in contacting everyone who needs to implement schedule changes, script changes, prop changes, and, indeed, everything "added" to the production plans between planning and production meetings. Indeed, cast members as well as designers and shop heads may have more one-on-one conversations with the stage management staff than with the director. As the communications hub, the PSM and his or her staff are absolutely central to the entire production.

Therefore, it is important that the director introduces the PSM at the first meeting, and does so proudly – stressing the PSM's importance to and authority over the production. For in today's theatre, the PSM is not the "Director's Assistant" as was the case in past decades, but the production's COO – its Chief Operating Officer.*

Stage managers

It's useful to understand the history of the PSM. Such positions have always existed, of course, but they became identified by title only in the eighteenth and nineteenth centuries. Mainly, they were considered the director's assistant and their main role was to do whatever the director said – and didn't want to do himself. When D.W. Waller was the stage manager for Booth's Theatre in New York in the 1870s, Edwin Booth was listed as director in the program – but Waller did most of what we call directing, including staging the plays!

These days, however, the stage management team takes care of all the duties mentioned above during rehearsals, plus many more when the production moves into technical rehearsals. There they record and then "call" the show's cues (sound, lighting, scene shifting, curtain risings and fallings, and actor entrances where necessary) that

---

*Few people realize it, but while stage managers are members of the same union as actors, the PSM's scale salary is approximately 30% higher than that of performers.

take place during the production. These often number into the several hundreds, and calling even one of them incorrectly (such as cueing a curtain to lower prematurely) could literally ruin the performance. And finally the PSM takes over the director's role after the production's opening, when the director (in most professional productions, at least) is no longer officially in residence or responsible for maintaining the show. This generally includes rehearsing understudies and actor replacements, giving notes and/or calling "refresher" rehearsals when actors deviate from their staging or pacing or even emotional commitments to the action, alerting production heads or the production manager when scenery, costumes, props, hardware, or lighting instruments are not working properly, and alerting the producer or production manager if there seems to be behavioral or morale problems developing among the cast, crews, or house staff. The PSM, therefore, is nothing less than the "director-in-waiting" for the entire production.

The PSM as COO

However, I wish to come back to the PSM as the production's Chief Operating Officer throughout the entire process, because it is the one most germane to the subject of this book.

The PSM's chief responsibility in this role is to provide the "human switchboard" that binds the collaboration, and maintain fluid and accurate communications within the entire production team. And since the individuals making up this team may perform their work in widely disparate locations – scene and costume shops may be elsewhere in town, designers may be emailing in updates from out-of-state or abroad, casting directors may be auditioning replacement actors in another city – the role of stage management is absolutely crucial in maintaining the production's integrity on a day-to-day basis.

And since almost every question posed in the rehearsal hall may turn out to have serious implications for the costume shop (since the actress has been asked to do a cartwheel, can she have some fancy bloomers underneath her skirt?), or for the scene shop (is the banister going to be sturdy enough for her to hop astride it the way the director has asked her to?), or for the lighting department (can she be lighted outside the upstage window that she just has been directed to peek through in act one?), or the hair and wig department (since five lines were cut from scene two, can she still make the wig change in time for scene three?), it is the PSM who must make certain these questions are conveyed *immediately* to the proper department, and then see to it that an answer is returned and relayed as soon as possible to the director in time for the next rehearsal.

And sometimes these questions will turn into decisions: Yes, the actress *will* do cartwheels and *does* need the bloomers, and she *will* be lighted outside the upstage window in act one – so the proper instruments should be hung and focused. In these cases, then, the PSM communicates the final decision – but first *making certain that it's indeed a decision* and not just an idea the director and actors are still exploring. Otherwise the idea may be discarded in the rehearsal room – while the bloomers and extra lights show up at tech and dress rehearsals.

If communication breaks down, and the scenery and costumes that are built in the shops do not reflect the actions that emerge from the rehearsals, the tech and dress rehearsals will be nightmares. Restaging scenes, rehanging lights, or rebuilding scenery at the last minute is costly and time-consuming, putting everybody on edge when they should be at their most confident.

So the stage management team's communications must be accurate – and they must be speedy. These days "as soon as possible" increasingly means "immediately," since the advent of smartphones and text-messaging has meant that queries sent from the rehearsal hall to production shops and vice-versa are nearly instantaneous – which means that the *replies* to such queries are often expected not by the end of the day but within the hour, if not the minute. Thus a permanent ongoing contact between the rehearsal hall, where stage management is recording moment-to-moment directorial decisions, and the production departments, which are charged with implementing these decisions, requires a communication system capable of interconnecting everyone, everywhere, in virtually warp speed – and stage managers willing to work at that speed.

But effective collaboration cannot wholly be limited to the electronic transmission of messages, questions, and answers. It also requires, at least from time to time, a *personal connection* – and sometimes an intense one – between the persons communicating. And this requires the PSM leave the rehearsal hall from time to time for face-to-face visits, wherever and whenever possible, between him or herself and the shops, studios, offices, and theatre spaces where scenery and props are constructed and painted, costumes and wigs are built and fitted, sound recordings are made, lights are hung, and publicity photos taken. There are two very good reasons why electronic communication should be supplemented by these more personal interactions. The first is obvious: only in the scene shop can the stage manager put together what he or she knows about the blocking scene with what's being built as the scenery for that scene. Yes, the dimensions of that scenery have been marked out with tape on the rehearsal floor since the first day of rehearsal, and renderings (drawings) of the scenery may also be hanging on the rehearsal hall wall, and a three-dimensional model of it may be sitting on a table nearby – but these are neither fully detailed nor in many cases fully up-to-date. Perhaps changes have been made between the rendering, developed during the design meetings, and the working drawings, made in the shop as construction began – and that change had not been fully communicated to the director or the PSM. Or perhaps there was a mistake in the original laying down of the tapes, or perhaps there wasn't room enough in the rehearsal hall to lay out the entire set, or maybe there were construction details added to the design (say a line of spikes on a garden fence that the director, unaware of, has staged a character to sit upon) which were not in the initial plans. Likewise costume renderings approved in the design meetings, and shown to the actors in early rehearsals and even posted in the rehearsal hall and/or the costume shop, may not be accurate representations of the actual costumes now being built or rented. Pictured only in one position, and as worn by an imaginary actor instead of the actual one (who had probably not been cast at the time the drawing was made), the rendering may look and feel quite different than what is now hanging on the costumer's hanger. How heavy is the fabric? How much does it sway when you dance in it? Where are its pockets? *Are* there pockets? How long does it take to button or unbutton? Does it "ride up" when the actor lifts both hands high in the air? What does it do when the actor sits on a small stool? Sinks into a cushy armchair? Falls to the floor? Stands on her head?

And while many of these costume questions may be addressed during fitting rehearsals, some will certainly be missed, since at the time of the fitting the costumers are not familiar with the blocking, and the actors may be preoccupied with how they look in the wedding scene and forget to ask about the scene where they tear down the stairs. No one hopes to have to deal with these issues for the first time at dress rehearsals, and it's the all-seeing, all-hearing stage manager's job to anticipate as many of them as possible.

Therefore, the PSM personally visits the shops on a regular basis, inspecting the units (scenery, props, costumes) where designs are being constructed, seeking to spot – and then address – any discrepancies that may appear between what the director is assuming in the rehearsal hall and production staffs are building in the various theatre shops. If carried out diligently, this process assures that technical and dress rehearsals will in fact *be* rehearsals, and not given over to restaging the play or rebuilding the scenery to make the one conform to the other. Fulfilling this function makes the PSM the production's Great Collaborator.

But the second reason for the PSM to visit the shops and studios is less obvious: it is to act as a *personal* liaison with the production heads so as to have the rapport necessary to avoid territorial warfare when any discrepancies arrive, as they almost always do. "Well, you never said the railing was to be sat upon" may be an entirely truthful statement, but it does little good to make that the sole basis of a solution. With a genuine personal rapport between the PSM and the production heads – easiest to obtain with regular face-to-face contact among people whose names you know and faces you recognize – leeway for even last-minute changes can be easily accommodated without necessarily assigning fault, and compromises can be negotiated in a helpful and friendly manner.* Making theatre is a human – and here we might say "humane" – art, after all, not just a process of calculated engineering, and the stage manager presides over all aspects of a profoundly personal – and not just an administrative – collaboration.

Stage managers have the acute responsibility of overseeing all the theatre's operations in production, which is why I think of them as COOs, but, contrary to the cardinal rule of management ("You can delegate authority, but not responsibility"), PSMs possess considerably less-than-COO authority during the rehearsal period. Though they are at the hub of the collaboration, they are not always, prior to the show's opening, as elevated in the hierarchy as are most of the "spokes" to which they are joined. Young actors, having begun their artistic work in educational institutions, may recall situations

---

* Fault may eventually be assigned, if the discrepancy is indeed due to mismanagement or incompetence, but the best time to do it is almost always after the production opens – at the exit interview, perhaps. See next chapter.

where their college's stage managers were simply those students not good enough to be cast as actors. No one in the professional theatre should make this mistake: PSMs are paid more than actors, for one thing, and they have day-to-day authority over all performances. But they also must rely on a ready reserve of good will, tactful diplomacy, and skillful negotiation to settle such discrepancies as may arrive between the various departments – as well as keep the players happy and the production on schedule.

But they also must be brave as well as humane. They must often speak truth to power (to the director, to the designer, to the shop foreman, even to the producer) and must doggedly point out discrepancies that no one really wants to acknowledge – in part because no one wants to be blamed for them. They must continually play the role of communicator of bad news: alerting the director that the prop being built will not work in the scene as staged, and alerting the prop shop that the director insists the prop be rebuilt – and then must monitor and report on the discussion as to how the discrepancy will be resolved, and how the additional shop time and money will be found and allocated. They must also enforce union rules: If the production operates under an Actors Equity contract, for example, they must end rehearsals at a precisely specified time, even in mid-speech, and even when the director may be imploring to let the actors at least finish the scene. Nothing they do is easy, and almost everything they do will encounter some moments of resistance.

In order to make the PSM effective, therefore, the director must privilege the stage management team in all artistic communications. The PSM should be copied on all written exchanges between the director and the designers and production heads, and the director should provide the PSM full opportunities to speak to the cast when the need arises, and to back up the PSM's authority except in cases where it has been clearly overstepped. And part of the reason for this is that the PSM rises to a substantially higher artistic *and* hierarchical level when the production moves into technical and dress rehearsals, at which point the PSM not only monitors the show but also begins calling it.

So to help stage managers master a delicate balancing act when dealing with the production "spokes," those spokes must collaborate humanely with the stage manager at their hub. I recall a director who would regularly blow up at "his" stage manager – usually for mistakes he had made himself. He inflicted irreparable harm to his productions, for if the hub is broken down, the spokes will fly apart.

Backstage and pit personnel

We've discussed "Shop Heads" for the first time in this section: these are the Heads (though other titles are common, including "Assistant Designer," "Prop Master," and the like) of the scene shop, costume shop, prop shop, craft shop, wig and hair studio, and perhaps others. They work together with the Master Electricians, Sound Technicians, Shift Crew Chiefs, Flymasters, Dressers (those who help actors make quick costume changes), and other technicians – all of whom may come under the oversight of those who may hold the titles such as Technical Director and/or Production Manager – and all those who work under them – along with many other titles in the many theatrical organizations and nomenclatures that exist around the world. Plus there may be "pit personnel" – the instrumental band or orchestra for a musical production – who are customarily located in an "orchestra pit" below the stage, or elsewhere on or around the stage proper. These folks are rarely if ever seen by the public, and rarely featured in reviews or newspaper columns. But *Washington Post* drama critic Peter Marks, who has reported from backstage for years, provides a welcome view of what he saw while observing Julie Andrews behind the curtain in the 1955 Broadway production of *Victor/Victoria*, in which Andrews played the title role. Marks writes, "A star does not come close to creating a performance on her own. From the stage managers to the prop men to the women who waited for Andrews in the shadows of the scenery with her next costume and a bottle of throat spray, the exertions of a small army of theater people, invisible to the paying customers out front, were making the imaginative universe of the show possible." Marks' interest in the theatrical backstage world has continued, and in early 2010 he expanded upon these observations: "In my theater-world travels, I've seen the collaborative ethos reinforced again and again. You'd think that ensuring that others looked good would be a thankless chore. But that is not the impression in talking to the people who do it for a living. There can be a parallel level of satisfaction in being the unseen hand, in participating in the allied arts of the stage. You know from the outset that there will be no fanfare for you, but the good of the whole is what matters."

For it is just these men and women who build the show in the shops, run the show from backstage, and play instruments in the show's pit that constitute the vast army of "offstage personnel" that are critical to every production. Each is absolutely crucial. If the scenery is poorly built and falls over during the scene change, or the curtain doesn't fall because the designated operator isn't there, or the police siren (or plot-activating clarinet solo) doesn't sound at the right time, the entire production will stop dead in its tracks – just as much as if Hamlet doesn't enter in the second scene. And so these individuals are theatre *artists* as well as theatre technicians. Many work directly with directors in rehearsals and designers in the planning, research, drawing and drafting, selecting and shopping for materials, and actual building of scenery, costumes, and properties. For costume designer Catherine Zuber, a six-time Tony Award winner, "Costume design is a real collaboration with those technicians who actually pattern, cut, drape and sew the costumes that she draws. We are very dependent on the people who make the clothes." But their work goes beyond this, Zuber insists, as exemplified by her relationship with assistant designer Patrick Bevilacqua: "Patrick and I have a great relationship. It's a true collaboration: I show him a sketch and he interprets it. And when really great assistant designers like Patrick take it a step further, it becomes a *great* collaboration!" And yet "backstage" personnel are not always made to *feel* as full members of the collaboration. They rarely receive acclamation or awards or even applause that are lavished on actors, directors, and designers. "For an art form so reliant on applause," says the wisely observant Peter Marx, "most of those who work in the theater only hear it as muffled noise from another room. Propping up a star's halo, the behind-the-scenes folks hardly bask in a sliver of reflected light."

Sometimes, however, backstage artists may be made to feel estranged from the director-designer-actor axis because they come from – or are given to believe they come from – different worlds. In high school and undergraduate drama programs, there is usually an informal social distinction between self-styled "artists" (chiefly actors) and "techies" (as backstage personnel are often called, often by their own choice). And stage instrumentalists generally come from the wholly different area of music. Such work distinctions, however, may lead to a social hierarchy quite apart from the job categories they represent, a juvenile caste system that may carry over from the high school level to the college, and then to the graduate school and even professional levels. This is much to the disadvantage of absolutely everyone.

And while few students are self-identified as directors or designers at the high school level, when they do so seek to so identify themselves, they are normally in advanced undergraduate or MFA training in their chosen areas of specialty, which means they are aiming at a high-profile and high-hierarchical positions from that time on – whereas carpenters, electricians, (costume) drapers, and milliners are more likely to receive their professional training through apprenticeships, rather than specialized graduate or conservatory programs. Thus, they customarily lack the abundance of longstanding colleagues that designers, directors, and actors usually enjoy.

Yet the collaborative collegiality and rapport among *all* these artists is vital for a production's well being, and must be carefully created and nurtured. Why? The great stage and film director Mike Nichols "believes in [collective] ownership of the work – that is, that everyone associated with the production creates a piece of it," as reported by Broadway PSM Peter Lawrence, who has often worked with him. Lawrence goes on to explain specifically what Nichols and he insist upon: "The actors must believe they have created their characters and staging, the designers must believe the same about the environment and clothes…. But also the press agents, stagehands, management, musicians – *everyone* – must believe they have contributed to the whole." Why is this so important? Because then, says Lawrence, "everyone on the production will fight for its survival."

But how do the individuals at the upper levels of the theatrical hierarchy (director, designers, actors) assure that those further down the ladder have this sense of ownership, this sense of full belonging?

They do it first by simply *learning their names.* Broadway star Brian Stokes Mitchell says he learned this from Chita Rivera when working with her on *Kiss of the Spider Woman,* and "Rivera made it a priority to learn the names of everyone on the crew and in the orchestra." Simple? Yes, but you will be surprised how few actors and even directors and designers learn the names of the shop heads and crews that build and run the shows in which they take their bows.

Learning the names makes the rest easy, because there will be plenty of interactions between the collaborators, and knowing each others' names and titles will quickly segue to developing personal as well as professional relationships. For personal relationships override hierarchical differences. Yes, the dresser will help the actress make her quick change whether they have a personal relationship or not, but each will enjoy it more, and fret about it less, if the two share a friendship that makes them familial equals – instead of creating a "mistress-servant" relationship as would exist if this scene were actually taking place in an aristocratic English mansion, rather than the backstage of a theatre production. Mitchell goes on to say that "next to the director, actors have the most collaborative job in theatre because we have to interface with so many different people: the director, the crew, the costume and prop people, the orchestra, the other actors, the house crew – [they] become your backstage family." If that interface is dissonant because of hierarchical or social distinctions, it is not a family but a class or corporate structure.

The second way to repair the high school rupture between the "artists" and the "techies" is for each to cultivate genuine interests in the various arts of the theatre beyond their own – both in regard to the production they are all working on together, and as a response to the splendor of theatre arts in its larger artistic sense. Certainly, a director should visit the shops on a regular basis, along with the PSM, and should personally see what is being built, not only to see if there are discrepancies but also to provide his or her personal support and appreciation for the work going on – and for those persons doing the work. This is also a time where questions can be raised and discrepancies yet-unnoticed by stage management can be discovered and addressed, but that is not the sole, or even the main, reason for directors to show appreciation where it is deserved: I have never experienced a case where the visit from a director to a prop shop, scene shop, or costume room has not elicited delight to those shops' staff when their hard work is recognized and appreciated from the person at the "top" of the production's hierarchy.

The costume room is a particularly lively center of collaboration, because when actors start taking their clothes off, the relationships between them and the wardrobe staff (designers, cutters, drapers, stitchers, dyers, first hands, and craft specialists) becomes *literally* intimate – both physically and emotionally. Issues of pride are invariably involved: the actors as to how they look partially disrobed and then in costume, and the costume staff as to how well they have built the garment and how much the actor likes it – or doesn't. Those actors who limit their interactions with costume staff to simply griping about how something doesn't fit, or doesn't look good, or might interfere with their stage movements, may so alienate the staff that they end up with these problems only halfheartedly resolved. Michael

Caine reminds actors why not to let this happen: "The makeup and hairdressing department is usually the hub of the universe, socially speaking, and word of your behavior there soon spreads." So think twice about your tone of voice when commenting sharply on the shade of your eyeliner or the length of your curls. Actors who, on the other hand, pose such issues in a collegial, collaborative, and affirmative manner – in ways that show their respect for the hard work and admiration for its successful aspects too – will receive the emotional as well as the professional commitment of the staff, making a resolution pleasant for all.

Assistants

And some theatre practitioners may have the generic title of "Production Assistant" or simply "Assistant." They may be assigned for a time to one staff member (e.g., "Assistant to the Director") or float between several, but their tasks may range from simply getting coffee to making phone calls to baby-sitting. You'd be wise to remember Twyla Tharp's advice here: "In any collaboration, assistants are as valuable as you allow them to be. Treat assistants with respect and you will gain valuable collaborators."

And, of course, the actors should also make friends, where possible, with the technical staff and their assistants in all the shops and with the running crews on and off the stage. After all, while actors get the applause at the curtain call, technicians, crews, and assistants work equally hard or harder in their less glamorous locales.* Politeness is essential everywhere in the adult world, of course, but mutually appreciative engagement between actors and all production staffers will pay particular dividends in the theatre, and may lead to long-term relationships – on many levels. "In the end, all collaborations are love stories," says Ms. Tharp.

Trust and respect, once again, become critical. Learn to have that respect – by understanding and learning to appreciate *all* the arts of the theatre in addition to your own – and you are well on your way to having great collaborations across the entire theatrical spectrum.

---

*Directors, including myself, may sometimes block the show's running crews into curtain calls these days, which certainly enhances the collaborative experience.

Publicists

There may be few theatre artists whose job is as hard as publicists.

The reason for this is that the marketing department, which generally plays no part in the creation of a production, nevertheless bears the responsibility to attract a large audience to come and see it. This is a tough assignment – and often a thankless one, for it is all too common for theatre artists to accept praise for attracting full houses while blaming the marketing staff for half-empty ones.

The fact is, however, that no publicist can do a decent job without, not just the cooperation, but the *proactive assistance* from the artistic team.

Granted, such assistance is not easily acquired. The production's directors, designers, and actors have their hands full directing, designing, and acting. That is what they are trained to do and, when in a professional production, are paid to do. Moreover, most theatre artists feel awkward publicly promoting themselves or their work – after all, that's why they have engaged (or hope to engage) agents to do it for them! And so most persons who work in a production are tempted to say, when asked for the second or third time to come up with material for the publicity department, "Hey, that's *their* job, isn't it?"

Yes, it is their job, but they can't do that job very well without *significant contributions from the artists* themselves. And that's for two different reasons: first, because the artists working on the show know it better than the publicists ever will, and second because the public wants to hear *from the artists* more than from (as they see it) their hired flacks.

So if the show is going to sell well, it's going to need a lot of input from the people who are *doing* the show, not just from those who are merely *representing* it. No one can explain why the theatre is producing this play as well as can the producer and director who chose it. At least they *should* be able to explain why they are doing this play, and doing it the way they are. And nothing will more engage the local public as to the show's visual excitement (whether majestic, delightful, shocking, gripping, or scary) as will actors photographed in action, in costume, before scenery, and under lights.

So even as they are making their decisions about play selection, producers and directors should be drafting sentences as to why they are making this particular choice, and thinking how they might "sell" it to the general public. Designers, for their part, should be drafting sentences about what impelled them to make their choices about the sets, lights, costumes, and sound. Such sentences can then be handed over to the marketing department to spark intriguing publicity blurbs in the subscription brochures, posters, TV promos, and other advertisements that will be key to drawing patrons other than the friends and relatives of the cast members. And while these tasks may be seen as onerous at the time, they are far easier to do at the points of conception than when the technical and dress rehearsals loom immediately ahead.

Moreover, it's not all that difficult. Many such sentences can simply be adapted from the communications between the artists during the production's preparatory and planning stages.

And once rehearsals begin, *all* participating artists – director, designers, actors, costume and scene shops – should work closely and eagerly with the marketing team to identify what will be the most intriguing preproduction photos to sell the show. That done, they should be quick to allot the needed time to take them and to adjust the scenery/costume building schedules, where possible, to ready the items needed at the photo-shoot.

Members of the artistic team also should be prepared to volunteer for press interviews and other publicity calls necessary to market the production successfully. None of this should be considered a sacrifice, nor is it undertaken just "to help out the marketing department." Rather, it is to help the production – which includes doing whatever possible to insure that the production is well attended and the audience is suitably prepared what to expect.

"Theatre," one remembers, is from the Greek word *teatron,* or "seeing place." If no one sees it, it's not theatre.

Fun

Finally, collaboration has values beyond those classed as purely professional. Theatre, after all, is a social activity as well as an artistic enterprise. Many if not most of your theatre colleagues first became attracted to the theatre – at least in part – for social reasons. "The reason most people do theater is because of the community," says Derek Cook, the technical director of Studio Theatre in Washington, D.C. "It is an art form where together you create something so much greater as an artist than you could do by yourself."

It's certainly a place to meet interesting people. And most people who work professionally in theatre do so – despite the infrequency of the work and the generally low remuneration of employment when it finally comes – because they simply love theatre and deeply enjoy "working together" with others who love it equally.

For the fact is that many people work in theatre, and stay in theatre, simply because it's fun. Cast parties, opening night parties, wrap parties, Oscar, Emmy, and Tony Award parties: these are familiar not just to theatre people but to just about everyone in America. Theatre restaurants and theatre bars are well known in Manhattan and London and other theatre centers around the world. They are usually jam-packed with theatre artists – and devoted audiences – after productions let out in such cities. If you want to see a representation of the social life of a theatre company, watch any episode of Canadian television's "Slings and Arrows," which portrays the fictional "Burbage Theatre Company" (obviously modeled on the Shakespeare Festival in Stratford, Ontario): Each episode of this series begins with the "Burbage Theatre" actors, directors, and theatre personnel hanging out at the local pub frequented by company members. They're all having a ton of fun. (Indeed, these episodes give one of the most honest and accurate portrayal of the lives of professional theatre artists, and the way they work – and play – together, that you are likely to encounter anywhere.)

It is important for any theatre group, even in the single-production mode, to have at least one event – either social or a combination of working and socializing – that involves *everyone connected with the production*. This way all the people who work onstage, offstage, backstage, or somewhere in between can identify with – and feel a sense of ownership of – the entire production. Everyone has an opportunity to meet everyone else, to talk to everyone else, and to hurdle the largely imaginary barriers surrounding their own – and everyone else's – professional discipline.

Some companies are especially proactive in fostering a broad social democracy. A popular way of getting this started is by posting, near the company callboard, a wall of photos of each person in the company, with their name and area of participation (as actor, wigmaker, and the like). Other companies have regular company meetings and parties; some (Broadway companies, notably) have softball teams that play in a league with teams from other shows. Yet other companies organize sign-up picnics, trips, and activities for off days.

All such activities are excellent ways to build rapport among company members, particularly when everyone on the artistic team is invited, so that the entire team – even those who choose not to participate – enjoys the welcoming spirit of a "family" ensemble in addition to their strictly professional association.

And, indeed, there is a larger theatre "family" that consists of theatre practitioners around the country. Theatre, even in a large country such as the United States, is a small world. Everyone who has spent time in more than one American theatre institution – a college department, a regional theatre, a Broadway show, a summer theatre festival – already knows this: "Oh, you acted at Milwaukee Rep, do you know Joe Bee?" "So, you designed at Oregon Shakes, did you run into Mary Cee?" It is rare to find *any* theatre practitioner who cannot (and does not) quickly discover, upon meeting a new colleague, at least one person that each has worked together with at another theatre company or theatre school.

And, given the globalization of theatre in the last two decades – mainly through international theatre festivals and artist exchanges – this extended theatre family now extends across national borders and language differences. Increasingly, theatrical participation has become an international meeting ground, where it has fostered a truly global theatre family.

And this means the company of friends as well as the collegiality of colleagues. For it is wise to remember that the word "company" has the same linguistic root as "companion" – and that both derive from the Latin words *com panis,* meaning "with bread" in the sense of "those we break bread with." And those of whom we request "the pleasure of your company."

PART THREE

7

Tones of Collaboration

Theatre companies have often been described as families in this book, but that does not mean that families escape without confronting misunderstandings, emotional conflicts, sibling rivalries, temper tantrums, parental resentments, and the imposition of longstanding power hierarchies handed down through generations. So honest, free-flowing, and open communications must be sufficiently lubricated to prevent unnecessarily hurt feelings, bruised egos, and eruptions of old "family" quarrels.

"I gotta' use words when I talk to you," said T.S. Eliot, in his play-poem "Sweeney Agonistes," and words, of course are the most crucial mode of theatre communications. But while words are effective communicators of specific facts, ideas, proposals, interpretations, queries, and answers – words can also hurt. And they can seduce. So one must choose wisely exactly which words to use.

But words are only one of the communicative modes of collaborative theatrical discourse. Images – sketches, renderings, photographs, and three-dimensional models – are another. "Acting out" – as by physical imitation of a proposed action or gesture or facial expression – is yet another. And sheer body language accompanying the words – a shrug, a wink, a snort, a snap of the fingers, a pat on the back – is sometimes the best communication of all. The British actor Brewster Mason – at least 6'-6" and 240 pounds in his prime and an international star of the Royal Shakespeare Company – would tower over the student actors he was directing on my campus many years ago, but he immediately made these

California undergraduates comfortable by reaching out and gently *taking their hands in his* as he spoke to them. They were enchanted; grateful that this giant of the world stage was treating them with proffered affection, not disdain. Conversely, a slightly built director I knew would often say to an actor, "It needs a bit more … (*Pause, then making a fist and, with a grunt, throwing an imaginary punch at an imaginary stomach)* Ya' know what I mean?" And yes, the actor knew exactly what he meant, which no word in the English language could have fully conveyed.

Volume, tone of voice, rapidity of speech, intensity of gaze, curl of the lip, fullness of the chest, tremor in the legs, extension of the finger – or fist: these often convey as much "content" as the semantics of the words in an oral face-to-face communication. Indeed, a basic principle of modern communication theory is that language conveys messages in two simultaneous forms: the *content* of the message, which is basically the words and their semantic meanings, and the *relationship* the speaker wishes to induce in the listener, which gives the listener a clue as to how to *process* that content. So if, say, a director says to an actor in a gentle voice, with a smile on her face and an open-palm gesture toward a chair, "I think you should sit over there," the statement comes off as a polite request, while if the director utters the identical words in a harsh voice, with a steely glance and an impatiently wagging forefinger pointing downward at the chair, no one cannot feel commanded to blindly follow suit or face unpleasant consequences.

So, whether you are director talking to actor, or designer to shop foreman, or shop foreman to carpenter, or usher to theatre patron, how do you maximize the impact of both the content and relationship aspects of your communication?

Learn the nomenclature

It's simply essential for every theatre worker to learn the basic nomenclature of the stage. No one wants to slow down tech rehearsal when somebody says "Cross upstage," or "Kill the house," or "Cheat out a bit," or "Where's the ASM?" and have someone holler back "*What*???" or "*Who*????" *Everyone* in theatre should be familiar with these terms, and be able to respond to them immediately.

And workers in any given field must know the specialized vocabularies – trade jargon – even if they haven't yet encountered them in practice. An actor in a verse play should be able to respond to the voice director's suggestion "why don't you start that line with a trochee instead of an iamb?" and a sound technician to the designer's request to "sweeten that reverb a bit, can you?" The use of such jargon is best limited to one-on-one conversations between partners well versed in each other's backgrounds, but when so employed it will speed things along and convey a mutual tone of professionalism. But those around them should also know what is being said, and stay abreast with what is being discussed in a production that involves everyone working on it.

For collaborators should, as much as possible, also know the basic techniques outside their own primary fields. Directors, for example, should really know how to "read" the designs in the same forms that designers normally prepare them. "It's hard for me when directors aren't visual; when, for example, they can't read a ground plan," says a scene designer.

And anyone who works with actors should understand the terms that they may use in their work, such as "goal," "objective," "action," "subtext," "center" – even if they themselves do not find such terms particularly useful. "You gotta *understand* the words when they're spoken to you," although not another line of Eliot's, is a requirement if quick, free-flowing communication is to take place.

And it is also crucial to understand the basic artistic methods, goals, and difficulties under which theatre artists work in their own field, which was the goal of Exercise 2 in Chapter 4. Directors who are sensitive to the actors' desires to find reasons (goals, motivations, objectives, intentions) for their actions, and with the designers' desires to have their work make an intellectual statement as well as a visual impact on the audience, will find collaborating with them easier. Actors who are sensitive to the ticking clock that the director must be hearing as tech rehearsals approach, and designers who seek to make costumes that are easy to move in and settings that are easy to walk on will save themselves and others unneeded exasperation when the production is put together in dress rehearsals.

And certainly everyone who requests the rebuilding of a prop or resewing of a costume should be aware of the amount of time it will take to undo what has been done and redo what remains. It is almost always acceptable for a director, stage manager, or even an actor to ask "Is it possible for you to redo this...?" But it becomes increasingly problematical when such requests are replaced by glowering demands.

The collaborative voice

Communicating is not solely about exchanging data. It's also about building various kinds of relationships: artistic, professional, and social. Here we will talk only of the first two, but the third can also be a catalyst for the others.

One thing communication experts have made clear is that the "relationship communication" mentioned above cannot *not* take place. It exists even in silence: We are *always* seeking to evoke, maintain, and improve our relationships with those within our gaze, whether or not we are speaking with them. Arched eyebrows, worrying shakes of the head, clenched teeth: these all indicate disapproval which, if not mediated by some suggestions how the disapproval may be alleviated, will quickly begin to fester in the minds of those who feel themselves targeted by them. Director Katie Mitchell has noticed that the way a director just *sits* in the rehearsal room may unconsciously impact the actors: "Sitting slouched with arms crossed makes them think you're judgmental; legs jigging up and down that you're tense or nervous; looking at your watch that you're bored."

So remember that when you ask a director a question, or convey a fact to a shop technician, or share an idea with a design colleague, you are always in the act of reinvoking your *artistic and professional relationship with that person.* Which may mean you are improving it – and may mean you are destroying it. For no communication – even electronic – is merely data transmission! No communication can be wholly impersonal. *Not* looking at someone can, in fact, be the most brutal "communication" under certain circumstances.

Thus phrasing and word choice in emails – and body language and vocal tone in face-to-face oral communications – are crucial in any exchange with colleagues. Everyone interested in good collaboration, therefore, must reckon with the dual-edged ego words, "I" and "My." There are plenty of times where these words are useful, even necessary. But anyone who finds himself saying "I" twice as much as "we" may soon be facing walls of resistance from all sides.

And the same goes with an abrupt "No" or "But" at the beginning of a response to a suggestion. As in:

> Lighting Designer: I'd like to lower the lights at this point.
> Director: No, Ellen! That would just make the stage look grim.

If this is the director's first interaction with the designer, it can be disheartening; if it's the director's routine style of responding it will be downright dismaying. How about, instead, in a first discussion of a scene:

> Lighting Designer: I'd like to lower the lights at this point.
> Director: That may work fine in scene two, Ellen, but are you sure it would sustain the buoyancy we're hoping to achieve here?

Phrasing this as a question rather than a blanket rejection, while it may be a bit cumbersome, is worth the few extra words. It encourages a discussion of the issue by projecting the *positive* goal (buoyancy) that the team has established for the scene rather than something to be avoided (grimness). It also maintains a sense of trust and respect between the two artists, without compromising anyone's dignity or authority.

And how about this exchange:

> Actor: Suppose I cross to the fireplace on this line?
> Director: No! Cross to the chair.
>
> Versus this one:
>
> Actor: Suppose I cross to the fireplace on this line?
> Director: Yes! And it might work better if you stopped at the chair.

In both cases the actor has asked the same question and the director has given the same answer – but in the second iteration it is phrased affirmatively rather than negatively. The second response will almost always produce the result the director wants, and at the same time confirm the actor's instinct to move. The first response, however, only signals that the director *wants everyone to know she's in charge.* And for a director to signal that he or she is in charge is only to display the director's *in*security – which most persons in the cast, at least unconsciously, will recognize.

Indeed, the idea of responding with "Yes! And…" instead of "No! But…" – at least in appropriate cases – which developed in the field of improvisational theatre, is becoming popular in business management circles as well.

Collaborative communication does not mean merely being polite and tactful, however, and it's just as easy to err on the side of over-politeness as the side of brusqueness. While tact can be the lubricant of collaboration, honesty remains absolutely fundamental to both collaboration and leadership. If the actor persists in asking the same sort of question several times, the director may need to clarify the production's core direction. Director Bonnie Monte explains that "On occasion I will say to an actor, 'That's taking the play down the wrong road. You can't do that. Please try this instead – you'll see how the payoff is going to happen.'" Monte calls this being "benignly dictatorial," but it's not dictatorial at all: it's merely firm. And firmness is essential to leadership in any field.

Certainly, where the director-designer relationship is well established and mutually trusting, cutting right to the chase is eminently desirable on both sides. "I want my directors to be honest," says lighting designer Lonnie Alcaraz, who urges directors, if they see something they don't like, "Don't pussyfoot around. Tell me what's wrong!" Lighting designer Tom Ruzika echoes this: "I actually prefer the director's straightforward gut reaction – such as 'What the hell is that lighting? That sucks!' When a director like Hal Prince says this, it's not at all embarrassing because *he does it in the right tone*." As always, honesty is always essential, and the "right tone" is crucial in delivering it successfully.

And when time is short, as it always is in technical rehearsals, undue politeness, far from enhancing communication, aborts it. In one such rehearsal long ago, the student lighting designer was conveying dimmer positions to the board operator upstairs by saying, over the intercom, "Would you please take dimmer fourteen to eight? Thank you very much, Michelle. Now, Michelle, would you please take dimmer fifteen to six? Thank you very much, Michelle. Now would you…" Figuring she had sixty dimmer positions to change for each cue, and maybe two hundred cues to set, I asked the designer to shortcut her instructions to simply "fourteen to eight; fifteen to six…" and so on. This saved us a *full hour* of the tech time – all by cutting out the unnecessary niceties. As scene designer Luke Cantarella says, "Politeness is important, but it does not require saying thank you all the time; once at the end of the day is quite enough. Real politeness is remembering people's names and treating them as equals."

The too-brusque to too-polite scale requires an acute calculation, however, and finding the balance takes some experience at judging both the situation and the individuals involved. As Robert Sternberg points out in *Successful Intelligence*, the optimum communication relies on "knowing what to say to whom, knowing when to say it, and knowing how to say it for maximum effect." That's all there is – but that's a lot!

The blame game

So a great collaboration means a production will encounter no mistakes, right? No, wrong! (In this case, this is the only possible response.)

There are *always* mistakes en route to an opening performance, and usually after the opening as well. Some are simple: the rehearsal schedule leaves off the name of a character that should have been called; the photo call does not give an actress sufficient time to put on her costume and makeup before the shoot; the prompter gives an actor the wrong line. And some are complex and serious. A latch on the setting's outside door jams, and the actor making his entrance cannot open it, leaving the actors standing helplessly on the stage. A railing installed on the set for tech rehearsal proves considerably shorter than the line that represented it on the rehearsal room floor, requiring that the scene be re-blocked or the railing rebuilt. A leading actress trips on her skirt each time she climbs the staircase on opening night and no one can figure out why. A leading actor falls asleep on stage and starts snoring, and the other actors onstage, unaware of it, cannot understand why the audience is starting to giggle. All of these I've seen on stage, two in Broadway productions and two in productions of my own. And the question always leaps to the minds of everyone in the company: "Who's to blame?"

But that's not the first question to be asked, or even to be addressed. "What needs to be *done*?" – *that* is the question when such mishaps occur. And while tracking down responsibility for the error eventually will become necessary, so as to insure it doesn't happen again, merely pointing a finger and assigning "blame" to someone rarely proves a wise idea.

This is not obvious, I'm afraid. When something goes wrong, most of us instinctively look around to see "who's at fault." Most of us will also overlook our *own* possible complicity at such a moment. But often the culprit is quite a bit less than obvious. And often, as Cassius says, "the fault, dear Brutus, is in ourselves...."

The railing error, for example, could possibly be attributed to the ASM who mis-taped the floor, or the tech director who misstated the dimension on the plan, or the designer who changed the design without letting the PSM know, or the welder who misread the dimensions when assembling the railing, or the director, who misread the taping and assumed a different line represented the railing (that would be me in this actual case). The broken door latch could be the fault of the carpenter who mis-installed it, the manufacturer who had built a defective product, the producer who didn't allocate enough money to buy a better-built product, the tech director who didn't alert the producer that his budget restricted him to buying only the cheapest model available, or perhaps even the actor who last exited the door – and slammed it so hard that its latch jammed.

"Who to blame," it turns out, is not as important a question at this moment as "How do we fix it?" Only when that's answered can we move to "How do we prevent it from happening again?"

And accusing a suspected perpetrator at this point may well begin an altercation that will make everybody uncomfortable and defensive. Worse, it will more likely delay than accelerate the search for a proper solution.

The best way to prevent a blame game, with everybody pointing fingers at somebody else, is for those persons at the highest level to *immediately accept a portion of the blame.* If, for example, a person's name is left off the rehearsal call and the director, discovering this, publicly lays the blame on the PSM, saying something like "Sorry, everybody! Ellen's made a mistake here, you were supposed to come at noon, not at eleven," Ellen will only feel embarrassed and the actors may lose confidence in her authority. But if instead the director says, "Oh, I'm sorry, we made a mistake here, you were supposed to come at noon," the director has assumed part of the responsibility, and no single person stands accused. "We" turns out to be a magic word here.

But is this "we" honest? Yes, absolutely, because it is based in the fundamental maxim of management referred to earlier: "You can delegate authority, but not responsibility." The director *does* have responsibility over the rehearsal call, because the director initiates it, oversees it, and oversees the PSM who posts it. And so the director certainly could have – and probably should have – noticed it. So what does the director lose by assuming part of the responsibility for the name omission? Nothing. What does the director gain? The confidence of the cast members, who realize that responsibility has been gracefully admitted and the problem has been addressed "at the top," and also the gratitude of the PSM for realizing that her authority has not been publicly impugned before the actors and his or her ASMs.

And if the PSM, at some convenient point in her announcements says, "I'm sorry I left your name off the call yesterday, Joe, I'll try to make sure it doesn't happen again," the episode becomes ancient history rather than an irritant that might fester. Plus, the PSM will be doing everything in her power to make certain that it *doesn't* happen again – and will feel an increased loyalty to the director. So the sharing of responsibility by the director is a completely win-win solution: nobody's hurt and everybody comes out on top. And the sharing of responsibility by the PSM becomes a welcome confirmation of the simple fact that mistakes will happen, and when they do in this production they will be quickly and fully addressed, and that the leaders of this company do not just duck for cover.

And why *shouldn't* a director take responsibility for the production's miscues? The director will certainly accept praise for the production's successes, its standing ovations, its great press reviews, and the year-end prizes that may come her way, even though she did not *herself* design the costume that so ravished the audience in act one, or deliver the monologue that had them weeping at the final curtain. And so to accept part of the blame for the flawed rehearsal call or the mis-measured railing is simply the flip side of the dual responsibility the director bears. People at the top of a hierarchy should therefore be quick, not reluctant, to say "it was our fault" or even "it was my fault" when things go wrong, in part because this moves things along faster than does mere finger pointing, in part because it looks to the future and not to the past, and in great part because director simply cannot cast off the responsibility that goes with their elevated positions. When, the day after an uninvited couple crashed President Obama's first state dinner in 2009, Secret Service director Mark Sullivan publicly acknowledged, "This is our fault and our fault alone," he garnered nothing but praise for his forthright acceptance of responsibility, though there were certainly others to whom he could have in part passed this particular buck. Indeed, an agency that should also have admitted its lapse of attention that evening but refused to do so received the very disdain its chief officer had tried to avoid by refusing phone calls.

So when mistakes happen, and they will, all members of the team are best advised to think first of the future – fixing the problem – and only then look back at the past to investigate what actually happened and what to do to prevent its recurrence. And a brief, non-mawkish apology is the best possible way to move into the future. It is also good for your mental health: As writer Beverly Engel reports, "The act of apology is not only beneficial to the person receiving it, but to the one giving it as well."

Mechanics of communication

We have spent a great deal of time discussing electronic communications in this book, and there is no question but email, teleconferencing, posted images and the like have been increasingly important in theatrical collaborations in the current era. This will undoubtedly increase as the electronics improve and the costs of physical transportation increase.

But nothing should alter the fact that *face-to-face* communication is and will probably remain unparalleled for rapid, clear, consistent, and friendly exchanges. As scene designer Jo Winiarski says, "In working up a design, I love to sketch on a napkin next to the director, talking and drawing at the same time, and get immediate feedback. Or when I work in model form I like to sit next to the director so I can rip the model up and tape it back together as we talk. This not only saves miscommunication, but it also allows us to read each other's facial expressions, to really understand where the other person is coming from. And the intimate tone of such communication is simply imperceptible in email."

Winiarski's sentiments are shared around the world. Indeed, email is probably the absolute *worst* way to settle serious disagreements, as it lacks the crucial interactions of eye contact, facial expression, tone of voice, and physical contact, which can collectively moderate such disagreements during face-to-face meetings. Email emoticons have of course been created for such purposes, but are only feeble ways of conveying the personal nuances by which we let people know that, while we are in disagreement with something that they've said or done, we don't hate them, don't hate their work, don't plan on quitting the collaboration, and are only seeking an agreeable and practical solution for this particular problem.

And there are other problems with email arguments. The sheer ease of whipping off a fiery response by simply hitting the "reply" button has destroyed more than a few careers in this business, in which artistic paranoia is not exactly unknown. And since email does not provide instant give-and-take as does a meeting, or even a phone conversation, the wounds the fiery response may inflict to their recipient will be left to smolder until a counter-reply is counter-counter-replied, which may be a day or two later – at which time they have erupted into a conflagration. Such occasions call for a meeting, or phone call, or pre-arranged chat-session in which the give-and-take can be in real-time, and the issue can be addressed by all parties simultaneously – or deferred to such time as a full meeting can be scheduled.

Remember too that, historically, the greatest collaborations have occurred over the proverbial breaking of bread discussed above. The founding of the Moscow Art Theatre began not with an email or text message but at a dinner conversation between Stanislavsky and Nemirovich-Dantchenko at the Slavik Bazaar in 1897. Their meeting lasted until breakfast the next day, and was certainly not the only time a theatre, or a theatre production, was chewed over along with food and wine. Nothing has changed about meeting face-to-face, shaking hands, breaking bread, and hugging bodies since those days, or since the many centuries preceding them.

But when push comes to shove

But once again, "be not too tame, neither." Thus far in this chapter, and in this book as a whole, our concentration has been mainly on those aspects of leadership and collaboration that may be called inductive. We have prioritized the leader who evokes, inspires, and who leads from the forefront as one who leads a parade, drawing all the others after her. We have prioritized the actor who requests rather than confronts, and the stage manager who pulls the cast together rather than pushes them back in line.

But while pulling is desirable, it is not always possible. For there are times, particularly when technical rehearsal looms ahead, that pushing becomes equally important. And when push comes to shove, as during technical rehearsals, pushing may be all there is, and the nudge from behind, or the proverbial crack of the whip or even kick in the backside may be necessary to accelerate the action and solidify the collaboration.

For at these points, the tone of leadership must be firm, decisive, and inarguable. The language of leadership may – and in healthy situations should – remain polite and tactful, but it cannot be timid, wishy-washy, or evasive. And this applies at every level of the hierarchy, not merely directors, producers, and stage managers but just about everyone else: There will be times when the stagehand must insist the actor not walk on the stage until the paint dries and the usher command the yakking patron to turn off his cellphone.

For the time comes where experiments can no longer be made and different options no longer investigated. A clear-cut decision as to which way to go must be firmly made at each of these artistic crossroads, and the decisions that emerge must be accepted and implemented by all collaborators. This is the moment where hierarchy takes over; indeed, it is the time when everyone must understand why a hierarchy exists.

Yet if the collaboration has been fruitful throughout the process, and the leadership has been exerted with grace, receptivity, and mutual understanding, the hierarchy will be accepted as *part of* the collaboration and not adverse to it. What is crucial for this to take place is that collaboration and leadership, and pushing and pulling, be *completely intertwined throughout the entire production process,* not switched back and forth according to the leader's mood of the moment, and certainly not because of the intervention of outside opinions. Many years ago, I was acting in a Shakespearean company where the young director was as encouraging as a director could possibly be. He joshed with the actors, laughed at our jokes, admired our speeches, took us out for coffee, and was all smiles as he gave us notes after rehearsals. But on the morning after the first dress rehearsal, he lit into us with a previously unseen fire: "You're acting is terrible! You're just saying lines! You're not audible! You're not believable! And everything's dragging! So pick it up, god-dammit!" And then he walked off the stage, leaving a bewildered cast behind him. What had happened was that the director's wife had seen our previous night's rehearsal and told him that his production sucked – and the director panicked. In the depth of his mind, he later told me, he had known this all along, but only now felt obliged to do what he could to "pump us up."

I am happy to say that we did get pumped up, and the production was reasonably successful. His wife may indeed have been right in her assessment. But it was a lousy way to get us to the finish line.

I am even happier to say that the young director learned his lesson and became an extraordinarily fine director, and an artistic director in his own right. He had learned the important lesson of this book – and in some ways taught it to me. He had learned that collaboration and leadership were not opposites; that you could not simply exhibit one at one point and the other at another; that he had to learn how to put them together at the same time. He had to realize that leadership does not stifle collaboration, it guides it, and that collaboration does not undermine leadership, it enhances it. He learned it, and I learned it, and now, as we've reached the end of this book, I hope you have learned it.

Nothing is more critical in creating productive leadership and fruitful collaboration than the sensitive personal communications among *all* the individuals involved, *all the time* throughout the production. Not just during the "fun" moments of exploration but in those moments when "push comes to shove." The collaboration is not a given: it is the result of a well-led production. And theatrical supremacy – as well as superb artistic leadership – is almost certainly best achieved through a beautifully collaborative process.

APPENDIX

The table below is a breakdown of roles and lines for the author's production of Molière's *The Misanthrope*. Each shows the scenes (as numbered in the stage manager's book rather than the literary edition), the characters appearing in each, the number of spoken lines each character has in each scene, and total numbers of spoken lines for each actor, for each scene and for the entire production. Such a breakdown, as described on page 72, proves very helpful to stage managers and directors in casting, scheduling rehearsals, determining the necessary times for costume changes, estimating the production's running time, and determining the best places where intermissions may be taken.

CHARACTERS	Total lines	1	2	3	4	5	6	7	8	9	10	11	12	13	14	15	16	17
Scene # Pages		2–10	10–19	19–23	23–30	30–32	33–35	35–36	36–40	40–43	43–45	45–48	48–52	52–55	55–58	58–61	61–63	63–66
Total lines		247	222	117	176	44	71	30	161	93	82	64	156	55	107	58	75	94
ALCESTE	746	129	122	68	36	23				43		44	104	22	75	21	3	56
PHILINTE	234	118	15			8					55	4				32			2
ORONTE	122		85													24	13	
CLITANDRE	50				16	0	20	2									12	
ACASTE	99				12	0	51	2									34	
GUARD/ DU BOIS	34					5								29				
BASQUE	8			2	0	4		2										
CELIMENE	337			47	88	4		24	86				52	4		13		19
ARSINOE	135								75	50							10	
ELIANTE	87				24						27	16					3	17
Total lines in play	1852																	

ENDNOTES

Citations in the text are listed by pages. Where a citation only cites a book title and page, the remaining publication information will be found in the Select Bibliography that follows these endnotes.

3 Malcolm Gladwell's quotation is from his *Outliers*, p. 115; Edward Dowling's quotation is from *The Journal for Stage Directors and Choreographers*, Spring/Summer 2000, pp. 20–21.

5 Giovanni Zoppé is quoted in *the New York Times*, August 1, 2005.

10 Willem Dafoe is quoted in Richard Eyre's *Talking Theatre*, p. 292; Denzel Washington is quoted in *Backstage West*, December 27–January 2, 2007.

11 John Kander's quotation is from "'A Little Night Music,' A Little Less Staging," *New York Times*, January 7, 2009.

13 Twyla Tharp as quoted in her *The Collaborative Habit*, p. 12.

17 The Steppenwolf statement is from the company website at www.steppenwolf.org as of August 18, 2010; Christopher Isherwood's comments are from his "Plays Well With Others," *New York Times*, December 5, 2007.

18 Stanislavsky's phrase appears repeatedly in the book, published by Theatre Arts Books, New York, 1938.

20 Stella Adler's comments are in Cole and Chinoy, *Actors on Acting*, p. 604; Arthur Miller's comments are from his *Timebends*, p. 230; Willem Dafoe's comments are cited by Richard Eyre in his *Talking Theatre*, p. 292.

21 Lev Dodin's comments are in Peter Lichtenfels' interview with him in Delgado, et. al., *Contemporary European Theatre Directors*, p. 76.

22 Peter Brook's comments are from his *The Shifting Point*, p. 17.

23 Garry Hynes is cited in L. Chambers et. al., eds., *Theatre Talk*, Dublin: Carysfort Press, Dublin, 2000, p. 196.

24 Willem Dafoe is cited in Richard Eyre's *Talking Theatre*, p. 292, emphasis added; the Wooster site was at www.thewoostergroup.org as of August 14, 2010.

37 The paraphrase of Sainte-Albine's remark is by Joseph Roach in his *The Players Passion*, Ann Arbor: University of Michigan Press, 1993.

39 Bill T. Jones is cited in his *Last Night on Earth*, New York: Pantheon, 1995, pp. 345–46.

40 Diana Rigg's book was published in London by Elm Tree Books, 1982.

55 Just as this book was going to press, South Coast Repertory's artistic directors (David Emmes and Martin Benson) announced their impending retirements from those positions.

56 Elia Kazan's remarks are in his autobiography, *A Life*, p. 61.

57 Richard Linklater is cited in his interview with Ann Hornaday, *Los Angeles Times*, Dec 25, 2009.

58 George Clooney's comments on this and the following page are from his interview in *Backstage West*, January 3, 2008; Neil Simon's report on Mike Nichols is cited by John Lahr in his "Making it Real," *The New Yorker*, February 21 and 28, 2000, p. 200; Kelsey Grammar's quotation is from *Backstage West*, February 25, 1999, p. 6; Elia Kazan's comments are from his autobiography, *A Life*, p. 299; and Charles Marowitz's quotations are from his review of *The Alchemy of Theatre of Theatre* in *Swann's Commentary*, November 17, 2008.

59 Mike Nichols' statement during the *Day of the Dolphin* appeared in Lahr's above-cited "Making it Real;" his following statement about the actor's need to trust was reported by Barbara Gelb in the *New York Times*, May 27, 1984; Ben Brantley's review was published on November 5, 2009; Harold Prince's comment (emphasis added) is from *Alchemy of Theatre*, p. 82.

60 Twyla Tharp's comment appears in her *Collaborative Habit*, p. 7.

61 James Burrows is cited in *American Way*, December 1, 1995, p. 94; John Travolta's comment is from *Backstage West*, January 3, 2008, p. 16.

62 Kathleen Chalfant's comment is in *Alchemy of Theatre*, p. 160.

64 Machiavelli's statement is from Chapter 17 of his *The Prince*.

65 Harold Prince's comment is in his *Contradictions*, p. 34.

66 Elia Kazan's statements (slightly abridged) in this and the next page can be found in his *A Life*, pp. 61–62.

68 George Bernard Shaw's statement is in the preface to his *Man and Superman*.

70 Ingmar Bergman is cited by John Lahr in "The Demon Lover," *The New Yorker*, May 31, 1999, p. 76; Peter Brook's comment on this and the next page is from his *The Open Door*, p. 43.

72 Susan Stroman's statement was published in *Theaterweek,* December 19, 1994, p. 16.

77 Terrance McNally's statement is from *Theaterweek,* February 27, 1995, p. 17; Elia Kazan's comments, slightly abridged, are from his "Author and Director: A Delicate Situation," in *Playbill* (September 30, 1957); reprinted in Brenda Murphy, *Tennessee Williams and Elia Kazan,* Cambridge: Cambridge University Press, 1992, p. 133, which is also the source of Williams' "explosive relationship" comment (p. 98).

78 Edward Albee's comment is in *Alchemy of Theatre,* pp. 19–20.

79 Jerry Patch's comments are from an interview with the author, July 21, 2009.

80 Mary Zimmerman's remarks are from her interview with Nicole Galland at www.mccarter.org/Education/secretinthewings/page10.htm as of August 14, 2010.

87 Danny Aiello is cited by Richard Covington in "Acid Washed Fashion," in the *Los Angeles Times,* August 14, 1994, p. 73.

88 Peter Brook's comment is from his *The Open Door,* p. 29.

94 Mary Zimmerman's comments are from her above-cited Nicole Galland interview; Daniel Ostling's comment is from his interview with Michael S. Eddy in *Live Design,* May 1, 2003.

95 Don Holder's remarks are from an interview with the author, January 23, 2009; Vince Olivieri's comments are from an interview with the author, March 15, 2009.

96 Quotations from Olivieri, Jaymi Smith, Luke Cantarella, and Tom Ruzika are from interviews with the author in March, 2009: Peter Brook's statement is from his *The Shifting Point,* p. 5.

97 Katie Mitchell's remarks are from her *The Director's Craft,* p. 120.

100 The (slightly edited) comment of Pamela Howard, currently Professor Emeritus at the University of Arts, London, is from her *What is Scenography,* second edition, London and New York: Routledge, 2009.

101 William Ivey Long's statement is from *Alchemy of Theatre,* p. 105.

104 Robin Wagner's comments are from *Alchemy of Theatre,* p. 105; comments on this and the following page by Jaymi Smith, Tom Ruzika, Jo Winiarski, Holly Poe Durbin and Janet Swenson are from interviews with the author in March 2009.

105 Gabriel Berry's comments are from her interview with Amy Reiter in *American Theatre,* March 1995, p. 42.

107 Susan Stroman comment is from *Alchemy of Theatre,* p. 97.

109 Harold Prince's conversation is as reported in his *Contradictions,* pp. 131–32; Gordon Perlman's comments are in *Entertainment Design,* March 1999, p. 58.

110 Comments from Jo Winiarski and Janet Swenson are from emails to the author in March, 2009; Susan Stroman is quoted in *Alchemy of Theatre,* p. 98.

111 George C. Wolfe is quoted in *Alchemy of Theatre*, p. 103; Jaymi Smith's comments from her interview with the author, March 2009.

114 Vince Olivieri and Jaymi Smith are quoted from interviews with the author, March 2009; Kathryn Bigelow is cited in an interview with Ryan Stewart, *Slant Magazine*, June 26,2009.

115 Susan Stroman is quoted in *Theatreweek*, December 19, 1994, p. 16.

121 Jeff Greenberg is quoted in interview with the author, February, 2001.

123 Kenny Leon's interview was online at www.langfieldentertainment. com/kennyleon.htm as of March 18, 2010.

124 Edward Norton's comments are from an interview with Rachel Abramowitz, *Los Angeles Times*, December 29, 2002; Peter Brook's citation is in *The Shifting Point*, p. 16; Stella Adler's citation is in Cole and Chinoy, *Actors on Acting*, p. 604.

125 The Michael Caine citation comes from his *Acting in Film*, p. 107.

129 Don Taylor's comment is from his *Directing Plays*, London: A & C Black, 1996, p. 101; Brian Stokes Mitchell's comment is from *Alchemy of Theatre*, p. 105.

130 Michael Caine's citation is from his *Acting in Film*, pp. 121–22.

131 Donald Sutherland is quoted in the *Los Angeles Times*, October 21, 2001.

133 Christine Ebersole is quoted in an interview in the *New York Times*, November 1, 2006; Meryl Streep is quoted in the *Los Angeles Times*, October 21, 2001.

134 James Burrows is cited in *The American Way*, December 1, 1995, p. 94.

135 David Mamet's comment is from his *True and False*, p. 63.

137 William Ivey Long's comments are from *Alchemy of Theatre*, p. 202.

140 On this and the next page, Peter Brook's comments are in his *Threads of Time*, p. 51 and Ingmar Bergman's comments, slightly edited, are from John Lahr's essay, "The Demon Lover," in *The New Yorker*, May 31, 1999, p. 77.

142 Katie Mitchell's comments are from her *The Director's Craft*, p. 126; Jason Reitman's comments are from his interview with Ann Hornaday, *Los Angeles Times*, December 25, 2009; Garry Hynes remarks are in her interview with Cathy Leeney in L. Chambers, et. al., *Theatre Talk*, Dublin: Carysfort Press, 2000, p. 198.

141 Deborah Warner cited in Richard Eyre, *Talking Theatre*, p. 300; emphasis added.

144 Ridley Scott is cited in the *Los Angeles Times*, December 28, 2001.

152 Arthur Miller, is cited in *Alchemy of Theatre*, p. 13; the report on rehearsals for Kushner's *Homosexual's Guide* was written by David Savan in *American Theatre*, October 2009.

154 Declan Donnellan's words are from his interview with Aleks Sierz in *Contemporary European Theatre Directors*, pp.153–54; Katie Mitchell's words appear in her *The Director's Craft*, p. 133.

155 Silviu Purcarete's remarks are from his interview with Aleksander Sasa Dunderovic in *Contemporary European Theatre Directors*, p. 95; Mary Zimmerman's comments on this and the following page are from the above-cited Nicole Galland interview.

156 Kathryn Bigelow's remarks are from her above-cited Ryan Stuart interview in *Slant.*

157 Roger Ebert's review is in the Chicago *Sun Times,* July 8, 2010; Anne Bogart's comments are from her book, *and then you act,* p. 122.

160 Anne Bogart's comments are from her *and then you act,* p. 39.

161 Bonnie Monte's words on this and the following page are from her interview with Charles Ney, published in *American Theatre,* April 2008, p. 85.

165 Harold Prince's remarks are from his *Contradictions,* p. 101–02; Martin Scorsese told this story in a nationally-televised speech honoring Robert De Niro at the 2009 Kennedy Awards Ceremony; it has also been reported, in slightly different language, in Andy Dugan, *Untouchable: A Biography of Robert De Niro,* New York: Thunder's Mouth Press, 1996.

166 Viola Spolin's main work, *Improvisation for the Theatre* (Evanston: Northwestern University Press, 1963), comprehensively covers her improvisational and theatre game techniques.

167 Katie Mitchell's comments are from her *Director's Craft,* p. 155.

168 Peter Brook's words are from his *The Open Door,* p. 155.

170 Stuart Wilson's, Ben Kingsley's and Sigourney Weaver's reports on this and the following page are from Lawrence Weschler's "Artist in Exile," *The New Yorker,* December 5, 1994, p. 104.

173 Peter Brook's comments, with emphasis added, are from his *Threads of Time,* p. 73.

182 Peter Marx's comments on this and the following page are from *The Washington Post,* March 1, 2010.

183 Catherine Zuber's remarks are from her interview with the author, February 22, 2009.

184 Peter Lawrence's remarks are from *Alchemy of Theatre,* p. 132, with emphasis added; Brian Stokes Mitchell's remarks on this and the next page are from *Alchemy of Theatre,* p. 148.

186 Michael Caine's comments are from his *Acting in Film,* p. 38; Twyla Tharp's remarks are from *The Collaborative Habit,* p. 56.

188 Derek Cook's remarks are from Peter Marx's above-cited essay in *The Washington Post,* March 1, 2010.

196 Katie Mitchell's remarks are from her *The Director's Craft,* p. 131.

198 Bonnie Monte's comments are from her interview with Charles Ney, *American Theatre,* April 2008, p. 88; comments by Lonnie Alcaraz, Tom Ruzika and Luke Cantarella are from interviews with the author, March 2009.

199 Robert Sternberg is cited in his *Successful Intelligence,* New York: Simon & Schuster, 1966, p. 88.

202 Beverly Engel's observations are from her *The Power of Apology,* New York: John Wiley and Sons, 2001, p.13; Jo Winiarsky's comments are from her interview with the author, March 2009.

SELECT BIBLIOGRAPHY

Bogart, Anne, *and then, you act: Making Art in an Unpredictable World,* New York and London: Routledge, 2007

Brook, Peter, *The Open Door,* London: Pantheon, 1991

——*The Shifting Point,* New York: Harper and Row, 1987

——*Threads of Time,* Washington, DC: Counterpoint, 1998

Caine, Michael, *Acting in Film,* New York: Applause Theatre Books, 1990, 1993

Cohen, Robert and Calleri, James, *Acting Professionally,* Seventh Edition, London and New York: Palgrave Macmillan, 2009

Cole and Chinoy, *Actors on Acting,* New York: Crown Publishers, 1954

Delgado, Maria M., and Dan Reballato, *Contemporary European Theatre Directors,* London: Routledge, 2010

Dugan, Andy, *Untouchable: A Biography of Robert De Niro,* New York: Thunder's Mouth Press, 1996

Engel, Beverly, *The Power of Apology,* New York: John Wiley and Sons, 2001

Eyre, Richard, *Talking Theatre,* London: Nick Hern Books, 2009

Gladwell, Malcolm, *Outliers,* New York: Little Brown, 2008

Kazan, Elia, *A Life,* New York: Borzoi Books, 1988

Kerrigan, Sheila, *The Performer's Guide to the Collaborative Process,* Portsmouth, NH: Heinemann, 2001

Mamet, David, *True and False,* New York: Pantheon, 1997

Miller, Arthur, *Timebends,* New York: Penguin, 1995

Mitchell, Katie, *Director's Craft,* New York: Routledge, 2009

Prince, Harold, *Contradictions,* New York: Dodd Mead, 1974

Rigg, Diana, *No Stone Unturned,* London: Elm Tree Books, 1982

Spolin, Viola, *Improvisation for the Theatre,* Chicago: Northwestern University Press, 1963

Stanislavsky, Konstantin, *An Actor Prepares,* New York: Theatre Arts Books, 1938

Sternberg, Robert, *Successful Intelligence,* New York: Plume, 1997

Taylor, Don, *Directing Plays,* London: A & C Black, 1996

Tharp, Twyla, *The Collaborative Habit,* New York: Simon and Schuster, 2009

Viagas, Robert, ed., *The Alchemy of Theatre of Theatre,* New York: Playbill Books, 2006

INDEX

215